60* More Quick Baby Knits

ADORABLE PROJECTS FOR NEWBORNS TO TOTS IN 220 SUPERWASH® SPORT FROM CASCADE YARNS *

sixth&springbooks
NEW YORK

sixth&springbooks

161 Avenue of the Americas, New York, NY 10013
sixthandspringbooks.com

Editorial Director
JOY AQUILINO

Senior Editor
MICHELLE BREDESON

Art Director
DIANE LAMPHRON

Yarn Editor
RENEE LORION

Associate Editor
ALEXANDRA JOINNIDES

Instructions Editors
LISA BUCCELLATO
PAT HARSTE
AMY POLCYN

Instructions
Proofreaders
CHARLOTTE PARRY
JUDY SLOAN

Copy Editor
LISA SILVERMAN

Technical Illustrations
ULI MONCH

Photography
JACK DEUTSCH

Stylist & Bookings Manager
SARAH LIEBOWITZ

Vice President, Publisher
TRISHA MALCOLM

Creative Director
JOE VIOR

Production Manager
DAVID JOINNIDES

President
ART JOINNIDES

Library of Congress
Control Number: 2011942091
ISBN: 978-1-936096-43-5

Manufactured in China
1 3 5 7 9 10 8 6 4 2
First Edition

CASCADE YARNS
DISTRIBUTOR OF FINE YARN

cascadeyarns.com

Quick Tip

Turn to the inside back cover to find abbreviations, an explanation of skill levels, illustrations of embroidery stitches, and even a handy ruler!

contents

✳ To locate retailers that carry 220 Superwash® Sport, visit cascadeyarns.com.

Picot Edge Cap

A pretty picot edging and a button accent make a dainty moss stitch cap even more precious.

DESIGNED BY LINDA VOSS PLUMMER

Size
Instructions are written for size 6–12 months.

Knitted Measurements
Head circumference 16½"/42cm
Depth 6½"/16cm

Materials
■ 1 1¾oz/50g hank (each approx 136yd/125m) of Cascade Yarns *220 Superwash Sport* (superwash merino wool) in #850 lime sherbet

■ Size 6 (4mm) circular needle, 16"/40cm long, *or size to obtain gauge*

■ One set (5) size 6 (4mm) double-pointed needles (dpns)

■ Spare size 6 (4mm) needle (for picot bind-off)

■ Stitch marker

■ One ⅝"/16mm button

Stitch Glossary
Ssp (slip, slip, purl) Sl first st knitwise, then sl next st knitwise. Slip these 2 sts back to LH needle, then purl them tog tbl.

Moss Stitch
(over a multiple of 2 sts)
Rnds 1 and 2 *K1, p1; rep from * around.
Rnds 3 and 4 *P1, k1; rep from * around.
Rep rnds 1–4 for moss st.

Cap
With circular needle, cast on 110 sts. Do not join. Work back and forth in garter st (knit every row) for 7 rows, end with a RS row.
Next row (WS) Bind off first 14 sts knitwise for button tab, knit to end—96 sts. Join and pm for beg of rnds. Work around in moss st until piece measures approximately 4½"/11.5cm from beg, end with rnd 4.

CROWN SHAPING
Change to dpns (dividing sts evenly between 4 needles).
Dec rnd 1 *K2tog, ssp, [k1, p1] 6 times; rep from * around 5 times more—84 sts.
Next rnd *K1, p1; rep from * around.
Dec rnd 2 *Ssp, k2tog, [p1, k1] 5 times; rep from * around 5 times more—72 sts.
Next rnd *P1, k1; rep from * around.
Dec rnd 3 *K2tog, ssp, [k1, p1] 4 times; rep from * around 5 times more—60 sts.

Next rnd *K1, p1; rep from * around.
Dec rnd 4 *Ssp, k2tog, [p1, k1] 3 times; rep from * around 5 times more—48 sts.
Next rnd *P1, k1; rep from * around.
Dec rnd 5 *K2tog, ssp, [k1, p1] twice; rep from * around 5 times more—36 sts.
Next rnd *K1, p1; rep from * around.
Dec rnd 6 *Ssp, k2tog, p1, k1; rep from * around 5 times more—24 sts.
Next rnd *P1, k1; rep from * around.
Dec rnd 7 [K2tog] 12 times—12 sts.
Cut yarn, leaving an 8"/20.5cm tail, and thread through rem sts. Pull tog tightly and secure end.

Finishing
PICOT EDGING
Turn cap so bottom edge is at top and RS is facing. Count 14 sts from front side edge of button tab. With circular needle, pick up and k 1 st in each rem st around bottom edge—96 sts. Work picot bind-off using spare needle as foll: Bind off first st, *transfer last st on RH needle to LH needle, cast on 4 sts to LH needle, bind off 4 sts on LH needle, bind off next 3 sts; rep from *, end bind-off last st (instead of 3 sts). Fasten off last st. Curve button tab onto hat as shown. Tack side edges in place. Sew on button. ■

Gauge
29 sts to 5"/12.5cm and 32 rnds to 4"/10cm over moss st using size 6 (4mm) circular needle.
Take time to check gauge.

✳ Pattern for Slip Stitch Cardigan is on page 130.

Checkered Blanket

The squares in this garter stitch blanket—or tablecloth for teddy's tea party—are knit diagonally, then sewn together. Change the arrangement to customize the blanket!

DESIGNED BY SANDI PROSSER

Knitted Measurements
Approx 26" x 32½"/66cm x 82.5cm

Materials
■ 5 1¾oz/50g hanks (each approx 136yd/125m) of Cascade Yarns *220 Superwash Sport* (superwash merino wool) in #871 white (MC)

■ 2 hanks each in #850 lime sherbet (A) and #1967 wisteria (B)

■ One pair size 6 (4mm) needles *or size to obtain gauge*

■ Size E/4 (3.5mm) crochet hook

Note
Squares are knitted on the diagonal.

Stitch Glossary
kf&b Inc 1 by knitting into the front and back of the next st.

Squares
With MC, cast on 3 sts. Use a contrasting-color yarn marker to mark center st for bottom left corner of square.
Row (inc) 1 (RS) K1, kf&b, k1—4 sts.
Row (inc) 2 K1, kf&b, knit to end of row—5 sts.
Rep row 2 until there are 52 sts on needle.
Next (dec) row K1, ktog, knit to end of row. Rep last row until 3 sts rem. Bind off knitwise. Make 9 more squares using MC, then 5 squares each using A and B.

Finishing
Block squares to measure 6½" x 6¾"/16.5cm x 16.5cm. Referring to placement diagram, arrange squares, making sure RS are facing and marked bottom corners are at left. Sew squares tog using MC.

EDGING
With RS facing and crochet hook, join MC with a sl st in any corner.
Rnd 1 (RS) Ch 1, making sure that work lies flat, sc evenly around entire edge, working 3 sc in each corner, join rnd with a sl st in first sc.
Rnd 2 (RS) Ch 1, working from left to right, reverse sc in each st around, join rnd with a sl st in first sc. Fasten off. ■

Placement Diagram

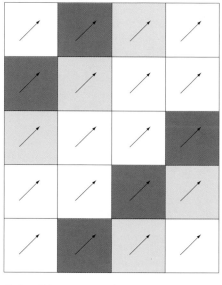

Color Key
□ White (MC)
□ Lime Sherbet (A)
■ Wisteria (B)

↑ = Direction of work

Gauge
22 sts and 46 rows to 4"/10cm over garter st (knit every row) using size 6 (4mm) needles.
Each square measures 6½" x 6½"/16.5cm x 16.5cm (after blocking). *Take time to check gauge.*

Lace Panel Pullover

A lovely lace panel and picot edgings give this chic pullover feminine flair. The body is knit in the round from the bottom to the underarm, then knit back and forth.

DESIGNED BY JOLENE TREACE

■■■■

Sizes

Instructions are written for size 6 months. Changes for 12 and 18 months are in parentheses. (Shown in size 6 months.)

Knitted Measurements

Chest 21 (22, 23)"/53.5 (56, 58.5)cm
Length 10¼ (11¼, 12)"/26 (28.5, 30.5)cm
Upper arm 7½ (8¼, 8½)"/19 (21, 21.5)cm

Materials

■ 3 (3, 4) 1¾oz/50g hanks (each approx 136yd/125m) of Cascade Yarns *220 Superwash Sport* (superwash merino wool) in #1941 salmon

■ One set (5) size 4 (3.5mm) double-pointed needles (dpns) *or size to obtain gauge*

■ Size 3 (3.25mm) circular needle, 16"/40cm long

■ One set (5) size 3 (3.25mm) double-pointed needles

■ Stitch markers

■ Three ½"/13mm buttons

Picot Point Cast-On

Using the knitted cast-on method, cast on 5 sts, then bind off 2 sts. *Slip st on right needle to left needle, cast on 6 sts, bind off 2 sts; rep from * to end, cast on 1 st more.

Notes

1) Sweater is made in one piece from bottom up.
2) To work in the round, always read chart from right to left.
3) To work back and forth, always read chart from right to left on RS rows and from left to right on WS rows.

Pullover

BODY

With smaller dpns, cast on 122 (128, 136) sts using picot point cast-on. Join, taking care not to twist sts on needles; pm for beg of rnds.
Rnd 1 Purl.
Rnd 2 Knit. Rep last 2 rnds for 1"/2.5cm, ending with rnd 2 and inc 6 (6, 4) sts evenly on last rnd—128 (134, 140) sts. Change to larger dpns.
Next rnd K23 (25, 27), pm, work row 1 of chart, pm, k23 (25, 27), pm (side marker), k65 (67, 69). Work even in pat as set until piece measures 6½ (7, 7½)"/16.5 (18, 19)cm from beg. Place all sts on holder. End of rnd is opposite side marker.

SLEEVES

With smaller dpns, cast on 32 (36, 36) sts using picot point cast-on. Join, taking care not to twist sts on needles, pm for beg of rnds.
Rnd 1 Purl.

Rnd 2 Knit. Rep last 2 rnds for 1"/2.5cm, ending with rnd 2 and inc 2 (0, 0) sts evenly on last rnd—34 (36, 36) sts. Change to larger dpns.
Next (inc) rnd K1, yo, knit to last st, yo, k1—36 (38, 38) sts. Rep inc rnd every 7 rnds 5 (6, 7) times—46 (50, 52) sts. Work even until piece measures 6½ (7½, 8)"/16.5 (19, 20.5)cm.
Next rnd Knit to last 4 sts, bind off next 8 sts (last 4 sts of this rnd and first 4 sts of next). Place rem sts on holder—38 (42, 44) sts.

JOIN BODY AND SLEEVES

Rnd 1 Drop beg of rnd marker on body and knit to 4 sts before side marker, bind off next 8 sts for underarm, k29 (30, 31) and pm to mark placket and new beg of rnds, knit to 4 sts before opposite side marker, bind off 8 sts for underarm, work in pat to new end of rnd—112 (118, 124) sts.
Rnd 2 *Work in pat to 1 st before underarm bind-off, p1, pm, p1 on sleeve, knit across sleeve sts to last st, p1, pm, p1 on body; rep from * for second sleeve, work in pat to end—188 (202, 212) sts.
Rnd 3 (dec) *Work in pat to 2 sts before sleeve marker, k2tog, slip marker, ssk; rep from * around—8 sts dec.
Rnd 4 Work even in pat, purling dec from previous rnd.
Work in pat until a total of 5 dec rnds

Gauge

24 sts and 32 rows to 4"/10cm over St st using size 4 (3.5mm) needles. *Take time to check gauge.*

8

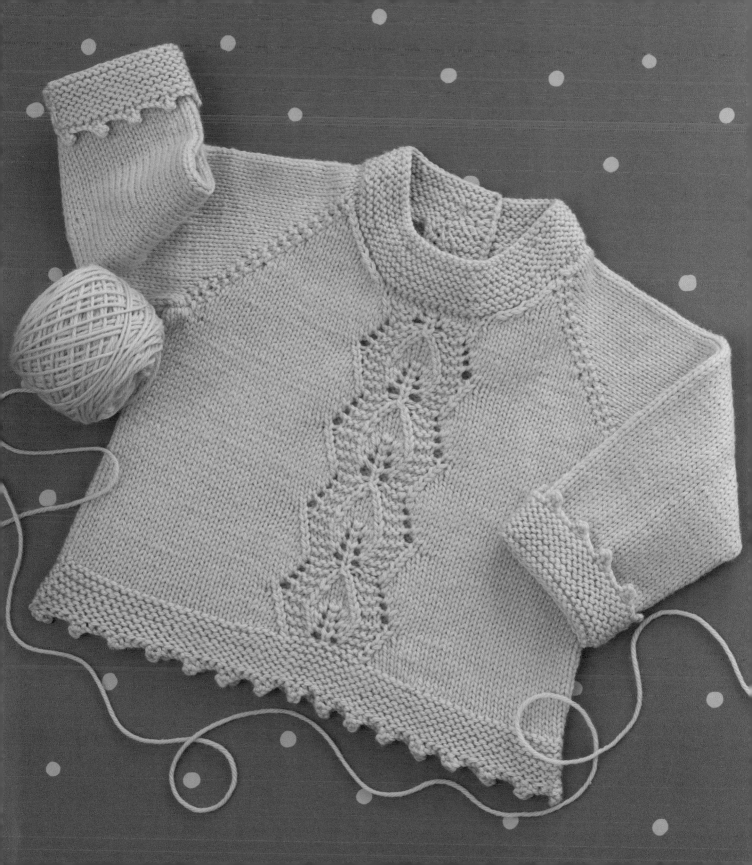

Lace Panel Pullover

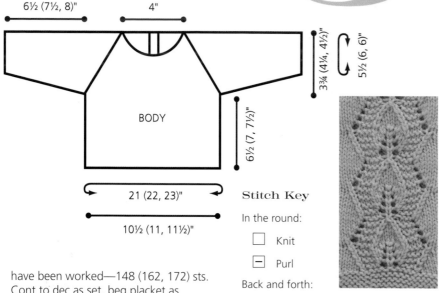

6½ (7½, 8)"   4"

3¾ (4¼, 4½)"   5½ (6, 6)"

BODY

6½ (7, 7½)"

21 (22, 23)"

10½ (11, 11½)"

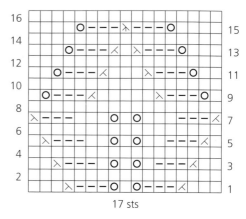

17 sts

Stitch Key

In the round:

☐ Knit

☐ Purl

Back and forth:

☐ K on RS, p on WS

☐ P on RS, K on WS

⊠ K2tog

⊠ Ssk

⊠ SK2P

⊙ Yo

have been worked—148 (162, 172) sts. Cont to dec as set, beg placket as follows:

PLACKET AND YOKE
Next rnd Working in pat as set, work to end of rnd marker at placket location, bind off 7 sts, work in pat to end. From this point forward, work back and forth in rows as follows. **Note** Work St st (k on RS, p on WS; work WS chart rows in purl).
Row 1 (dec) *Work in pat to 2 sts before sleeve marker, k2tog, slip marker, ssk; rep from * across—8 sts dec.
Row 2 Work even in pat, knitting dec from previous rnd.

NECK SHAPING
Cont dec as set until a total of 15 (17, 18) dec rows have been worked (sizes 12 and 18 months only, omit dec on front and back on last dec rnd only, working only sleeve dec), and, AT THE SAME TIME, when piece measures 1"/2.5cm from placket bind-off, ending with a WS row, shape neck as follows:

Next row (RS) Work in pat to center 9 sts of front, join a second ball of yarn and bind off center 9 sts, work in pat to end. Working both sides at once, cont in pat, dec 2 sts at each neck edge every other row once, then dec 1 st each neck edge every other row twice. When all dec rnds are complete, bind off—44 (46, 48) sts.

Finishing
PLACKET AND NECKBAND
With circular needle and RS facing, pick up and knit 16 sts along right placket edge, cont around neck, pick up 1 st in each bound-off st, and 34 (35, 36) sts along front neck shaping. Cont to pick up 1 st in each bound-off st around, pick up and knit 16 sts along left placket edge.

Turn work, cast on 8 sts using knitted cast-on.
Next row (WS) Sl 1, k6, k2tog (last cast-on st and first st of placket), turn.
Next row Sl 1, k7, turn.
Rep last 2 rows a total of 16 times—32 rows. Break yarn. Cast on 8 sts on smaller dpns and work as for first placket on right placket edge as follows:
Next row (RS) Sl 1, k6, k2tog (last cast-on st and first st of placket), turn.
Next row Sl 1, k7, turn. Rep last 2 rows a total of 16 times—32 rows. At the same time, add buttonholes every 12 rows as follows twice:
Next (buttonhole) row (RS) Sl 1, k1, k2tog, yo, k3, k2tog.
Next row Sl 1, k7, turn. Work even until placket measures same as first placket. Work across all sts in garter st (knit all rows), slipping the first st of each row, for 4 rows—94 (97, 100) sts.
Next row (dec) Sl 1, knit, dec 6 (7, 8) sts evenly across—88 (90, 92) sts.
Work 1 more buttonhole as before at beg of RS row, then work even until neckband measures 1"/2.5cm. Bind off. Sew underarm seams. Sew buttons opposite buttonholes. Fold up sleeve cuffs. ■

Elephant Onesie

A band of Fair Isle elephants makes a plain onesie big-top ready. It's unforgettable.

DESIGNED BY DANIELA NII

Sizes

Instructions are written for 3 months. Changes for 6 months are in parentheses. (Shown in size 6 months.)

Knitted Measurements

Chest 18 (21)"/45.5 (53.5)cm
Length 15 (16¼)"/38 (41)cm (with shoulders and crotch buttoned)

Materials

■ 2 (3) 1¾oz/50g hanks (each approx 136yd/125m) of Cascade Yarns *220 Superwash Sport* (superwash merino wool) in #897 baby denim (MC)

■ 1 hank each in #845 denim (A) and #871 white (B)

■ One pair size 6 (4mm) needles *or size to obtain gauge*

■ Size 6 (4mm) circular needle, 16"/40cm long

■ Stitch holder

■ Stitch markers

■ Seven ⁷⁄₁₆"/11mm buttons

■ Sewing needle and light blue sewing thread

Note

Lower front and lower back are worked separately, then the body is worked in the round to underarms.

Onesie

FRONT

Beg at crotch, with straight needles and MC, cast on 19 (21) sts. Work in garter st (knit every row) for 4 rows, end with a WS row. **Next row (RS)** K3, pm, k13 (15), pm, k3. **Next row** K3, sl marker, p13 (15), sl marker, k3. Keeping 3 sts each side in garter st and rem sts in St st (k on RS, p on WS), cont as foll: **Next (inc) row (RS)** K3, sl marker, k1, M1, knit to 1 st before next marker, M1, k1, sl marker, k3. **Next row** K3, sl marker, purl to next marker, sl marker, k3. Rep last 2 rows 6 (7) times more—33 (37) sts.

LEGBANDS

Row 1 (RS) Cast on 7 (9) sts, knit to end, dropping markers, cast on 7 (9) sts—47 (55) sts. **Row 2** K10 (12), purl to last 10 (12) sts, k10 (12). **Row 3** Knit. **Row 4** Rep row 2. Place sts on holder.

BACK

Beg at crotch, with straight needles and MC, cast on 19 (21) sts. Work in garter st (knit every row) for 4 rows, end with a WS row. **Next row (RS)** K3, pm, k13 (15), pm, k3. **Next row** K3, sl marker, p13 (15), sl marker, k3. **Next (button-hole) row (RS)** K3, sl marker, *k2tog, yo, k3 (4); rep from * once more, end k2tog, yo, k1, sl marker, k3. Keeping 3 sts each side in garter st and rem sts in St st, cont as foll:

Next (inc) row (RS) K3, sl marker, k1, M1, knit to 1 st before next marker, M1, k1, sl

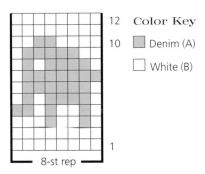

12

10

1

8-st rep

Color Key

▨ Denim (A)

☐ White (B)

Gauge

21 sts and 27 rows to 4"/10cm over St st using size 6 (4mm) needles. *Take time to check gauge.*

Elephant Onesie

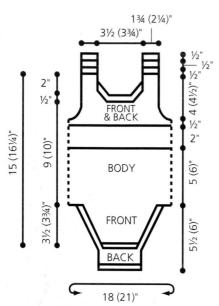

1¾ (2¼)"
3½ (3¾)"
2"
½"
15 (16¼)"
9 (10)"
FRONT & BACK
½"
½"
½"
4 (4½)"
½"
2"
BODY
5 (6)"
3½ (3¾)"
FRONT
BACK
5½ (6)"
18 (21)"

marker, k3. **Next row** K3, sl marker, purl to next marker, sl marker, k3. Rep last 2 rows 10 (11) times more—41 (45) sts.

LEGBANDS
Row 1 (RS) Cast on 4 (6) sts, knit to end, dropping markers, cast on 4 (6) sts—49 (57) sts. **Row 2** K7 (9), purl to last 7 (9) sts, k7 (9). **Row 3** Knit. **Row 4** Rep row 2. Leave sts on needle.

BODY
Next rnd With circular needle and MC, k 47 (55) sts from front holder, then k 49 (57) sts from back needle—96 (112) sts. Join and pm for beg of rnd. **Next rnd** Knit to 1 st before rnd marker, pm for new rnd marker, knit to end of rnd, dropping first rnd marker. **Next rnd** K48 (56), pm for side marker, knit to end of rnd. Cont in St st (knit every rnd) until piece measures 5 (6)"/12.5 (15cm) from legband cast-on. Change to A. Knit one rnd, purl one rnd for bottom garter st ridge.

BEG CHART PAT
Rnd 1 Work 8-st rep 12 (14) times. Cont to foll chart in this way to rnd 12. Change to A. Knit one rnd, purl one rnd for top garter st ridge. Change to MC.

DIVIDE FOR FRONT AND BACK

FRONT
Change to straight needles.

ARMBANDS
Row 1 (RS) K48 (56); leave rem 48 (56) sts on needle for back. **Row 2** K6 (7), purl to last 6 (7) sts, k6 (7).**Row 3** Knit. **Row 4** Rep row 2.

ARMHOLE SHAPING
Row 1 Bind off first 3 (4) sts, knit to end. **Row 2** Bind off first 3 (4) sts, purl to last 3 sts, k3—42 (48) sts. **Row 3** K3, pm, knit to last 3 sts, pm, k3. **Row 4** K3, sl marker, purl to last marker, sl marker, k3. **Row (dec) 5 (RS)** K3, sl marker, ssk, knit to 2 sts before last marker, k2tog, sl marker, k3. **Row 6** K3, sl marker, purl to last marker, sl marker, k3. Rep rows 5 and 6 once more—38 (44) sts. Keeping 3 sts each side in garter st and rem sts in St st, work even until armhole measures 1 (1½)"/2.5 (4)cm, end with a WS row.

NECK BORDER
Row 1 (RS) K3, sl marker, k8 (10), pm, k16 (18), pm, k8 (10), sl marker, k3. **Row 2** K3, sl marker, p8 (10), sl marker, k16 (18), sl marker, p8 (10), sl marker, k3. **Row 3** Knit. **Row 4** Rep row 2.

NECK SHAPING
Row 1 (RS) K14 (16), dropping markers, join a 2nd ball of yarn and bind off center 10 (12) sts, knit to end—14 (16) sts each

side. **Row 2** With first ball of yarn, k3, pm, p8 (10), pm, k3; with 2nd ball of yarn, k3, pm, p8 (10), pm, k3. **Row (dec) 3 (RS)** With first ball of yarn, k3, sl marker, knit to 2 sts before next marker, k2tog, sl marker, k3; with 2nd ball of yarn, k3, sl marker, ssk, knit to next marker, sl marker, k3. **Row 4** With first ball of yarn, k3, sl marker, purl to next marker, sl marker, k3; with 2nd ball of yarn, k3, sl marker, purl to next marker, sl marker, k3. Rep rows 3 and 4 three times more—10 (12) sts each side. Work even until armhole measures 4 (4½)"/10 (11.5)cm, end with a WS row, dropping all markers.

BUTTONBANDS
Work even in garter st for 4 rows. Bind off each side knitwise.

BACK
Work armbands and armhole shaping as for front—38 (44) sts. Work even until armhole measures 1½ (2)"/4 (5)cm, end with a WS row. Work neckband and neck shaping as for front—10 (12) sts each side. Work even until armhole measures 4¾ (5¼)"/12 (13.5)cm, end with a WS row.

BUTTONHOLE BANDS
Next row (RS) With first ball of yarn, k3, yo, k2tog, k0 (2), k2tog, yo, k3; with 2nd ball of yarn, k3, yo, k2tog, k0 (2), k2tog, yo, k3. **Next row** With first ball of yarn, k3, p4 (6), k3; with 2nd ball of yarn, k3, p4 (6), k3. Work even in garter st for 4 rows. Bind off each side knitwise.

Finishing
Block piece lightly to measurements. Sew legband and armband seams. Sew on buttons. ∎

5

Boatneck Pullover

A hint of texture dresses up a simple design, and the wide boatneck
makes dressing baby quick and easy.

DESIGNED BY ANN MCCAULEY

Sizes
Instructions are written for size 6 months.
Changes for 12 and 18 months are in
parentheses. (Shown in size 6 months.)

Knitted Measurements
Chest 19½ (22, 23½)"/49.5 (56,
59.5)cm
Length 10 (11, 12)"/25.5 (28, 30.5)cm
Upper arm 9 (10, 11)"/23 (25.5, 28)cm

Materials
■ 2 (3, 3) 1¾oz/50g hanks (each approx
136yd/125m) of Cascade Yarns *220
Superwash Sport* (superwash merino
wool) in #1910 summer sky heather

■ One pair size 5 (3.75mm) needles *or
size to obtain gauge*

Note
Sweater is made in one piece from lower
edge of front to lower edge
of back.

Broken Twisted Rib
(over a multiple of 2 sts)
Row 1 (RS) K1, *p1, k1tbl;
rep from *, end k1.
Row 2 K1, *p1tbl, p1;
rep from *, end k1.
Rep rows 1 and 2 for broken twisted rib.

Pattern Stitch
(over a multiple of 4 sts plus 2)
Row 1 and all WS rows K1 (selvage st),
purl to last st, end k1 (selvage st).
Row 2 (RS) Knit.
Row 4 K1, *k3, p1; rep from *, end k1.
Row 6 Knit.

Row 8 K2, *p1, k3; rep from * to end.
Rep rows 1–8 for pattern st.

Pullover
BACK
Cast on 58 (66, 70) sts. Work in broken
twisted rib for 9 rows, end with a RS row.
Cont in pattern st until piece measures
5½ (6, 6½)"/14 (15, 16.5)cm from beg,
end with a WS row.

SLEEVE SHAPING
Working new sts into pattern st,
cont as foll:
Cast on 6 sts at beg of next 0 (4, 12)
rows, 5 sts at beg of next 8 (8, 0) rows,
then 4 sts at beg of next 4 (0, 0) rows—
114 (130, 142) sts. Work even for 2 (2½,
3)"/5 (6.5, 7.5)cm, end with a WS row.
Cont in broken twisted rib for 9 rows,
end with a RS row.

NECK OPENING
Next row (WS) Work in broken twisted
rib over first 37 (45, 51) sts, join a 2nd
ball of yarn and bind off center 40 sts in
rib, work to end. Working both sides at
once, work next row even.

Gauge
23 sts and 33 rows to 4"/10cm over pattern st using size 5 (3.75mm) needles.
Take time to check gauge.

Boatneck Pullover

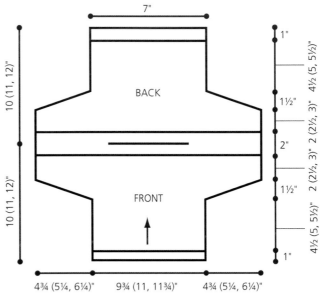

Diagram labels:
- 7"
- BACK
- FRONT
- 10 (11, 12)"
- 10 (11, 12)"
- 1"
- 4½ (5, 5½)"
- 1½"
- 2 (2½, 3)"
- 2"
- 2 (2½, 3)"
- 1½"
- 4½ (5, 5½)"
- 1"
- 4¾ (5¼, 6¼)"
- 9¾ (11, 11¾)"
- 4¾ (5¼, 6¼)"

 = Direction of work

Next row (WS) With first hank of yarn, work in broken twisted rib over first 37 (45, 51) sts, knit or cable cast-on 40 sts, with same hank of yarn, work to end—114 (130, 142) sts. Cut 2nd hank of yarn. Cont in broken twisted rib for 9 rows, end with a RS row. Cont in pattern st and work even for 2 (2½, 3)"/5 (6.5, 7.5)cm, end with a WS row.

SLEEVE SHAPING
Bind off 4 sts at beg of next 4 (0, 0) rows, 5 sts at beg of next 8 (8, 0) rows, then 6 sts at beg of next 0 (4, 12) rows—58 (66, 70) sts. Work even for 4½ (5, 5½)"/ 11.5 (12.5, 14)cm, end with a WS row. Cont in broken twisted rib for 9 rows. Bind off loosely in rib.

Finishing
Block piece lightly to measurements.

CUFFS
With RS facing, pick up and k 34 (38, 42) sts evenly spaced across sleeve edge. Beg with row 2, cont in broken twisted rib for 6 rows. Bind off in rib. Sew side and sleeve seams. ■

Quick Tip
To make sure a garment will fit your baby before knitting, measure a favorite sweater and choose the size that's closest.

Simple Sleep Sack

Two are better than one! Knit a pair of sleep sacks as a sweet gift for twins.

DESIGNED BY JEANNIE CHIN

Size
Instructions are written for newborn–3 months.

Knitted Measurements
Chest (closed) 20"/51cm
Length 20"/51cm

Materials
■ 3 1¾oz/50g hanks (each approx 136yd/125m) of Cascade Yarns *220 Superwash Sport* (superwash merino wool) in #1946 silver grey (MC)

■ 1 hank each in #897 baby denim (CC) or #894 strawberry cream (CC)

■ One pair each sizes 5 and 6 (3.75 and 4mm) needles *or size to obtain gauge*

■ Size 5 (3.75mm) circular needle, 29"/74cm long

■ Eight size 1 metal snap fasteners

■ Sewing needle and sewing thread

Stitch Glossary
Inc 3 (on RS row) Work (k1, M1, k1) in same stitch.
Inc 3 (on WS row) Work (p1, M1 p-st, p1) in same stitch.

K1, P1 Rib
(over a multiple of 2 sts plus 1)
Row 1 (RS) K1, *p1, k1; rep from * to end.
Row 2 P1, *k1, p1; rep from * to end.
Rep rows 1 and 2 for k1, p1 rib.

Back
With larger needles and MC, cast on 38 sts. Purl next row. Beg with a knit row, cont in St st (k on RS, p on WS) as foll:

BOTTOM SHAPING
Cast on 5 sts at beg of next 2 rows, then 3 sts at beg of next 6 rows—66 sts.
Inc row (RS) K1, M1, knit to last st, M1, k1—68 sts. Purl next row. Rep last 2 rows 8 times more, end with a WS row—84 sts. Work even until piece measures 5¾"/14.5cm from beg, end with a WS row.

SIDE SHAPING
Dec row (RS) K1, k2tog, knit to last 3 sts, ssk, k1—82 sts.
Rep dec row every 8th row 7 times more, then every 6th row 3 times—62 sts. Work even until piece measures 16"/40.5cm from beg, end with a WS row.

ARMHOLE SHAPING
Bind off 4 sts at beg of next 2 rows.
Dec row (RS) K1, k2tog, knit to last 3 sts, ssk, k1. Purl next row. Rep last 2 rows 4 times more—44 sts. Work even until armhole measures 3½"/9cm, end with a WS row.

Gauge
25 sts and 33 rows to 4"/10cm over St st using larger needles.
Take time to check gauge.

Simple Sleep Sack

NECK SHAPING
Next row (RS) K15, join a 2nd ball of yarn and bind off center 14 sts, k15. Working both sides at once, bind off 3 sts from each neck edge twice. Work even on 9 sts each side until armhole measures 4"/10cm. Bind off each side for shoulders.

Right Front
Work as for back to side shaping—84 sts. Work even until piece measures 5½"/14cm from beg, end with a WS row.

SIDE SHAPING
Next row (RS) Bind off first 4 sts, knit to end—80 sts. Work next row even.
Dec row (RS) K1, k2tog, knit to last 3 sts, ssk, k1—78 sts.
Rep dec row every 8th row 6 times more—66 sts.

CONT SIDE SHAPING AND BEG NECK SHAPING
Cont to dec 1 st at side edge (end of RS rows) every 8th row once more, then every 6th row 3 times. AT THE SAME TIME, shape neck as foll:
Row 1 (RS) K1, k3tog, work to end.
Row 2 Purl.
Row 3 Knit, working neck edge even.
Row 4 (WS) Purl to last 4 sts, p3tog, p1.
Row 5 Knit, working neck edge even.
Row 6 Purl.
Rep rows 1–6 ten times more. AT THE SAME TIME, when piece measures same length as back to underarm, end with a RS row. Shape armhole at side edge as for back. When all shaping has been completed, work even on 9 sts until piece measures same length as back to shoulder, end with a WS row. Bind off.

Left Front
With larger needles and MC, cast on 2 sts.

FRONT EDGE AND SIDE SHAPING
Row 1 (RS) Knit.
Row 2 Purl.
Row 3 Knit.
Row 4 (WS) Inc 3 in first st, p1—4 sts.
Row 5 Knit.
Row 6 Purl.
Row 7 K1, k2tog, inc 3 in last st—5 sts.
Row 8 Purl.
Row 9 Knit.
Row 10 Inc 3 in first st, p4—7 sts.
Row 11 Knit.
Row 12 Purl.
Row 13 K1, k2tog, k3, inc 3 in last st—8 sts.
Row 14 Purl.
Row 15 Knit.
Row 16 Inc 3 in first st, p7—10 sts.
Row 17 Knit.
Row 18 Purl.
Row 19 K1, k2tog, k6, inc 3 in last st—11 sts.
Row 20 Purl.
Row 21 Knit.
Row 22 Inc 3 in first st, p10—13 sts.
Row 23 Knit.
Row 24 Purl.
Row 25 K1, k2tog, k9, inc 3 in last st—14 sts.
Row 26 Inc 3 in first st, p13—16 sts.
Rows 27 and 29 Knit.
Rows 28 and 30 Purl.
Row 31 K15, inc 3 in last st—18 sts.
Row 32 Purl.

CONT FRONT SHAPING AND BEG ARMHOLE SHAPING
Row 33 (RS) Bind off first 4 sts, k13—14 sts.
Row 34 Inc 3 in first st, p13—16 sts.
Row 35 K1, k2tog, k13—15 sts.
Row 36 Purl.
Row 37 K1, k2tog, k11, inc 3 in last st—16 sts.
Row 38 Purl.
Row 39 K1, k2tog, k13—15 sts.
Row 40 Inc 3 in first st, p14—17 sts.
Row 41 K1, k2tog, k14—16 sts.
Row 42 Purl.
Row 43 K15, inc 3 in last st—18 sts.
Row 44 Purl.
Row 45 K1, k2tog, k15—17 sts.
Row 46 Inc 3 in first st, p16—19 sts.
Row 47 Knit.
Row 48 Purl.
Row 49 K18, inc 3 in last st—21 sts.

NECK SHAPING
Row 50 P1, p3tog-tbl, p17—19 sts.
Row 51 Knit.
Row 52 Purl.
Row 53 Knit to last 4 sts, k3tog-tbl, k1—17 sts.
Row 54 Purl.
Row 55 Knit.
Row 56 P1, p3tog-tbl, p13—15 sts.
Row 57 Knit.
Row 58 Purl.
Row 59 Knit to last 4 sts, k3tog-tbl, k1—13 sts.
Row 60 Purl.
Row 61 Knit.
Row 62 P1, p3tog-tbl, p9—11 sts.
Row 63 Knit.
Row 64 Purl.
Row 65 Knit to last 4 sts, k3tog-tbl, k1—9 sts.
Row 66 Purl. Bind off.

6 Simple Sleep Sack

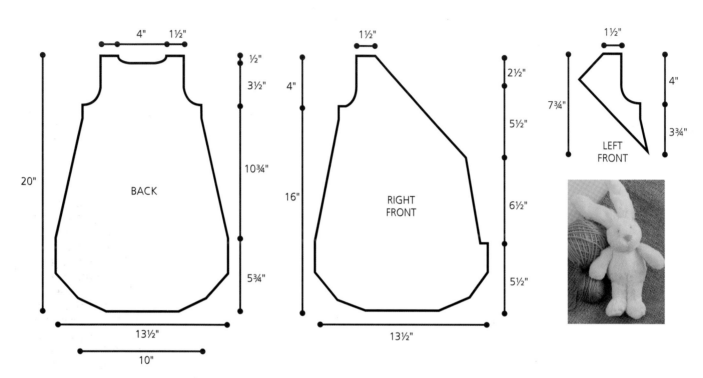

Finishing

Block piece lightly to measurements. Sew shoulder seams.

ARMBANDS

With RS facing, smaller needles, and CC, pick up and k 63 sts evenly spaced along armhole edge. Beg with row 2, cont in k1, p1 rib for 4 rows. Bind off in rib.

RIGHT FRONT BAND AND NECKBAND

With RS facing, circular needle, and CC, beg at 4 bound-off sts, pick up and k 113 sts evenly spaced along right front and neck edge to right shoulder, 32 sts across back neck to left shoulder, then 18 sts along left front neck—163 sts. Beg with row 2, work in k1, p1 rib for 4 rows. Bind off loosely in rib. Sew seams in order as foll: sew right armband and right side seam, bottom seam, then bottom left side seam to 4 bound-off sts on right front. Sew left armband and left side seam.

LEFT FRONT BAND

With RS facing, circular needle, and CC, pick up and k 5 sts across side edge of right front band, then 92 sts evenly spaced to bound-off 4 sts on right front—97 sts. Beg with row 2, work in k1, p1 rib for 4 rows. Bind off in rib. Sew side edge of right front band to 4 bound-off sts. Sew side edge of left front band to side edge of right front band. Place markers for top halves of 8 snaps on WS of right front band, with the first 1"/2.5cm from bottom edge of band, the last 3"/7.5cm from shoulder seam, and 6 more evenly spaced between. Sew on top halves of snaps. Sew on bottom halves along left front band. ■

Ruffled Pants

Pretty ruffles that are picked up and knit take pants from plain to fiesta-ready. Olé!

DESIGNED BY MARY SCOTT HUFF

Sizes
Instructions are written for size 6 months. Changes for 12 and 18 months are in parentheses. (Shown in size 6 months.)

Knitted Measurements
Waist 19 (20, 20½)"/48 (51, 52)cm
Length 14 (15½, 17)"/35.5 (39.5, 43)cm
Rise 5¼ (6, 6½)"/13.5 (15, 16.5)cm

Materials
■ 2 (2, 3) 1¾oz/50g hanks (each approx 136yd/125m) of Cascade Yarns *220 Superwash Sport* (superwash merino wool) in #1940 peach (MC)

■ 2 hanks in #827 coral (CC)

■ Size 3 (3.25mm) circular needle, 16"/40cm long, *or size to obtain gauge*

■ One set each (5) sizes 2 (2.75mm) and 3 (3.25mm) double-pointed needles (dpns)

■ Stitch markers

■ Stitch holders

■ Waste yarn

■ ¾"/19mm elastic, 1yd/1m

Stitch Glossary
M1R (make 1 right) Insert left needle from back to front into the horizontal strand between the last st worked and the next st on left needle. Knit this strand through the front loop to twist the st.
M1L (make 1 left) Insert left needle from front to back into the horizontal strand between the last st worked and the next st on left needle. Knit this strand through the back loop to twist the st.

Pants
LEGS (make 2)
With smaller dpns and CC, cast on 60 (63, 67) sts. Join, taking care not to twist sts on needles, pm for beg of rnds. Work in St st (k all rnds) for 8 rnds. Purl next rnd (turning ridge). Change to larger dpns. Work in St st for 8 rnds. Change to MC. Work even in St st until piece measures 3"/7.5cm from turning ridge. **Next (inc) rnd** *K1, M1L, knit to last st, M1R, k1—62 (65, 69) sts. Rep inc rnd every 4 rows 7 times—76 (79, 83) sts. Work even until piece measures 8 (8¾, 9¾)"/20.5 (22, 25)cm from turning ridge. Working back and forth in rows on dpns, dec 1 st each end of row once—74 (77, 81) sts. Work even until piece measures 8¾ (9½, 10½)"/22 (24, 26.5)cm from turning ridge. Bind off 3 (3, 4) sts at beg of next 2 rows—68 (71, 73) sts.
Set aside.

Gauge
28 sts and 38 rows to 4"/10cm over St st using size 3 (circular or dpn) (3.25mm) needles.
Take time to check gauge.

Ruffled Pants

Body

With circular needle, knit across one leg, then the other—136 (142, 146) sts. Join, taking care not to twist sts on needle, pm for beg of rnds. Work even in St st until piece measures 13 (14½, 16)"/33 (37, 40.5)cm from turning ridge.

WAISTBAND

Change to CC. Knit 8 rnds. Purl next rnd (turning ridge). Knit 8 rnds more. Bind off. Fold band to inside and sew in place, leaving 1"/2.5cm open to insert elastic.

GUSSET

Holding pants upside down, pick up and knit 4 (4, 6) sts at base of crotch opening [2 (2, 3) sts from each leg], turn.
Next row (WS) Purl.
Next row K1, M1R, knit to last st, M1L, k1. Rep last 2 rows until there are 20 (20, 22) sts, ending with a WS row. Work 2 rows even in St st (k on RS, p on WS).
Next row (RS) K1, ssk, knit to last 3 sts, k2tog, k1.
Next row Purl. Rep last 2 rows until there are 4 (4, 6) sts, ending with a WS row. Bind off. Cut yarn, leaving a long tail for sewing. Sew rem 3 sides of gusset to upper edges of legs.

RUFFLES

Mark 1"/2.5cm, 2¼"/5.5cm, and 3½"/9cm down from bottom of waistband on back of pants to mark location of ruffles. With RS facing,

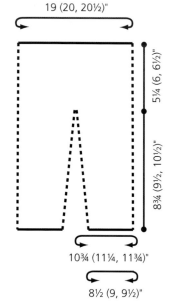

circular needle, and CC, pick up and knit 68 (70, 72) sts across back of pants at first marker.
Next row Knit into front and back of each st across—136 (140, 144) sts. Continuing with a purl row, work in St st for 8 rows. Knit 3 rows. Bind off. Rep for rem 2 ruffles.

Finishing

Weave in ends. Cut a 19 (20, 20½)"/48 (51, 52)cm length of elastic. Thread through waistband, overlap ends, and sew securely. Sew opening in waistband closed. Fold up ends of cuffs along turning ridge and sew in place. ■

19 (20, 20½)"

5¼ (6, 6½)"

8¾ (9½, 10½)"

10¾ (11¼, 11¾)"

8½ (9, 9½)"

Striped Socks

Alternating light and dark stripes create a subtle color pattern; use contrasting colors for a more graphic look. Reversing the order of the colors between the socks creates a fun surprise.

DESIGNED BY HOLLI YEOH

Size
Instructions are written for size 6 months.

Knitted Measurements
Foot circumference 6"/15cm
Foot length 4½"/11.5cm

Materials
- 1 1¾oz/50g hank (approx 136yd/125m) of Cascade Yarns *220 Superwash Sport* (superwash merino wool) each in #893 ruby (MC) and #808 sunset orange (CC)
- One set (5) size 2 (2.75mm) double-pointed needles (dpns) *or size to obtain gauge*
- Stitch marker

Notes
1) For 2nd sock, use sunset orange as MC and ruby as CC. **2)** When working stripes, carry color not in use up WS.

K2, P2 Rib
(over a multiple of 4 sts)
Rnd 1 (RS) *K2, p2; rep from * around. Rep rnd 1 for k2, p2 rib.

First Sock
CUFF
With MC, cast on 44 sts. Divide sts over 4 needles (11 sts on each). Join, taking care not to twist sts, pm for beg of rnds. Work in k2, p2 rib for 6 rnds. Cont in St st and stripe pat as foll: 1 rnd CC and 1 rnd MC. Rep these 2 rnds until piece measures 1¾"/4.5cm from beg, end with 1 rnd CC. Cont with CC as foll:

BEG HEEL FLAP
Note Heel flap is worked back and forth on one needle over half the sts; rem 22 sts are on hold. **Next row (RS)** With CC, sl 1, k21; turn—22 sts for heel flap. **Next row (WS)** *Sl 1, p1; rep from * to end of heel flap. **Next row (RS)** Sl 1, knit to end of row. Rep last 2 rows until there are 11 edge chain sts on selvages each side, ending with a WS row.

TURN HEEL
Row 1 (RS) Sl 1, k12, ssk, k1; turn.
Row 2 Sl 1, p5, p2tog, p1; turn. **Row 3** Sl 1, knit to 1 st before gap, ssk, k1; turn.
Row 4 Sl 1, purl to 1 st before gap, p2tog, p1; turn. Cont in this manner until all sts have been worked, ending with a RS row—14 heel sts. Cut yarn.

GUSSET
Next rnd With free needles and MC, pick up and k 11 sts into edge chain sts along right side of heel, k7 across turned heel sts—this is now Needle 4. *Needle 1* Knit rem half of turned heel sts, then pick up and k 11 sts into edge chain sts along opposite side of heel. *Needle 2* Knit sts from next needle. *Needle 3* Knit sts from next needle. *Needle 4* Knit sts from next needle—58 sts. Pm for beg of rnds. You will now be working in a stripe pat of 8 rnds MC, 9 rnds CC, and 9 rnds MC. AT THE SAME TIME, work as foll: **Dec rnd** *Needle 1* Knit to last 3 sts, k2tog, k1; *Needles 2 and 3* Knit; *Needle 4* K1, ssk, knit to end—56 sts. Knit next rnd. Rep last 2 rnds 6 times more—44 sts.

FOOT
Work even until stripe pat is completed. Change to CC and cont as foll:

TOE
Dec rnd *Needle 1* Knit to last 3 sts, k2tog, k1; *Needle 2* K1, ssk, knit to end; *Needle 3* Knit to last 3 sts, k2tog, k1; *Needle 4* K1, ssk, knit to end—40 sts. Knit next rnd. Rep last 2 rnds 3 times more—28 sts. Rep dec rnd only 3 times more—16 sts. Cut yarn, leaving a 12"/30.5cm tail, and graft toe sts tog using Kitchener stitch. Sew holes at beg of gussets closed.

Second Sock
Work as for first sock, using sunset orange as MC and ruby as CC. ■

Gauge
31 sts and 42 rnds to 4"/10cm over St st (k every rnd) using size 2 (2.75mm) dpns. *Take time to check gauge.*

Wave Motif Pullover

Two shades of blue dotted on a white background create sparkle above the ocean waves. Seed stitch edgings add depth and texture.

DESIGNED BY LOIS S. YOUNG

Sizes
Instructions are written for size 6 months. Changes for 12 and 18 months are in parentheses. (Shown in size 6 months.)

Knitted Measurements
Chest 19½ (22, 24)"/49.5 (56, 61)cm
Length 10 (11, 12)"/25.5 (28, 30.5)cm
Upper arm 9 (10, 11)"/23 (25.5, 28)cm

Materials
■ 2 (3, 3) 1¾oz/50g hanks (each approx 136yd/125m) of Cascade Yarns *220 Superwash Sport* (superwash merino wool) in #871 white (MC)

■ 1 hank each in #813 blue velvet (A) and #845 denim (B)

■ Sizes 4 and 6 (3.5 and 4mm) circular needles, 16"/41cm long, *or size to obtain gauge*

■ One pair each sizes 4 and 6 (3.5 and 4mm) needles

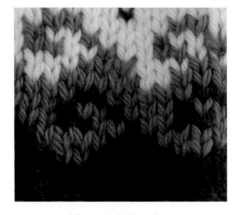

■ One set (5) size 4 (3.5mm) double-pointed needles (dpns)

■ Stitch holders

■ Stitch marker

Notes
1) Body is worked in one piece to the underarms.
2) Sleeves are worked back and forth.
3) To work in the rnd, always read chart from right to left.
4) To work back and forth, always read charts from right to left on RS rows and from left to right on WS rows.

Seed Stitch
(over a multiple of 2 sts)
Rnd 1 *K1, p1; rep from * around.
Rnd 2 *P1, k1; rep from * around. Rep rnds 1 and 2 for seed st.

Body
With smaller circular needle and A, cast on 112 (126, 140) sts. Join and pm for beg of rnds. Work around in seed st for 9 rnds. Change to larger circular needle and St st (knit all rnds).

BEG CHART PAT 1
Rnd 1 Work 7-st rep 16 (18, 20) times. Cont to foll chart in this way through rnd 34 (38, 42).

DIVIDE FOR BACK AND FRONT
Change to larger straight needles.
Row 35 (39, 43) (RS) Work across first 56 (63, 70) sts. Leave rem 56 (63, 70) sts on circular needle for front.

BACK
Cont to work back and forth foll chart through row 70 (78, 86).

Gauge
23 sts and 32 rnds to 4"/10cm over St st and chart pats using larger circular needle.
Take time to check gauge.

Wave Motif Pullover

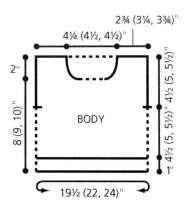

NECK AND SHOULDER SHAPING
Next row (RS) With MC only, bind off first 16 (19, 22) sts for shoulder, knit until there are 24 (25, 26) sts on RH needle, place these sts on holder for back neck, bind off rem 16 (19, 22) sts.

FRONT
Change to larger straight needles.
Row 35 (39, 43) (RS) Work across rem 56 (63, 70) sts. Cont to work back and forth foll chart through row 56 (64, 72).

NECK SHAPING
Row 55 (59, 63) Work across first 19 (22, 25) sts, place next 18 (19, 20) sts on holder for front neck, join a 2nd ball of color in progress and work to end. Working both sides at once, work next row even.
Next (dec) row (RS) With first hank of yarn, work to last 3 sts, with MC, k2tog, k1; with 2nd hank of MC, k1, ssk, work to end. Work next row even. Rep last 2 rows twice more. Work even on 16 (19, 22) sts each side through row 70 (78, 86). With MC only, bind off each side for shoulders.

Sleeves
With smaller straight needles and A, cast on 29 (31, 35) sts. Cont in seed st as foll:
Next row (RS) K1, *p1, k1; rep from * to end. Rep this row 8 times more, end with a RS row.
Next (inc) row (WS) Purl across, inc 4 (6, 6) sts evenly spaced—33 (37, 41) sts. Change to larger straight needles and St st (knit on RS, purl on WS).

BEG CHART 2
Row 1 (RS) Beg chart where indicated for size being made and work to rep line, work 7-st rep 4 times, then end chart where indicated for size being made. Work even for 3 rows. Inc 1 st each side on next row, then every 4th row 8 (9, 10) times more—51 (57, 63) sts. Work even foll chart through row 47 (51, 59). With MC, bind off purlwise.

Finishing
Block pieces lightly to measurements. Sew shoulder seams.

NECKBAND
With RS facing, dpn and A, beg at left shoulder seam and pick up and k 13 sts evenly spaced along left neck edge, k 18 (19, 20) sts from front neck holder, pick up and k 13 sts evenly spaced along right neck edge to shoulder, k 24 (25, 26) sts from back neck holder—68 (70, 72) sts. Divide sts evenly between 4 needles. Join and pm for beg of rnds. Work around in seed st for 7 rnds. Bind off loosely in seed st. Sew sleeve seams. Set in sleeves. ■

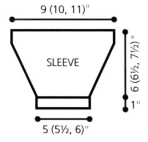

2¾ (3¼, 3¾)"

4¼ (4½, 4½)"

2"

8 (9, 10)"

BODY

4½ (5, 5½)" 4½ (5, 5½)"

1"

19½ (22, 24)"

9 (10, 11)"

SLEEVE

6 (6½, 7½)"

1"

5 (5½, 6)"

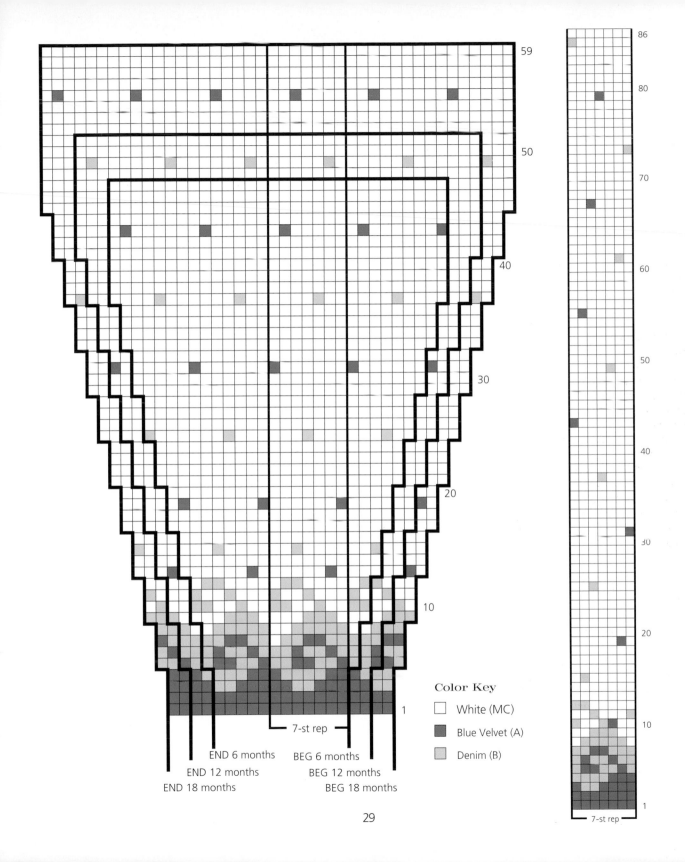

59

50

40

30

20

10

1

7-st rep

END 6 months

END 12 months

END 18 months

BEG 6 months

BEG 12 months

BEG 18 months

Color Key

☐ White (MC)

■ Blue Velvet (A)

▨ Denim (B)

86

80

70

60

50

40

30

20

10

1

7-st rep

29

Sleeveless Lace Dress

With a stockinette stitch bodice and eyelet skirt, this little dress would look lovely on its own as a sundress or over a blouse or T-shirt.

DESIGNED BY GRACE AKHREM

Sizes

Instructions are written for size 3 months. Changes for 6 and 12 months are in parentheses. (Shown in size 3 months.)

Knitted Measurements

Chest (closed) 17 (19, 21)"/43 (48, 53)cm
Length 14½ (16, 18)"/37 (40.5, 46)cm

Materials

- 3 (4, 5) 1¾ oz/50g hanks (each approx 136yd/125m) of Cascade Yarns *220 Superwash Sport* (superwash merino wool) in #826 tangerine
- Size 4 (3.5mm) circular needle, 16"/40cm long, *or size to obtain gauge*
- Size 5 (3.75mm) circular needle, 16"/40cm long, *or size to obtain gauge*
- Scrap yarn
- Stitch marker
- One ¾"/19mm button
- Size E/4 (3.5mm) crochet hook
- ⅜"/10mm ribbon, 24"/61cm long

Lace Pattern

(multiple of 4 sts)
Rnd 1 Knit around.
Rnd 2 *Yo, ssk, p2; rep from * around.
Rnd 3 *K2, p2; rep from * around.
Rnd 4 *K2tog, yo, p2; rep from * around.
Rnd 5 *K2, p2; rep from * around.
Work rnds 2–5 for lace pattern.

Provisional Method Cast-on

Using scrap yarn and crochet hook, ch the number of sts to cast on plus a few extra. Cut a tail and pull the tail through the last chain. With knitting needle and yarn, pick up and knit the stated number of sts through the "purl bumps" on the back of the chain. To remove waste chain, when instructed, pull out the tail from the last crochet stitch. Gently and slowly pull on the tail to unravel the crochet stitches, carefully placing each released knit stitch on a needle.

Dress

SKIRT
Using provisional method and larger needle, cast on 100 (112, 124) sts. Place marker (pm) and join, being careful not to twist sts.
Next rnd Work rnd 1 of lace pat.

Cont in lace pat (rnds 2–5) until piece measures 8 (9, 10)"/20 (23, 25.5)cm from beg, end with a rnd 3 or 5. Bind off in pat.

BODICE
Carefully remove scrap yarn and place 100 (112, 124) sts on smaller needle. Pm and work in St st (k every rnd) for 2¾(3, 3½)"/7 (7.5, 9)cm.

DIVIDE FOR ARMHOLES
Next row (RS) K to last 7 sts, bind off 14 sts, removing marker, k until there are 36 (42, 48) sts on RH needle and place on st holder for front, bind off 14 sts, k to end of row for back. Turn to work back in St st rows.

BACK
Cont in St st (knit on RS, purl on WS), bind off 3 sts at beg next 2 rows—30 (36, 42) sts. Purl one row on WS.
Next (dec) row (RS) K2, ssk, work across to last 3 sts, k2tog, k2—28 (34, 40) sts.
Next row Work even.
Rep last 2 rows once more— 26 (32, 38) sts.
Work even until armhole measures 2 (2½, 3)"/5 (6.5, 7.5)cm, end with a WS row. Bind off.

Gauges

24 sts and 34 rnds to 4"/10cm over St st using size 4 (3.5mm) needle.
24 sts and 34 rnds to 4"/10cm over lace pattern using size 5 (3.75mm) needle. *Take time to check gauges.*

10 Sleeveless Lace Dress

FRONT

Rejoin yarn and purl 1 row on WS.
Next (dec) row (RS) K2, ssk, work across to last 3 sts, k2tog, k2—34 (40, 46) sts.
Next row Work even.
Rep last 2 rows once more—32 (38, 44) sts.
Work even until armhole measures 1 (1½, 2)"/2.5 (4, 5)cm, end with a WS row.

NECK SHAPING

Next row (RS) K11, join second ball of yarn and bind off center 10 (16, 22) sts, knit to end—11 sts each strap.
Next row Work even.
Next (dec) row (RS) [Knit across to last 3 sts, k2tog, k2] on left strap; [k2, ssk, k to end] on right strap.
Rep last 2 rows twice more—8 sts each strap.
Work even until straps measure 5 (5½, 6)"/13 (14, 15)cm above first armhole bind-off. Bind off.

Finishing

Sew left shoulder seam.

ARMHOLE AND NECK EDGING

With RS facing and crochet hook, work sc around left armhole. Beg at shoulder seam and work sc around front neck edge to bound-off edge of right strap, sc in next 3 sts, ch 6 for button loop, sc in next 3 sts, work sc around armhole edge and back neck edge, join with a sl st in first sc. Fasten off.
Sew button to right back shoulder.
Thread ribbon through first row of lace pat. ■

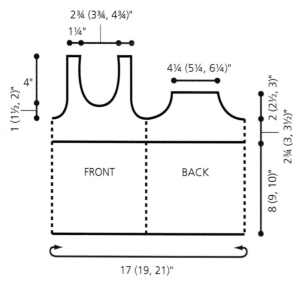

2¾ (3¾, 4¾)"
1¼"
4¼ (5¼, 6¼)"
4"
1 (1½, 2)"
2 (2½, 3)"
2¾ (3, 3½)"
8 (9, 10)"

FRONT   BACK

17 (19, 21)"

Hooded Onesie

11

With its contrasting colors, textured pattern, and pompom "ears," this snuggly onesie is bursting with cuteness.

DESIGNED BY DEVIN COLE

Sizes
Instructions are written for size 6 months. Changes for 12 and 18 months are in parentheses. (Shown in size 6 months.)

Knitted Measurements
Chest 21 (22, 23)"/53.5 (56, 58.5)cm
Length 14 (15, 16)"/35.5 (38, 41)cm
Upper Arm 7½ (8, 8½)"/19 (20.5, 21.5)cm

Materials
■ 4 (5, 6) 1¾oz/50g hanks (each approx 136yd/125m) of Cascade Yarns *220 Superwash Sport* (superwash merino wool) in #845 denim (MC)
■ 1 hank in #871 white (CC)
■ One pair size 5 (3.75mm) needles *or size to obtain gauge*
■ Cable needle
■ Stitch holders
■ Eight ½"/13mm snaps
■ 2 " (5cm) pompom maker

Stitch Glossary
MB (Make Bobble) (K1, yo, k1) in same st, turn. P3, turn. K3, turn. P3, turn. K3tog—1 st.
4-st LPC Sl 2 sts to cable needle and hold in front, p2, k2 from cable needle.
4-st RPC Sl 2 sts to cable needle and hold in back, k2, p2 from cable needle.

K2, P2 Rib
Row 1 (RS) *K2, p2; rep from * across, end k2. **Row 2** *P2, k2; rep from * across, end p2. Rep rows 1 and 2 for k2, p2 rib.

Seed Stitch
Row 1 (RS) *K1, p1; rep from * across.
Row 2 Purl the knit sts and knit the purl sts as they appear.
Rep row 2 for seed st.

Onesie
RIGHT SLEEVE
With CC, cast on 32 sts.
Rows 1–13 Work in k2, p2 rib. Change to MC.
Row 14 (RS) Knit.
Row 15 Work 6 seed sts, p5, k12, p3, work 6 seed sts.
Row 16 Work 6 seed sts, work chart 1 over next 20 sts, work 6 seed sts. Keeping new sts each side in seed st, cont to follow chart in this way to row 28, then repeat rows 1–28 to end. AT THE SAME TIME, inc 1 st each end of row every 10 (8, 8) rows 3 (4, 5) times—38 (40, 42) sts. Work even until piece measures 6½ (7½ , 8)"/16.5 (19, 20.5)cm, ending with a WS row.

CAP SHAPING
Bind off 2 sts at beg of next 2 rows—34 (36, 38) sts. Dec 1 st at each end of row

Gauge
20 sts and 28 rows to 4"/10cm over St st using size 5 (3.75mm) needles.
Cable panel = 2¾"/7cm wide using size 5 (3.75mm) needles. *Take time to check gauge.*

every other row until 14 sts rem. Bind off in pat.

LEFT SLEEVE
Work rows 1–14 as for first sleeve.
Row 15 Work 6 seed sts, p3, k12, p5, work 6 seed sts. **Row 16** Work 6 seed sts, work chart 2 over next 20 sts, work 6 seed sts. Cont as for right sleeve.

BACK
With MC, cast on 13 sts.
Row 1 (RS) P1, k3, work 5 seed sts, k3, p1.
Row 2 Cast on 2 sts, k1, p3, work 5 seed sts, p3, k1, cast on 2 sts—17 sts.
Row 3 P3, k3, work 5 seed sts, k3, p3.
Row 4 Cast on 2 sts, k3, p3, work 5 seed sts, p3, k3, cast on 2 sts—21 sts.
Row 5 P5, k3, work 5 seed sts, k3, p5.
Row 6 Cast on 2 sts, k5, p3, work 5 seed sts, p3, k5, cast on 2 sts—25 sts.
Row 7 P7, k3, work 5 seed sts, k3, p7.
Row 8 Cast on 2 sts, k7, p3, work 5 seed sts, p3, k7, cast on 2 sts—29 sts.
Row 9 P9, k3, work 5 seed sts, k3, p9.
Row 10 Cast on 2 sts, k9, p3, work 5 seed sts, p3, k9, cast on 2 sts—33 sts.
Row 11 P11, k3, work 5 seed sts, k3, p11.
Row 12 Cast on 2 sts, k11, p3, work 5 seed sts, p3, k11, cast on 2 sts—37 sts.
Row 13 K1, p12, k3, work 5 seed sts, k3, p12, k1.
Row 14 Cast on 2 sts, p1, k12, p3, work 5 seed sts, p3, k12, p1, cast on 2 sts—41 sts.
Row 15 K3, p12, k3, work 5 seed sts, k3, p12, k3.
Row 16 Cast on 2 sts, p3, k12, p3, work 5 seed sts, p3, k12, p3, cast on 2 sts—45 sts.
Row 17 Work row 1 of chart 2, work 5 seed sts, work row 1 of chart 1.
Row 18 Cast on 2 sts, work row 2 of chart 1, work 5 seed sts, work row 2 of chart 1, cast on 2 sts. Cont to cast on 2 sts each end of each WS row, working charts as set

and rem sts in seed st until there are 65 (69, 73) sts. Work even in pat until piece measures 10 (10¾, 11½)"/25.5 (27, 29)cm, ending with a WS row.

ARMHOLE AND NECK SHAPING
Bind off 2 sts at beg of next 2 rows—61 (65, 69) sts. Dec 1 st at each end of row every other row until 41 (43, 45) sts rem. Work even in pat until armholes measure 4 (4¼, 4½)"/10 (11, 11.5)cm. Bind off in pat.

FRONT
Work as for back until piece measures 5"/12.5cm shorter than back, ending with a WS row.

SHAPE PLACKET
Next row (RS) Work in pat to center 5 sts, join a second ball of yarn and bind off center 5 sts, work in pat to end. Working both sides separately at the same time, work even until piece measures same as back to armholes. Shape armholes as for back, and AT THE SAME TIME, dec 1 st each neck edge every 4 rows until 11 (11, 12) sts rem, then work even until piece measures same as back.

HOOD
With MC, cast on 24 sts.
Next row (RS) K2, work row 1 of chart 2, k2. Working in pat as set, cast on 1 st on each side of row every 5 rows, working new sts in seed st until piece measures 7½ (8, 8½)"/19 (20.5, 21.5)cm, ending with a WS row.
Next row (RS) Work across first set of seed sts, place center 24 sts on holder, place rem seed sts on another holder. Working on first set of sts only, work next row even in seed st.
Next row (RS) Bind off 1 st, work in seed

st to last st, M1, work last st. Work next row even in seed st.
Next row (RS) Bind off 3 sts, work in seed st to end. Work 2 rows even in seed st. Bind off in pat.
Place center 24 sts on needles and work in pat for approx 2"/5cm more or until long enough to cover bound-off seed st edge. Bind off in pat.
Place rem seed sts on needles. Work 1 row even (RS). Shape as for opposite side, binding off on WS rows.

Finishing
Sew shoulder seams. Set in sleeves, sew side and sleeve seams. Sew seed st sections to sides of center extension on hood. Sew hood to neck opening.

PLACKET TRIM
With RS facing and CC, pick up and knit 46 sts along left side of placket opening. Work in k2, p2 rib for 1"/2.5cm. Bind off in pat. Rep on right side of opening. Lap left side over right and sew lower edge of each trim to bound-off sts.

LEG TRIM
With RS facing and CC, pick up and knit 58 (58, 62) sts along leg opening. Work in k2, p2 rib for 2"/5cm. Bind off in pat.

HOOD TRIM
With RS facing and CC, pick up and knit 106 (110, 114) sts around hood. Work in k2, p2 rib for 2"/5cm. Bind off in pat. Sew edges of band to fronts.
Set 4 snaps along crotch opening and 4 snaps on placket, evenly spaced. With CC and pompom maker, make two 2" (5cm) pompoms, following package instructions, and sew to hood as shown. Weave in ends. ∎

Hooded Onesie

CHART 1

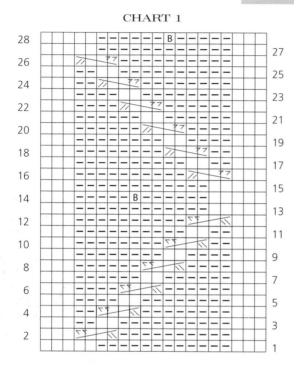

CHART 2

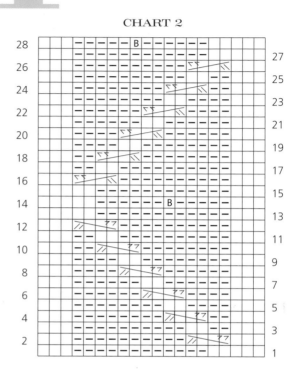

Stitch Key

☐	K on RS, p on WS
—	P on RS, k on WS
B	Make bobble
	4-st RPC
	4-st LPC

2¼ (2¼, 2½)"

3½ (4, 4)"

4 (4¼, 4½)"

5"

7 (7½, 8)"

3 (3¼, 3½)"

BACK
&
FRONT

10½ (11, 11½)"

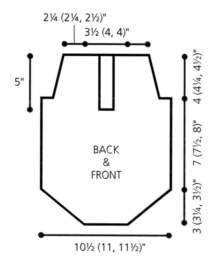

7½ (8, 8½)"

3 (3¼, 3½)"

6½ (7½, 8)"

SLEEVE

6½"

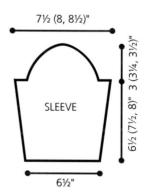

HOOD

7½ (8, 8½)"

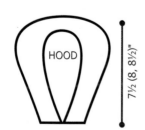

Tie-Front Cardigan

This A-line cardigan features stylish ties at the neck and a subtle chevron stitch pattern. It's an instant classic.

DESIGNED BY THERESE CHYNOWETH

Sizes
Instructions are written for size 6 months. Changes for 12 and 18 months are in parentheses. (Shown in size 6 months.)

Knitted Measurements
Chest (closed) 23 (25, 28)"/58 (63.5, 71)cm
Length 11½ (12½, 13½)"/29 (32, 34)cm
Upper arm 10 (11, 12)"/ 25 (28, 30.5)cm

Materials
■ 4 (5, 6) 1¾oz/50g hanks (each approx 136yd/125m) of Cascade Yarns 220 Superwash Sport (superwash merino wool) in #807 raspberry

■ Size 6 (4mm) needles *or size to obtain gauge*

■ One set (4) size 6 (4mm) double-pointed needles (dpns)

■ Size 6 (4mm) circular needle, 24"/60cm long

■ Scrap yarn

■ Stitch holders

■ Stitch markers

■ Three ½"/13mm buttons

Provisional Method Cast-on
Using scrap yarn and crochet hook, ch the number of sts to cast on plus a few extra. Cut a tail and pull the tail through the last chain. With knitting needle and yarn, pick up and knit the stated number of sts through the "purl bumps" on the back of the chain. To remove waste chain, when instructed, pull out the tail from the last crochet stitch. Gently and slowly pull on the tail to unravel the crochet stitches, carefully placing each released knit stitch on a needle.

Seed Stitch
(worked over 3 sts)
Row 1 (RS) K1, p1, k1.
Repeat row 1 for seed st.

Cardigan
BACK
Using provisional method and straight needles, cast on 71 (77, 83) sts. Purl 1 row on WS.

BEG CHART
Row 1 (RS) K1 (selvage st), beg with st 9 (6, 3) and work to end of 12-st rep, then work 12-st rep 6 times more, ending last repeat with st 5 (8, 11), k1 (selvage st).
Row 2 K1 (selvage st), working chart from left to right beg with st 5 (8, 11) and work across 12-st rep to st 1, then work 12-st rep 6 times more, ending last repeat with st 9 (6, 3), k1 (selvage st). With garter selvage sts at side edges, follow chart and work 4 rows even.
Next (dec) row (RS) K1 (selvage st), k2tog (or p2tog to maintain pat), work as established to last 3 sts, k2tog (or p2tog to maintain pat), k1 (selvage st)—69 (75, 81) sts. Repeat dec row every 6th row 5 more times—59 (65, 71) sts. Work even until piece measures 5 (5½, 6)"/12.5 (14, 15)cm from beg, end with a WS row.

ARMHOLES
Bind off 3 sts at beg of next 2 rows, then 2 sts at beg of next 2 rows. Dec 1 st each end every RS row 3 times—43 (49, 55) sts. Work even until piece measures 10 (11, 12)"/25 (28, 30.5)cm from beg, end with a WS row.

Gauge
20 sts and 32 rows to 4"/10cm over chart pattern using size 6 (4mm) needle. *Take time to check gauge.*

Tie-Front Cardigan

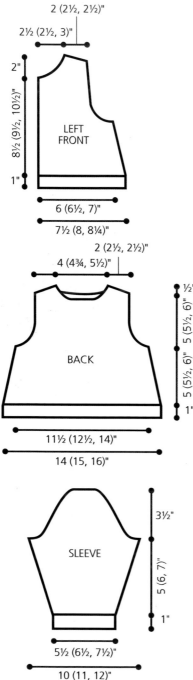

2 (2½, 2½)"

2½ (2½, 3)"

2"

8½ (9½, 10½)"

1"

LEFT FRONT

6 (6½, 7)"

7½ (8, 8¼)"

2 (2½, 2½)"

4 (4¾, 5½)"

½"

5 (5½, 6)"

5 (5½, 6)"

BACK

1"

11½ (12½, 14)"

14 (15, 16)"

3½"

SLEEVE

5 (6, 7)"

1"

5½ (6½, 7½)"

10 (11, 12)"

NECK AND SHORT ROW SHOULDERS
Next row (RS) Work 15 (17, 17) sts for right shoulder, turn and leave rem 28 (32, 38) sts on hold. **Next (short) row (WS)** Bind off 3 sts, work 8 sts, turn and work back to neck edge. **Next (short) row (WS)** Bind off 1 st, work 4 sts, turn and work back to neck edge. Bind off rem 11 (13, 13) sts. Cut yarn.

With RS facing, slip next 13 (15, 21) sts to holder for neck. Rejoin yarn to armhole edge of left shoulder. Work 1 WS row even. **Next (short) row (RS)** Bind off 3 sts, work 8 sts, turn and work back to neck edge. **Next (short) row (RS)** Bind off 1 st, work 4 sts, turn and work back to neck edge. **Next row (RS)** Bind off rem 11 (13, 13) sts.

LEFT FRONT
Using provisional method and straight needles, cast on 39 (41, 43) sts.
Purl 1 row on WS.

BEG CHART PAT
Row 1 (RS) K1 (selvage st), beg with st 9 (7, 5) and work to end of 12-st rep, then work 12-st rep 3 times more, ending last repeat with st 7, then [k1, p1, k1] for front band. **Row 2** [K1, p1, k1] for front band, working chart from left to right beg with st 7 and work across 12-st rep to st 1, then work 12-st rep 3 times more, ending last repeat with st 9 (7, 5), k1 (selvage st). With front band in seed st and garter selvage st at side edge, follow chart and work 4 rows even. **Next (dec) row (RS)** K1 (selvage st), k2tog (or p2tog to maintain pat), work as established to last 3 sts, [k1, p1, k1] for front band—38 (40, 42) sts. Rep dec row every 6th row 5 more times—33 (35, 37) sts. Work even until piece measures 5 (5½, 6)"/12.5 (14, 15)cm from beg, end with a WS row.

ARMHOLE
Bind off 3 sts at beg of next RS row, then 2 sts at beg of next RS row. Dec 1 st at beg of every RS row 3 times—25 (27, 29) sts. Work even until piece measures 8½ (9½, 10½)"/21.5 (24, 26.5)cm from beg, end with a RS row.

FRONT NECK
Next row (WS) Bind off 4 sts, place the resulting st on holder, work to end of row—20 (22, 24) sts. Work 1 row even on RS. **Next row (WS)** Work 3 (3, 4) sts and place on holder, work to end of row—17 (19, 20) sts. Work 1 row even on RS. **Next row** Work 2 (2, 3) sts and place on holder, work to end of row—15 (17, 17) sts on needle, 6 (6, 8) sts on holder. Dec 1 st at neck edge every RS row 4 times. AT THE SAME TIME, when piece measures 10 (11, 12)"/25 (28, 30.5)cm from beg, end with a RS row and work short row shoulder as foll: **Next (short) row (WS)** Complete final neck decrease, work to last 3 sts, turn and work back to neck edge. **Next (short) row** Work to last 8 sts, turn and work back to neck edge—11 (13, 13) sts. Bind off.

RIGHT FRONT
Using provisional method and straight needles, cast on 39 (41, 43) sts. Purl 1 row on WS.

BEG CHART PAT
Row 1 (RS) [K1, p1, k1] for front band, beg with st 7 and work to end of 12-st rep, then work 12-st rep 3 times more, ending last repeat with st 5 (7, 9), k1 (selvage st). **Row 2** K1 (selvage st), working chart from left to right beg with st 5 (7, 9) and work across 12-st rep to st 1, then work 12-st rep 3 times more,

Tie-Front Cardigan

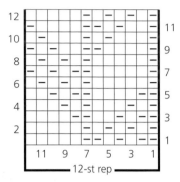

Stitch Key

☐ K on RS, p on WS

⊟ P on RS, k on WS

ending last rep with st 7, then [k1, p1, k1] for front band. With front band in seed st and garter selvage st at side edge, foll chart and work 4 rows even.

Next (dec) row (RS) K1, p1, k1, work as established to last 3 sts, k2tog (or p2tog to maintain pat), k1 (selvage st)—38 (40, 42) sts. Rep dec row every 6th row 5 more times—33 (35, 37) sts. Work even until piece measures 5 (5½ , 6)"/12.5 (14, 15)cm from beg, end with a RS row.

ARMHOLE AND BUTTONHOLES
Bind off 3 sts at beg of next WS row, then 2 sts at beg of next WS row. Dec 1 st at the end of every RS row 3 times AT THE SAME TIME, when piece measures 6 (6½ , 7)"/15 (16.5, 18)cm from beg, end with a WS row and work buttonholes as follows: **Next (buttonhole) row (RS)** K1, p1, yo, p2tog, work to end of row. Work remaining armhole shaping and rep buttonhole row every 10 rows twice more—25 (27, 29) sts. Work even until piece measures 8½ (9½ ,10½)"/21.5 (24, 26.5)cm from beg, end with a WS row.

FRONT NECK
Next row (RS) Bind off 4 sts, place resulting st on holder, work to end of row—20 (22, 24) sts. Work 1 row even. **Next row** Work 3 (3, 4) sts and place on holder, work to end of row—17 (19, 20) sts. Work 1 row even. **Next row** Work 2 (2, 3) sts and place on holder, work to end of row—15 (17, 17) sts on needle, 6 (6, 8) sts on holder. Dec 1 st at neck edge every RS row 4 times. AT THE SAME TIME, when piece measures 10 (11, 12)"/25 (28, 30.5)cm from beg, end with WS row and work short-row shoulder as foll: **Next (short) row (RS)** Complete final neck dec, work to last 3 sts, turn and work back to neck edge. **Next (short) row** Work to last 8 sts, turn and work back to neck edge—11 (13, 13) sts. Bind off.

SLEEVES
Using provisional method and straight needles, cast on 31 (37, 41) sts. Purl 1 row on WS.

BEG CHART PAT
Row 1 (RS) K1 (selvage st), beg with st 5 (2, 12) and work to end of 12-st rep, then work 12-st rep 2 (2, 4) times more, ending last rep with st 9 (12, 2), k1 (selvage st). **Row 2** K1 (selvage st), working chart from left to right beg with st 9 (12, 2) and work across 12-st rep to st 1, then work 12-st rep 2 (2, 4) times more, ending last rep with st 5 (2, 12), k1 (selvage st). **Next (inc) row (RS)** K1 (selvage st), M1, work to last st, M1, k1 (selvage st)—33 (39, 43) sts. With garter selvage sts at side edges, follow chart and rep inc row every 4th row 7 times, then every other row 3 times more, work new sts into pat—53 (59, 63) sts. Work even until sleeve measures 5 (6, 7)"/ 12.5 (15, 18)cm from beg, end with a WS row.

SHAPE CAP
Bind off 3 sts at beg of next 2 rows, then 2 sts at beg of next 2 rows—43 (49, 53) sts. Dec 1 st each end every RS row 8 times—27 (33, 37) sts. Bind off 3 sts at beg of next 2 rows, then 4 sts at beg of next 2 rows—13 (19, 23) sts. Bind off.

Finishing
Weave in ends. Gently block pieces to measurements. Sew shoulder seams.

LOWER BAND
Carefully remove scrap yarn from fronts and back, placing sts on straight needles with markers between back and front sts. **Next row (WS)** [Knit to 1 st before marker, remove marker and k2tog] twice. Knit 13 rows more. Bind off knitwise.

NECKBAND
With circular needle, use long-tail method to cast on 72 sts for right neck tie. With RS facing, k 6 (8, 10) sts from right front neck holder, pick up and k 17 sts along right neck to back holder, k 13 (17, 21) sts from back holder, pick up and k 17 sts along left neck to holder, k 6 (8, 10) sts from left front neck holder, holding a 2nd strand of yarn tog with working yarn, use long-tail method to cast on 72 sts for left neck tie—203 (211, 219) sts. Do not join. Knit 6 rows. Bind off knitwise on RS. Sew buttons to left front band opposite buttonholes. Set sleeves into armholes. Sew side and sleeve seams.

SLEEVE CUFFS
Remove scrap yarn from sleeve, placing sts evenly divided on 3 dpns. Place marker for beg of rnd. [Purl 1 rnd, knit 1 rnd] 5 times. Bind off purlwise. Rep on rem sleeve. ■

13

Lace Blanket

This beautiful lace blanket is sure to become an heirloom. Knit from the center out, it's easy to make it larger or smaller.

DESIGNED BY ANNA AL

■■■■

Knitted Measurements
Approx 31" x 31"/78.5cm x 78.5cm

Materials
■ 7 1¾oz/50g hanks (each approx 136yd/125m) of Cascade Yarns *220 Superwash Sport* (superwash merino wool) in #1941 salmon

■ Size 5 (3.75mm) circular needles, 24"/61cm and 36"/91cm long, *or size to obtain gauge*

■ One set (5) size 5 (3.75mm) double-pointed needles (dpns)

■ Stitch markers

Note
Blanket is worked in the round from the center out.

Stitch Glossary
sssk (slip, slip, slip, knit) Slip next 3 sts knitwise, one at a time, to RH needle. Insert tip of LH needle into fronts of these sts, working from left to right, then k3tog.

Blanket
With dpns, cast on 8 sts. Divide sts over 4 needles (2 sts on each). Join, taking care not to twist sts on needles, pm for beg of rnds.

Rnd 1 (RS) [Yo, k1] 8 times—16 sts.
Rnd 2 and even rnds Knit.
Rnd 3 [Yo, k3, yo, k1, pm for corner] 3 times, end yo, k3, yo, k1—24 sts.
Rnd 5 [Yo, k5, yo, k1] 4 times—32 sts.
Rnd 7 *Yo, k1, yo, ssk, k1, k2tog, [yo, k1] twice; rep from * around 3 times more—40 sts.
Rnd 9 *Yo, k3, yo, SK2P, yo, k3, yo, k1 (corner st); rep from * around 3 times more—48 sts.
Rnd 11 *Yo, k3, k2tog, yo, k1, yo, ssk, k3, yo, k1 (corner st); rep from * around 3 times more—56 sts.
Rnd 13 *[Yo, k1, yo, ssk, k1, k2tog] twice, [yo, k1] twice; rep from * around 3 times more—64 sts.
Rnd 15 *[Yo, k3, yo, SK2P] twice, yo, k3, yo, k1 (corner st); rep from * around 3 times more—72 sts.
Rnd 17 *Yo, k3, [k2tog, yo, k1, yo, ssk, k1] twice, k2, yo, k1 (corner st); rep from * around 3 times more—80 sts.
Rnd 19 *Yo, k1, yo, ssk, k1, [k2tog, yo, k1, yo, ssk, k1] twice, k2tog, [yo, k1] twice; rep from * around 3 times more—88 sts.

Gauge
24 sts and 30 rnds to 4"/10cm over lace pat using size 5 (3.75mm) circular needle.
Take time to check gauge.

Lace Blanket

Rnd 21 *[Yo, k3, yo, SK2P] 3 times, yo, k3, yo, k1 (corner st); rep from * around 3 times more—96 sts.
Rnd 23 *Yo, k3, [k2tog, yo, k1, yo, ssk, k1] 3 times, k2, yo, k1 (corner st); rep from * around 3 times more—104 sts.
Rnd 25 *Yo, k1, yo, ssk, k1, [k2tog, yo, k1, yo, ssk, k1] 3 times, k2tog, [yo, k1] twice; rep from * around 3 times more—112 sts.
Rnd 27 *[Yo, k3, yo, SK2P] 4 times, yo, k3, yo, k1 (corner st); rep from * around 3 times more—120 sts.
Rnd 29 *Yo, k3, [k2tog, yo, k1, yo, ssk, k1] 4 times, k2, yo, k1 (corner st); rep from * around 3 times more—128 sts.
Rnd 31 *Yo, k1, yo, ssk, k1, [k2tog, yo, k1, yo, ssk, k1] 4 times, k2tog, [yo, k1] twice; rep from * around 3 times more—136 sts.
Rnd 33 *[Yo, k3, yo, SK2P] 5 times, yo, k3, yo, k1 (corner st); rep from * around 3 times more—144 sts. Change to shorter circular needle.

Rnd 35 *Yo, k3, [k2tog, yo, k1, yo, ssk, k1] 5 times, k2, yo, k1 (corner st); rep from * around 3 times more—152 sts.
Rnd 37 *Yo, k1, yo, ssk, k1, [k2tog, yo, k1, yo, ssk, k1] 5 times, k2tog, [yo, k1] twice; rep from * around 3 times more—160 sts.
Rnd 38 Knit. Changing to longer circular needle when necessary, cont in pat st as established, rep sts between [ ]'s (red brackets) one more time every other rnd until there are 128 sts between corner markers, end with a knit rnd—512 sts. *Do not remove st markers.*

BORDER
Rnd 1 [Yo, purl to next corner st, yo, k1 (corner st)] 4 times.
Rnd 2 and all even rnds Knit.
Rnd 3 [Yo, *k1, yo, k3, sssk, k3, yo; rep from * to 1 st before corner st, k1, yo, k1] 4 times.
Rnd 5 [Yo, k1, *k1, yo, k3, sssk, k3, yo; rep from * to 2 sts before corner st, k2, yo, k1] 4 times.
Rnd 7 [Yo, k2, *k1, yo, k3, sssk, k3, yo; rep from * to 3 sts before corner st, k3, yo, k1] 4 times.
Rnd 9 [Yo, k3, *k1, yo, k3, sssk, k3, yo; rep from * to 4 sts before corner st, k4, yo, k1] 4 times.
Rnd 11 [Yo, k4, *k1, yo, k3, sssk, k3, yo; rep from * to 5 sts before corner st, k5, yo, k1] 4 times.
Rnd 13 [Yo, k5, *k1, yo, k3, sssk, k3, yo; rep from * to 6 sts before corner st, k6, yo, k1] 4 times. Bind off all sts loosely purlwise.

Finishing
Block piece lightly to measurements. ∎

42

14

Lollipop Sweater

What could be sweeter than a pink pullover with a candy motif?
The multicolored lollipops are crocheted separately, then sewn on.

DESIGNED BY MARY BONNETTE

Sizes
Instructions are written for size 6 months. Changes for 12 and 18 months are in parentheses. (Shown in size 12 months.)

Finished Measurements
Chest 21 (23, 25)"/53.5 (58.5, 63.5)cm
Length 10½ (11½ ,12½)"/26.5 (29, 31.5)cm
Upper arm 8 (9, 10)"/20.5 (23, 25.5)cm

Materials
■ 2 (3, 3) 1¾oz/50g hanks (each approx 136yd/125m) of Cascade Yarns *220 Superwash Sport* (superwash merino wool) in #836 pink ice (B)

■ 1 hank each in #901 cotton candy (A), #844 periwinkle (C) and #807 raspberry (D)

■ One pair size 6 (4mm) needles *or size to obtain gauge*

■ One set (5) size 6 (4mm) double-pointed needles (dpns)

■ Size G/6 (4mm) crochet hook

■ Stitch marker

Note
Sweater has rolled hems. To measure accurately, measure length from the bottom edge of the roll. Do not unroll the hem to measure.

Back
With A, cast on 60 (66, 70) sts. Work in St st (k on RS, p on WS) for 6 rows.
**Next row (RS) With B, *k1, p1; rep from * to end. Beg with a purl row, cont in St st using B for 5 rows, end with a WS row. Change to C and work in St st for 8 rows. Change to A and work in St st for 4 rows.
Next row (RS) With B, *p1, k1; rep from * to end. Beg with a purl row, cont in St st using B for 5 rows, end with a WS row. Change to C and work in St st for 8 rows. Change to A and work in St st for 4 rows.** Rep from ** to ** once more.
Next row (RS) With B, *k1, p1; rep from * to end. Beg with a purl row, cont in St st using B only until piece measures 10½ (11½ ,12½)"/26.5 (29, 31.5)cm from beg, end with a WS row.

SHOULDER AND NECK SHAPING
Next row (RS) Bind off first 15 (18, 20) sts, knit until there are 30 sts on RH needle, place these 30 sts on holder for

back neck, bind off last 15 (18, 20) sts.

Front
With A, cast on 60 (66, 70) sts. Work in St st for 6 rows.
Next row (RS) With B, *k1, p1; rep from * to end. Beg with a purl row, cont in St st using B for 5 rows, end with a WS row. Change to C and work in St st for 8 rows. Change to A and work in St st for 4 rows.
Next row (RS) With B, *p1, k1; rep from * to end. Beg with a purl row, cont in St st using B only until piece measures 9 (9½, 10)"/23 (24, 25.5)cm from beg, end with a WS row.

NECK SHAPING
Next row (RS) K18 (21, 23), place center 24 sts on holder for front neck, join a 2nd hank of B, k18 (21, 23). Working both sides at once, purl next row.
Next (dec) row (RS) With first hank of B, knit to last 3 sts, k2tog, k1; with 2nd hank of B, k1, ssk, knit to end. Purl next row. Rep last 2 rows twice more—15 (18, 20) sts. Work even until piece measures same length as back to shoulder, end with a WS row. Bind off each side for shoulders. Sew shoulder seams. Place markers 4 (4½, 5)"/10 (11.5, 12.5)cm down from shoulders on back and front.

Gauge
22 sts and 30 rows to 4"/10cm over St st using size 6 (4mm) needles.
Take time to check gauge.

Lollipop Sweater 14

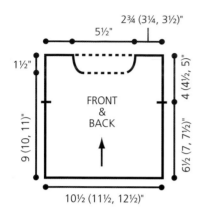

2¾ (3¼, 3½)"
5½"
1½"

FRONT & BACK

4 (4½, 5)"
6½ (7, 7½)"
9 (10, 11)"

10½ (11½, 12½)"

8 (9, 10)"

SLEEVE

7 (7½, 8½)"

7 (8, 9)"

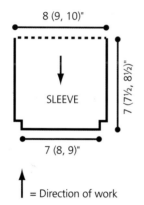

↑ = Direction of work

Sleeves
With RS facing and B, pick up and k 46 (52, 58) sts evenly spaced between markers. Beg with a purl row, cont in St st for 4 (4½, 5½)"/10 (11.5, 14)cm, end with a WS row.
Next row (RS) With A, *k1, p1; rep from * to end. Beg with a purl row, cont in St st using A for 3 rows, end with a WS row. Change to C and work in St st for 8 rows. Change to B and work in St st for 6 rows.
Next row (RS) With A, *p1, k1; rep from * to end.
Next row Purl.
Next row Knit.
Next (dec) row (WS) Purl across, dec 8 sts evenly spaced—38 (44, 50) sts. Cont in St st for 4 rows. Bind off knitwise.

Finishing
Block piece lightly to measurements.

NECKBAND
With RS facing, dpn and B, beg at left shoulder seam and pick up and k 8 sts evenly spaced along left neck edge, k 24 sts from front neck holder, pick up and k 8 sts along right neck edge, k 30 sts from back neck holder—70 sts. Divide sts evenly between 4 needles. Join and pm for beg of rnds. **Next rnd** *K1, p1; rep from * around. **Next 4 rnds** Knit. Bind off loosely knitwise.

STEMS (make 3)
With crochet hook and A, ch 12, leaving a long tail for sewing. Fasten off, leaving a long tail for sewing. Position first stem vertically on center front of sweater with bottom edge of chain just above last row of stripe. Sew in place using tails. Measure and sew 2nd stem 1¾"/4.5cm to the right of center stem, then sew 3rd stem 1¾"/4.5cm to the left of center stem.

LOLLIPOPS
Note When changing colors, draw new color through last 2 lps on hook to complete sc.

RIGHT LOLLIPOP
With crochet hook and C, ch 103, leaving a long tail for sewing.
Row 1 Sc in 2nd ch from hook and in next 58 ch, changing to D; with D sc in next 35 ch, changing to C; with C sc in last 8 ch—102 sc. Fasten off, leaving a long tail for sewing. With fasten-off end in center and top loops of sc facing up, coil strip into a 2"/5cm diameter circle; pin coils in place. Turn over to WS and sew rnds tog using tails. Sew to top of right stem, as shown.

LEFT LOLLIPOP
With crochet hook and D, ch 107, leaving a long tail for sewing.
Row 1 Sc in 2nd ch from hook and in next 34 ch, changing to C; with C sc in next 28 ch, changing to D; with D sc in next 22 ch, changing to C; with C sc in next 14 ch, changing to D; with D sc in last 7 ch—106 sc. Fasten off, leaving a long tail for sewing. Working same as right lollipop, make a 2⅛"/5.5cm diameter circle. Sew to top of left stem, as shown.

CENTER LOLLIPOP
With crochet hook and A, ch73, leaving a long tail for sewing.
Row 1 Sc in 2nd ch from hook and in next 28 ch, changing to C; with C sc in next 21 ch, changing to D; with D sc in next 14 ch, changing to A; with A sc in last 8 ch—72 sc. Fasten off, leaving a long tail for sewing. Working same as right lollipop, make a 1¾"/4.5cm diameter circle. Sew to center stem, as shown. Sew side and sleeve seams. ∎

Striped Top & Pants

This chic suit really stripes it rich! The top is knit from side to side in garter ridge stripes, while the coordinating bottoms are knit in stockinette stitch stripes.

DESIGNED BY JACQUELINE VAN DILLEN

Size
Instructions are written for size 6 months.

Knitted Measurements
TOP
Chest (closed) 20"/51cm
Length 11"/28cm
Upper arm 8"/20.5cm
PANTS
Waist 21"/53cm
Length 11¾"/30cm
Inseam 3½"/9cm

Materials
■ 4 1¾oz/50g hanks (each approx 136yd/125m) of Cascade Yarns *220 Superwash Sport* (superwash merino wool) in #873 extra creme cafe (A)

■ 3 hanks in #878 lazy maize (B)

■ 2 hanks in #871 white (C)

■ Size 6 (4mm) needles *or size to obtain gauge*

■ Size 5 (3.75mm) needles

■ Cable needle (cn)

■ Stitch holders ■ Stitch markers

■ Size 6/G (4mm) crochet hook

■ One ¾"/2cm button

■ One sew-on snap

Notes
1) Body of top is worked sideways in one piece.
2) When working stripes, carry color not in use up WS of work.
3) Pants are worked in 2 pieces, then sewn tog along the middle of the front and back; then the inseams are sewn.

Stitch Glossary
M1 Insert LH needle under the strand between last st worked and the next st on the LH needle. Knit into the front loop to twist the st—1 st increased.
Kfb Knit into front and back of st—1 st increased.
4-st RC Sl 2 sts to cn and hold to back, k2, k2 from cn.

Cuff Cable
(multiple of 6 sts plus 2)
Row 1 *P2, k4; rep from *, end p2.
Rows 2 and 4 *K2, p4; rep from *, end k2.
Row 3 *P2, 4-st RC; rep from *, end p2.
Rep rows 1–4 for cuff cable pat.

Neckband Cable
(worked over 8 sts)
Row 1 (RS) P2, k4, p1, k1.
Rows 2 and 4 K2, p4, k2.
Row 3 P2, 4-st RC, p1, k1.

Rep rows 1–4 for neckband cable pat.

Garter Stripes
Row 1 (RS) Knit with B.
Row 2 (WS) Knit with B.
Rows 3 and 4 Knit with C.
Rep rows 1–4 for garter stripes.

K1, P1 Rib
(worked over an odd number of sts)
Row 1 (RS) P1, *k1, p1; rep from * to end.
Row 2 K1, *p1, k1; rep from * to end.
Rep rows 1 and 2 for k1, p1 rib.

St St Stripes
Rows 1 and 3 (RS) Knit with A.
Rows 2 and 4 Purl with A.
Row 5 Knit with B.
Row 6 Purl with B.
Rep rows 1–6 for St st stripes.

Crochet Edging
Sc in first st, *ch 3, join with sl st to second ch, skip 2 sts, sc in next st; rep from *, end sc in last st.

Top
LEFT SLEEVE
With A, cast on 40 sts.

BEG CUFF CABLE
Next row (WS) K3, [p4, k2] 5 times, p4, k3.

Gauges
24 sts and 32 rows to 4"/10cm over St st using size 6 (4mm) needles.
24 sts and 44 rows to 4"/10cm over garter st using size 6 (4mm) needles. *Take time to check gauges.*

Row 1 P1, work row 1 of cuff cable to last st, p1. Work even in cuff cable with first and last st in Rev St st until 4-row rep has been worked 3 times, work rows 1 and 2 once more; piece measures approx 1½"/3.5cm.

BEG GARTER STRIPES
Row 1 (RS) Work row 1 of garter stripes. Work next row even on WS.
Next (inc) row (RS) K1, M1, k to last st, M1, k1—42 sts. Cont in garter stripes and rep inc row every 6th row 3 times more—48 sts. Work even until piece measures approx 5½"/14cm from beg, end with a row 2.

BEG RAGLAN DECREASES
Bind off 3 sts at beg of next 2 rows—42 sts. Work next row even on WS.
Next (dec) row K2, ssk, k to last 4 sts, k2tog, k2—40 sts.
Next row P3, k to last 3 sts, p3.
Next row Knit.
Next row P3, k to last 3 sts, p3.
Rep last 4 rows 11 times more—18 sts.*

SLEEVE TOP SHAPING
Next (dec) row (RS) K2, ssk, k to end—17 sts.
Next (dec) row (WS) Bind off 5 sts, k to last 3 sts, p3—12 sts.
Rep last 2 rows once more—6 sts.
Next (dec) row (RS) K2, ssk, k2—5 sts. Bind off. With A, pick up and knit 15 sts across top edge of sleeve. Bind off.

RIGHT SLEEVE
Work same as for right sleeve to *.

SLEEVE TOP SHAPING
Next (dec) row (RS) K to last 4 sts, k2tog, k2—17 sts.
Next row P3, k to last 3 sts, p3.

Next (dec) row (RS) Bind off 5 sts, k to last 4 sts, k2tog, k2—11 sts.
Next row P3, k to end.
Next (dec) row (RS) Bind off 5 sts, k to last 4 sts, k2tog, k2—5 sts. Bind off. With A, pick up and knit 15 sts across top edge of sleeve. Bind off.

BODY
LEFT FRONT
With A, cast on 8 sts for neckband cable; with B, cast on 36 sts for garter st stripes.

BEG NECK SHAPING
Row (inc) 1 (RS) Work row 1 of garter stripe pat to last 2 garter stripe sts, M1, k2—37 garter stripe sts; with A, work row 1 of neckband cable.
Next row With A, work row 2 of neckband cable; work row 2 of garter stripe to end.
Next row (RS) Work row 3 of garter stripe; with A, work row 3 of neckband cable pat.
Next row With A, work row 4 of neckband cable; work row 4 of garter stripe to end. Rep last 4 rows 11 times more—48 garter stripe sts. Work inc row 1 once more—49 sts.
Next row (WS) Work neckband cable sts and place on holder; work to end of row.

BEG RAGLAN DECREASES
Next (dec) row (RS) K to last 3 sts, k2tog, k1—48 sts. Work next row even on WS.
Next (dec) row (RS) K to last 4 sts, k3tog, k1—46 sts.
Work next row even on WS.
Rep last 4 rows 8 times more—22 sts. Work 4 rows even.

BACK
BEG RAGLAN INCREASES
Next (inc) row (RS) K to last st, M1,

k1—23 sts.
Work next row even on WS.
Next (inc) row (RS) K to last st, M1, kfb—25 sts. Work next row even on WS. Rep last 4 rows 10 times more, end with a WS row—55 sts. Set aside back sts to be worked later.

CABLE BAND
Return to neckband cable on holder, cont in pat until this section fits along the top of left sleeve, approx 3"/7.5cm, end with a WS row.

CENTER BACK
Next (joining) row (RS) Work even across 55 back sts, work neckband cable.
Work next row even on WS.
Work even on all sts for 15 more rows.
Next row (WS) Work neckband cable sts and place on holder; work to end of row.

BEG RAGLAN DECREASES
Next (dec) row (RS) K to last 3 sts, k2tog, k1—54 sts.
Work next row even on WS.
Next (dec) row (RS) K to last 4 sts, k3tog, k1—52 sts. Work next row even on WS. Rep last 4 rows 10 times more—22 sts. Work 4 rows even.

RIGHT FRONT
BEG RAGLAN INCREASES
Next (inc) row (RS) K to last st, M1, k1—23 sts.
Work next row even on WS.
Next (dec) row (RS) K to last st, M1, kfb—25 sts. Work next row even on WS. Rep last 4 rows 8 times more—49 sts. Set aside front sts to be worked later.

CABLE BAND
Return to neckband cable on holder, cont in pat until this section fits along the top

of right sleeve, approx 3"/7.5 cm, end with a WS row.

Next (joining) row (RS) Work even across 49 front sts; work neckband cable. Work next WS row even over all sts.

BEG NECK SHAPING

Next (dec) row (RS) Work to last 4 sts of garter stripe, k2tog, k2—48 sts; work neckband cable. Work 3 rows even. Rep last 4 rows 12 times more—36 sts. Bind off garter strip with B, neckband cable with A. Mark last st of A for snap placement.

CABLE RIBBING

With A, and RS facing, pick up and knit 146 sts along lower edge of sweater.
Next row (WS) K2, [p4, k2] 24 times.
Row 1 (RS) Work cuff cable rib row 1. Work 3 rows even. Change to smaller needles, work rows 1–4 of cuff cable rib once more. Bind off.

BUTTON LOOP

With crochet hook, join A to top edge of neckband cable cast-on row. Ch 8, join with sl st to first B st, fasten off.

Finishing

Set in sleeves, sew neckband cables to top of sleeves. Sew sleeve and underarm seams. Sew button to right front, opposite buttonloop. Sew one half of snap in place at marker, the other half to corresponding spot on WS of left front raglan seam.

Pants
RIGHT LEG
With A, cast on 67 sts.

BEG ST ST STRIPES
Row 1 (RS) Work row 1 of St st stripes.

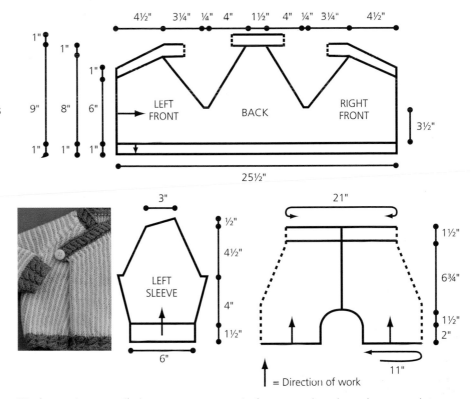

Work even in pat until piece measures 2"/5cm from beg, end with a WS row.

INSEAM SHAPING
Next (inc) row (RS) K1, M1, k to last st, M1, k1—69 sts.
Work next row even on WS. Rep inc row once more—71 sts.
Next row (WS) Work to end of row, cast on 2 sts. Turn.
Next row (RS) Work to end of row, cast on 2 sts—75 sts. Turn.
Rep last 2 rows 3 times more—87 sts, piece meas approx 3½"/ 9 cm from beg.

HIP SHAPING
Next (dec) row (RS) Work 9 sts, place marker (pm), k2tog, work to last 11 sts, ssk, pm, work to end—85 sts. Work next row even on WS.
Next (dec) row (RS) Work to first marker, slip marker (sm), k2tog, work to 2 sts

before second marker, ssk, sm, work to end—83 sts.
Rep last dec row every 4th row 10 times more—63 sts. Work even until piece measures 10¼"/ 26cm from beg.

WAISTBAND
Work in k1, p1 rib for 1½"/4cm. Bind off in rib.

LEFT LEG
Work same as right leg.

Finishing
Gently block pieces to measurements.

CROCHET EDGING
With crochet hook and A, work picot edging along cast-on edge of each leg. Fasten off. Sew pant halves tog from ribbed waist to inseam, sew inseams. ■

16

Bubble Hat

This cute topper is bursting with fun design details including a rolled brim, a textured bubble stitch, and an I-cord "stem."

DESIGNED BY AMY POLCYN

Size
Instructions are written for size 12–18 months.

Knitted Measurements
Head circumference 16"/40.5cm
Depth 6"/15cm (excluding I-cord)

Materials
■ 1 1¾oz/50g hank (approx 136yd/125m) of Cascade Yarns *220 Superwash Sport* (superwash merino wool) in #859 lake chelan heather

■ Size 5 (3.75mm) circular needle, 16"/40cm long, *or size to obtain gauge*

■ One set (5) size 5 (3.75mm) double-pointed needles (dpns)

■ Stitch marker

Stitch Glossary
K5B Slip next st off LH needle and unravel for 4 rows. Insert tip of RH needle through dropped st and under the 4 horizontal strands above the unraveled stitch. Insert LH needle into dropped st from left to right (as if to knit an ssk) and knit the stitch, trapping the 4 strands.

Bubble Pattern Stitch
(over a multiple of 4 sts)
Rnds 1–4 Knit.
Rnd 5 *K5B, k3; rep from * around.
Rnds 6–10 Knit.
Rnd 11 K2, *K5B, k3; rep from * to last 2 sts, K5B, k1.
Rnd 12 Knit.
Rep rnds 1–12 for bubble pat st.

Hat
With circular needle, cast on 92 sts. Join and pm for beg of rnds. Work around in St st (knit every rnd) for 1½"/4cm. Cont in bubble pat st and work even until piece measures 5"/12.5cm from beg.

CROWN SHAPING
Change to dpns (dividing sts evenly between 4 needles).
Next (dec) rnd Knit, dec 4 sts evenly spaced around—88 sts. Knit next rnd.
Dec rnd 1 *K6, k2tog; rep from * around—77 sts. Knit next rnd.
Dec rnd 2 *K5, k2tog; rep from * around—66 sts. Knit next rnd.
Dec rnd 3 *K4, k2tog; rep from * around—55 sts. Knit next rnd.
Dec rnd 4 *K3, k2tog; rep from * around—44 sts. Knit next rnd.
Dec rnd 5 *K2, k2tog; rep from * around—33 sts. Knit next rnd.
Dec rnd 6 *K1, k2tog; rep from * around—22 sts. Knit next rnd.
Dec rnd 7 [K2tog] 11 times—11 sts.
Dec rnd 8 K1, [k2tog] 5 times—6 sts.
Dec rnd 9 [K2tog] 3 times—3 sts.

I-CORD EMBELLISHMENT
Work I-cord as foll: *Next row (RS)** With 2nd dpn, k3, do not turn. Slide sts back to beg of needle to work next row from RS; rep from * for 3½"/9cm. Cut yarn, leaving an 8"/20.5cm tail. Thread tail in tapestry needle, then thread through rem sts. Pull tog tightly, secure end and weave in. Tie cord in an overhand knot at base. ■

Gauge
23 sts and 40 rnds to 4"/10cm over bubble pat st using size 5 (3.75mm) circular needle.
Take time to check gauge.

✻Pattern for Asymmetrical Stripes Cardigan is on page 136.

Plaid Jacket

Knit horizontal stripes and vertical stripes created in duplicate stitch form a rustic plaid pattern in this tiny lumberjack coat.

DESIGNED BY LINDA MEDINA

■■■■

Sizes

Instructions are written for size 6 months. Changes for 12 and 18 months are in parentheses. (Shown in size 12 months.)

Knitted Measurements

Chest 21 (22, 23)"/53.5 (56, 58.5)cm
Length 10½ (11¾, 12½)"/26.5 (30, 31.5)cm
Upper Arm 8 (9, 9½)"/20.5 (23, 24)cm

Materials

■ 1 (1, 1) 1¾oz/50g hanks (each approx 136yd/125m) of Cascade Yarns *220 Superwash Sport* (superwash merino wool) in each of #904 colonial blue heather (MC), #1944 westpoint blue heather (A), #864 christmas green (B), and #854 navy (C)
■ Size 6 (4mm) circular needle, 24" (61cm) long, *or size to obtain gauge*
■ Spare size 6 (4mm) needle
■ Stitch holders
■ Lockable stitch markers or safety pins
■ ¾yd/0.75m grosgrain ribbon, ⅞"/22mm wide
■ Sewing needle and thread
■ Eight ⁷⁄₁₆"/11mm snaps

Note

Body is worked in one piece to the underarms.

K1, P1 Rib

(over a multiple of 2 sts plus 1)
Row 1 (RS) *K1, p1; rep from * to last st, k1.
Row 2 *P1, k1; rep from * to last st, p1.
Rep rows 1 and 2 for k1, p1 rib.

Stripe Pattern

Row 1 (RS) With A, knit.
Row 2 Purl.
Row 3 Knit.
Row 4 With B, purl.
Row 5 Knit.
Row 6 With C, purl.
Row 7 Purl.
Row 8 With B, purl.
Row 9 Knit.
Row 10 With A, purl.
Row 11 Knit.
Row 12 Purl.
Row 13 With MC, knit.
Row 14 Knit.
Rep rows 1–14 for pat.

Note

Carry color not in use loosely up the side of the work.

Jacket

BODY
With MC, cast on 113 (119, 125) sts. Work in k1, p1 rib for 8 rows. Change to St st (k on RS, p on WS). Work in stripe pat until piece measures 6½ (7¼, 7¾)"/16.5 (18.5, 19.5)cm from beg, ending with a RS row.

DIVIDE FOR FRONTS AND BACK
Next row (WS) Cont in stripe pat, p23 (25, 27), place these sts on holder for left front. Bind off next 6 sts for underarm, p55 (57, 59) (back), bind off next 6 sts for underarm. P23 (25, 27) and place these sts on holder for right front. Cont on 55 (57, 59) back sts only.

BACK
Cont in stripe pat, dec 1 st each end of row every row 4 times—47 (49, 51) sts. Work even in stripe pat until armholes measure 4 (4½, 4¾)"/10 (11.5, 12)cm, ending with a RS row.

NECK SHAPING
Next row (WS) P14, join a second ball of yarn and bind off center 19 (21, 23) sts, purl to end. Working both sides

Gauge

22 sts and 28 rows to 4"/10cm over St st using size 6 (4mm) needles. *Take time to check gauge.*

Plaid Jacket

neck edge on next RS row 1 (2, 3) times. Work even in stripe pat until piece measures same as back. Place sts on holder.

LEFT FRONT
Place held left front sts on needles. Work as for right front, reversing all shaping.

SLEEVES
With MC, cast on 33 (33, 35) sts. Work in k1, p1 rib for 8 rows. Change to St st. Work in stripe pat, inc 1 st each end of row every 5 rows 4 times, then every 4 rows 2 (4, 4) times—45 (49, 51) sts. Work even until piece measures 6 (7, 7½)"/15 (18, 19)cm, ending with a WS row.

CAP SHAPING
Bind off 3 sts at beg of next 2 rows—39 (43, 45) sts. Cont in stripe pat, dec 1 st each end of row every other row 5 (7, 8) times, then every row 6 times. Bind off 4 sts at beg of next 2 rows—9 sts. Bind off.

Finishing
DUPLICATE STITCH DETAIL
On body, place a marker or safety pin 2 sts in from left front edge, then *skip 1 st, place a second pin, skip 4 sts, place a pin; rep from * across. At first pin, with B, work a vertical column of duplicate

stitch through entire striped section. Rep at rem pins, alternating C and B. With C only, do not work duplicate st over garter ridges; instead, slide needle underneath the ridge and resume duplicate st on the opposite side (work over garter ridges in B). Rep on sleeves, beg in center of piece and working out toward the side edges.
Join shoulders using 3-needle bind-off. Set in sleeves, sew sleeve seams.

FLAPS (make 2)
With MC, cast on 13 sts. Work in St st for 3 rows. Dec 1 st each end of row every row until 3 sts rem.
Next row (RS) K3tog—1 st. Fasten off. Cut yarn, leaving a long tail for sewing.

FRONT BANDS
With RS facing and MC, pick up and knit 53 (59, 63) sts along right front. Work in k1, p1 rib for 8 rows. Bind off. Rep on left front.

NECKBAND
With RS facing and MC, pick up and knit 81 (83, 85) sts beginning at center of right front band and ending at center of left front band. Work in k1, p1 rib for 8 rows. Bind off.

Cut 2 pieces of grosgrain ribbon ½"/1cm longer than front bands. Fold ends in ¼"/0.5cm, then sew in place on WS of bands with sewing needle and thread. Sew a small piece of ribbon on the center of each flap, on the WS. Install one top section of snap to middle of each flap. Sew flaps to body as shown. Set six snaps on front bands. ∎

separately, dec 1 st at neck edge every row twice, then work 2 rows even—12 sts per shoulder. Place sts on holders.

RIGHT FRONT
Place 23 (25, 27) held right front sts on needles. Cont in stripe pat, dec 1 st at armhole edge every row 4 times—19 (21, 23) sts. Work even in stripe pat until armhole measures 2½ (3, 3¼)"/6.5 (7.5, 8)cm, ending with a WS row.

NECK SHAPING
Bind off 4 (5, 6) sts at neck edge once, then 2 sts at neck edge once. Dec 1 st at

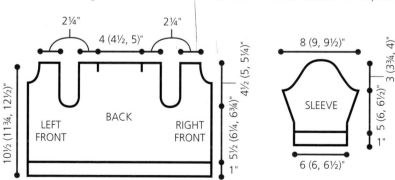

18

V-neck Onesie

Buttons along the inside legs of this handsome onesie make for easy dressing. A decorative pocket and ribbed edges complete the look.

DESIGNED BY VERONICA MANNO

Sizes
Instructions are written for size 3 months. Changes for 6 and 12 months are in parentheses. (Shown in size 6 months.)

Knitted Measurements
Chest 24 (26, 28)"/61 (66, 71)cm
Length 16½ (18, 19)"/42 (46, 48)cm

Materials
■ 4 (5, 6) 1¾ oz/50g hanks (each approx 136yd/125m) of Cascade Yarns *220 Superwash Spor*t (superwash merino wool) in #897 baby denim
■ Size 6 (4mm) needles *or size to obtain gauge*
■ Size 5 (3.75mm) needles
■ 10½"/13mm buttons
■ Stitch holder

K2, P2 Rib
(multiple of 4 sts)
Row 1 (RS) *K2, p2; rep from * to end.
Row 2 Rep row 1.
Rep rows 1 and 2 for k2, p2 rib.

Onesie
BACK
With smaller needles, cast on 36 (40, 44) sts. Work in k2, p2 rib for 2"/5cm, increase 7 (9, 9) sts evenly spaced across last WS row—43 (49, 53) sts. Change to larger needles. Work even in St st (knit on RS, purl on WS) until piece measures

Gauge
24 sts and 32 rows to 4"/10cm over St st using size 6 (4mm) needles.
Take time to check gauge.

V-neck Onesie

3 (4, 4)"/7.5 (10, 10) cm from beg, end with a WS row. Place sts on holder, set aside, and make second back leg in same manner.

JOIN LEGS

Next row (RS) K 43 (49, 53) sts from one leg, cast on 6 (8, 8) sts, work across 43 (49, 53) sts from second leg—92 (106, 114) sts. Work even in St st for 1"/2.5cm. Dec 1 st at each side on next RS row—90 (104, 112) sts. Cont to dec at each side every 4th row 10 (13, 14) times more—70 (78, 84) sts. Work even until piece measures 12½ (13½, 14½)"/32 (34, 37)cm from beg, end with a RS row.

ARMHOLE SHAPING

Bind off from each side 6 sts once, 3 sts once, 2 sts once, 1 st twice—44 (52, 58) sts. Work even until armhole measures 4 (4½, 4½)"/10 (11.5, 11.5)cm. Bind off.

FRONT

Work same as back until piece measures 10½ (11½, 12½)"/26.5 (29, 32)cm from beg, end with a WS row.

PLACKET OPENING

Mark center 6 sts.
Next row (RS) Work to marker, join second ball of yarn and bind off center 6 sts, work to end of row—32 (36, 39) sts each side. Work even over both sides of neck until same length as back to armhole shaping.

SHAPE ARMHOLES

Working both sides of neck at once, shape armholes same as for back—19 (23, 26) sts each side of neck.

SHAPE NECK

Working both sides of neck at once, decrease 1 st at both sides of neck opening 7 (9, 9) times—12 (14, 17) sts each side of neck.
Work even until armhole measures 4 (4½, 4½)"/10 (11.5, 11.5)cm. Bind off both sides of neck.

Finishing

Block pieces to measurements. Sew shoulder seams.

NECKBAND

With smaller needles and RS facing, pick up and knit 44 (46, 48) sts along right front edge, 20 (24, 24) sts along back neck, 44 (46, 46) sts along left front edge—108 (116, 116) sts. Work in k2, p2 rib for 2 rows.
Next (buttonhole) row (WS) [Work 6 sts, k2tog, yo] 3 times, rib to end. Work 2 more rows in rib. Bind off. Place buttonhole band over button band, sew

edges of both bands to bound-off edge of neck opening. Sew buttons opposite buttonholes.

POCKET

With larger needles, cast on 30 (36, 36) sts. Work in St st for 2 rows. Dec 1 st each side on next row, then every 4th row 4 (6, 6) times more—20 (22, 22) sts. Work 3 rows even. Bind off. With smaller needles and RS facing, pick and knit 20 (24, 24) sts evenly along one angled edge of pocket. Work in k2, p2 rib for ¾"/2cm. Bind off. Work rib on other angled edge. Using photo as guide, place pocket in center of front below placket opening. Sew pocket in place, leaving ribbed edges open. Sew side seams.

ARMHOLE BANDS

With smaller needles and RS facing, pick up and k 76 (80, 80) sts around each armhole edge. Work in k2, p2 rib for ¾"/2cm. Bind off.

INSEAM BUTTON BANDS

With smaller needles and RS facing, beg at cast-on row of ribbing, pick up and k 56 (64, 64) sts along inner edge of back legs. Work in k2, p2 rib for ¾"/2cm. Bind off.
Pick up and k along inner edge of front legs in same manner. Work in k2, p2 rib for 2 rows.
Next (buttonhole) row (WS) Rib 6 (7, 7), [yo, k2tog, rib 5 (6, 6)] 7 times, k1. Work in k2, p2 rib for 2 rows. Bind off. Sew buttons to WS of back button band, opposite buttonholes. ∎

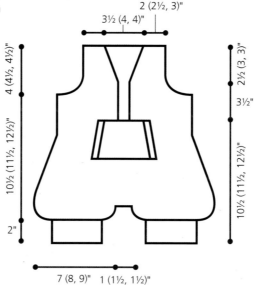

2 (2½, 3)"

3½ (4, 4)"

4 (4½, 4½)"

2½ (3, 3)"

3½"

10½ (11½, 12½)"

10½ (11½, 12½)"

2"

7 (8, 9)"   1 (1½, 1½)"

Lined Blanket

Adding a fabric lining and quilt batting to a simple knit blanket transforms it into something extra-special and extra-warm. "Whoo" wouldn't love that?

DESIGNED BY SANDI PROSSER

Knitted Measurements
Approx 30" x 30"/76cm x 76cm

Materials
■ 8 1¾oz/50g hanks (each approx 136yd/125m) of Cascade Yarns *220 Superwash Sport* (superwash merino wool) in #802 green apple
■ Size 6 (4mm) circular needle, 36"/91cm long *or size to obtain gauge*
■ Size E/4 (3.5mm) crochet hook
■ 1 yd/1m lightweight cotton fabric
■ 1 yd/1m low-loft fusible batting
■ Sewing needle and sewing thread

Blanket
Cast on 183 sts.
Row 1 (RS) Knit.
Row 2 K1, purl to last st, end k1.
Row 3 K1, *[p1, k1] 5 times, p10; rep from * to last 2 sts, end p1, k1.
Row 4 K2, *k10, [p1, k1] 5 times; rep from * to last st, end k1.
Row 5 K1, *p1, [p1, k1] 4 times, p2, k9; rep from * to last 2 sts, end p1, k1.
Row 6 K2, *p9, k1, [k1, p1] 4 times, k2; rep from * to last st, end k1.
Rows 7–22 Rep rows 3–6 four times more.
Rows 23 and 25 Knit.

Rows 24 and 26 K1, purl to last st, end k1.
Row 27 K1, *p11, [k1, p1] 4 times, k1; rep from * to last 2 sts, end p1, k1.
Row 28 K2, *[p1, k1] 4 times, p1, k11; rep from * to last st, end k1.
Row 29 K1, *p1, k9, p1, [p1, k1] 4 times, p1; rep from * to last 2 sts, end p1, k1.
Row 30 K2, *k1, [p1, k1] 4 times, k1, p9, k1; rep from * to last st, end k1.
Rows 31–46 Rep rows 27–30 four times more.
Row 47 Knit.
Row 48 K1, purl to last st, end k1.
Rep rows 1–48 four times more, then rows 1–24 once. Bind off all sts loosely knitwise. Piece should measure approximately 30"/76cm from beg.

Finishing
Block piece lightly to measurements.

EDGING
With RS facing and crochet hook, join yarn with a sl st in any corner.
Rnd 1 (RS) Ch 1, making sure that work lies flat, sc evenly around entire edge, working 3 sc in each corner, join rnd with a sl st in first sc. Fasten off.

LINING
Cut one 36"x 36"/91.5cm x 91.5cm square each of cotton fabric and batting. Fuse batting to WS of cotton fabric following package directions. Place lining/batting, batting side up, on work surface. Place WS of blanket on top of batting. Center blanket carefully and pin around the perimeter, working from the center out along each edge. Trim lining/batting so it's ½"/1.3cm wider all around than blanket. Remove pins. Fold each edge of lining/batting ½"/1.3cm to WS and press. Place blanket WS up on work surface. Place lining/batting, lining side up, on top of blanket. Center lining/batting carefully and pin in place, working from the center out along each edge. Butting edge of lining to bottom edge of sc edging, slipstitch lining to blanket. ■

Gauge
24 sts and 34 rows to 4"/10cm over pat st using size 6 (4mm) circular needle. *Take time to check gauge.*

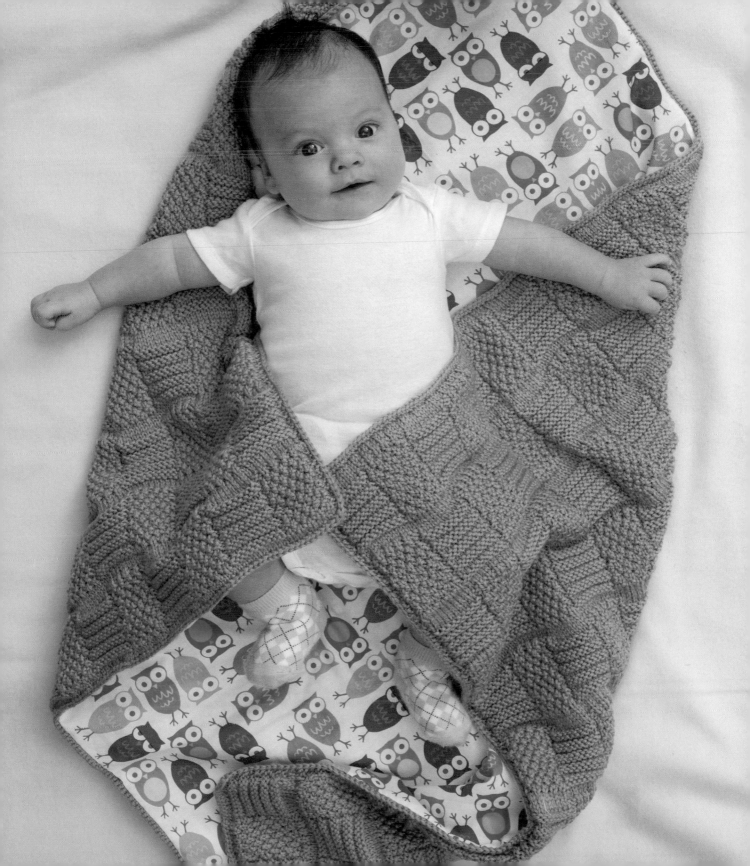

Summer Sunsuit

This cute combo is as summery as mint chocolate chip ice cream. Pair the separates with other pieces for even more stylish looks.

DESIGNED BY MARY BONNETTE

Sizes
Instructions are written for size 6 months. Changes for 12 and 18 months are in parentheses. (Shown in size 12 months.)

Knitted Measurements
TOP
Chest 21 (22, 23)"/53 (56, 58)cm
Length 7¾ (8½, 9½)"/19.5 (21.5, 24)cm

PANTS
Waist 19 (20, 20½)"/48 (50.5, 52)cm
Length 9 (10, 11)"/23 (25.5, 28)cm

Materials
■ 3 (3, 4) 1¾oz/50g hanks (each approx 136yd/125m) of Cascade Yarns *220 Superwash Sport* (superwash merino wool) in #1942 mint (MC)
■ 1 hank in #1946 silver grey (CC)
■ Size 6 (4mm) circular needle, 24"/61cm length *or size to obtain gauge*
■ Size E/4 (3.5mm) crochet hook
■ Stitch markers
■ Stitch holders
■ Two ⅝"/16mm buttons

K1, P1 Rib
Rnd 1 *K1, p1; rep from * across.
Rep rnd 1 for k1, p1 rib.

Seed Stitch
Row 1 (RS) * K1, p1; rep from * across.
Row 2 Purl the knit sts and knit the purl sts as they appear. Rep row 2 for seed st.

Pants
LEGS (make 2)
With MC, cast on 144 (150, 156) sts.
Row 1 (RS) Knit.
Row 2 Purl.
Row 3 K3tog across—48 (50, 52) sts.
Row 4 Purl.
Rows 5–10 With CC, work in St st (k on RS, p on WS).
Row 11 With MC, knit, inc 1 st each end of row—50 (52, 54) sts.
Rows 12–16 Work in St st.
Row 17 With CC, knit, inc 1 st each end of row—52 (54, 56) sts. Size 6 months only; cont to crotch shaping.

SIZES 12 AND 18 MONTHS
Rows 18–22 (24) Work in St st in stripe pat as set.

ALL SIZES
Piece measures approx 2½ (3, 3½)"/ 6.5(7.5, 9)cm, ending with a WS row.

CROTCH SHAPING
Continuing in stripe pat, inc 1 st each end of row every row 3 times—58 (60,62) sts. Place sts on holder; make second leg. For size 6 months only, work one row even.

JOIN LEGS
Next row (WS) Purl across first leg, cast on 3 sts, purl across second leg, cast on 3 sts—122 (126, 130) sts. Knit next row. Pm and join in the rnd. Work in stripe pat and St st (knit every rnd), changing colors every 6 rnds, until piece measures 8 (9, 10)"/20.5 (23, 25.5)cm from beg.

WAISTBAND
Next rnd Dec 18 (16, 18) sts evenly around—104 (110, 112) sts. Knit next rnd. With MC, work in k1, p1 rib for 10 rnds. Bind off in rib.

Finishing
Weave in ends. Sew inseams. With crochet hook and MC held double, work a ch approx 30"/76cm long. Fasten off. Thread several 3"/7.5cm lengths through ends of chain, fold in half and tie in overhand knot to form tassels. Weave chain through ribbing at waist.

Gauge
22 sts and 28 rows to 4"/10cm over St st using size 6 (4mm) needles.
Take time to check gauge.

20 Summer Sunsuit

BACK

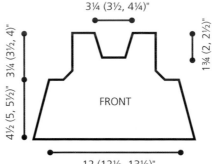

3¼ (3½, 4¼)"

4½ (5, 5½)" 3¼ (3½, 4)"

1¾ (2, 2½)"

FRONT

12 (12½, 13½)"

RIGHT BACK

6 (6½, 6¾)"

Top

FRONT

With MC, cast on 68 (70, 74) sts. Work back and forth in seed st for 8 rows. Change to St st, dec 1 st each end of row every 6 rows 5 times—58 (60, 64) sts. Work even until piece measures 4½ (5, 5½)"/11.5 (12.5, 14)cm, ending with a WS row.

ARMHOLE SHAPING

Bind off 6 sts at beg of next 2 rows—46 (48, 52) sts. Cont in St st, dec 1 st each end of row every other row 3 times—40 (42, 46) sts. Work even until piece measures 6 (6½, 7)"/15 (16.5, 17.5)cm from beg, ending with a WS row.

NECK SHAPING

Next row (RS) K14 (14, 15), join a second ball of yarn and bind off center 12 (14, 16) sts, knit to end. Working both sides in St st at the same time, dec 1 st each neck edge every other row 3 (3, 4) times—11 sts. Work even until piece measures 7¾ (8½, 9½)"/19.5 (21.5, 24)cm. Bind off.

RIGHT BACK

With MC, cast on 34 (35, 37) sts. Work back and forth in seed st for 8 rows. Change to St st.
Next row (RS) Ssk, knit to last 7 sts, work in seed st over next 6 sts, M1, work last st.

Next row Work first 8 sts in seed st, purl to end. Rep last 2 rows, and, AT THE SAME TIME, work an additional dec at side edge every 6 rows 5 times—29 (30, 32) sts. Rep last 2 rows without additional dec until piece measures 4½ (5, 5½)"/11.5 (12.5, 14)cm, ending with a WS row.

ARMHOLE SHAPING

Bind off 6 sts at beg of row—23 (24, 26) sts. Cont in St st, and maintaining shaping and seed st edge as before, dec 1 additional st at beg of row every other row 3 times—20 (21, 23) sts. Work even until piece measures 6 (6½, 7)"/15 (16.5, 17.5)cm from beg, ending with a WS row.

NECK SHAPING

Work as for front, keeping seed st edge as set. Do not bind off.

TAB SHAPING

Note Work buttonhole on left side strap only; on right side strap, work across row without binding off.
Next (buttonhole) row (RS) K6, bind off 2 sts, work in pattern to end. On next row, work in pattern, casting on 2 sts over gap. Work 2 rows more, binding off 1 st at beg of each row—9 sts. Bind off.

LEFT BACK

With MC, cast on 34 (35, 37) sts. Work

back and forth in seed st for 8 rows. Change to St st.
Next row (RS) K1, M1, work next 6 sts in seed st, knit to last 2 sts, k2tog.
Next row Purl to last 8 sts, work in seed st. Rep last 2 rows, and, AT THE SAME TIME, work an additional dec at side edge every 6 rows 5 times—29 (30, 32) sts. Rep last 2 rows without additional dec until piece measures 4½ (5, 5½)"/11.5 (12.5,14)cm, ending with a RS row. Finish as for right back, reversing all shaping. Work buttonhole on same strap as right back.

Finishing

Block pieces. Sew side seams. With crochet hook and MC, work 1 rnd of sc around neck, armholes, and tabs (through both thicknesses of back). Fasten off. Weave in ends. Sew button opposite buttonhole. On right strap sew button in place decoratively. ∎

19 (20, 20½)"

9 (10, 11)" 5½ (6, 6½)"

2½ (3, 3½)"

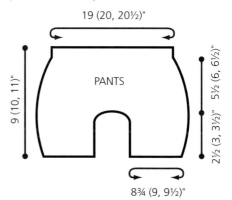

PANTS

8¾ (9, 9½)"

21

Fringed Poncho

Your little girl will love to skip off to school or jump in a pile
of leaves wearing this hippie-chic poncho.

DESIGNED BY LOREN CHERENSKY

■◀■■▷

Sizes

Instructions are written for size 12 to 18
months. Changes for 2 to 3 years are in
parentheses. (Shown in size 2 to 3 years.)

Knitted Measurements

Width 16 (18)"/40.5 (45.5)cm
Length 10 (11)"/25.5 (28)cm (excluding
fringe)

Materials

■ 4 (5) 1¾oz/50g hanks (each approx
136yd/125m) of Cascade Yarns *220
Superwash Sport* (superwash merino
wool) in #1942 mint (MC)

■ 1 (2) hank in #808 sunset orange (CC)

■ One pair size 6 (4mm) needles *or size
to obtain gauge*

■ Size D/3 (3.25mm) crochet hook

■ Stitch markers

■ Bobbins

Note

When working chart pat, use a separate
bobbin of color for each color section.

Back

With MC, cast on 3 sts.
Row 1 (RS) Knit.
Row 2 Purl.
Row (inc) 3 K1, M1, k1, M1, k1—5 sts.
Row (inc) 4 P1, M1 p-st, p3, M1 p-st,
p1—7 sts.
Row (inc) 5 K1, M1, knit to last st, M1,
k1—9 sts.
Row (inc) 6 P1, M1 p-st, purl to last st,

M1 p-st, p1—11 sts. Rep rows 5 and 6
until there are 97 (109) sts on needle,
end with a WS row. Piece should
measure approximately 6½ (7)"/16.5
(18)cm from beg. Work even for 28 (32)
rows. Piece should measure
approximately 10 (11)"/25.5 (28)cm from
beg. Bind off all sts knitwise.

Front

With MC, cast on 3 sts.
Row 1 (RS) Knit.
Row 2 Purl. Mark for center st as foll:
Row (inc) 3 K1, M1, pm, k1, pm, M1,
k1—5 sts.
Row (inc) 4 P1, M1 p-st, p1, sl marker,
p1, sl marker, p1, M1 p-st, p1—7 sts.
Slipping markers *every* row, cont to work
as for back until piece measures 6 (7)"/15
(18)cm from beg, end with a WS row.

NECK OPENING
FOR SIZE 12 MONTHS ONLY
Next row (RS) Work across to first
marker, drop marker, join a 2nd hank of
MC, bind off center st, drop 2nd marker,
work to end. Working both sides at once,
cont to inc each side every row until
there are 48 sts each side, end with a WS

Gauge

24 sts and 30 rows to 4"/10cm over St st using size 6 (4mm) needles.
Take time to check gauge.

Fringed Poncho

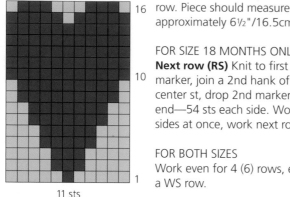

16

10

1

11 sts

Color Key

Mint (MC)

Sunset Orange (CC)

row. Piece should measure approximately 6½"/16.5cm from beg.

FOR SIZE 18 MONTHS ONLY
Next row (RS) Knit to first marker, drop marker, join a 2nd hank of MC, bind off center st, drop 2nd marker, knit to end—54 sts each side. Working both sides at once, work next row even.

FOR BOTH SIZES
Work even for 4 (6) rows, end with a WS row.

BEG CHART PAT
Row 1 (RS) With first hank of MC, k26 (30), work 11 sts of chart, with MC, k11 (13); with 2nd hank of MC, knit to end. Working both sides at once, cont to foll chart in this way to row 16, end with a WS row. Work neck shaping as foll:

NECK SHAPING
Bind off 5 (6) sts from each neck edge once, then 2 sts twice. Work even on 39 (44) sts each side for 2 rows. Bind off each side knitwise.

Finishing
Block pieces lightly to measurements. Sew shoulder seams.

NECK EDGING
With RS facing and crochet hook, join MC with a sl st in left shoulder seam.
Rnd 1 (RS) Ch 1, making sure that work lies flat, sc evenly around entire neck edge, working 3 sc in each corner and 1 sc in bound-off st at beg of neck opening, join rnd with a sl st in first st. Fasten off.

TASSELS (MAKE 2)
Wrap MC 11 times around a 2¼"/5.5cm piece of cardboard. Slip a 10"/25.5cm strand of MC under strands and tightly knot at one end of cardboard. Remove cardboard. Wrap another length of MC 4 times around the tassel about ½"/1.3cm down from top. Cut loops at opposite end. Trim ends even.

TIES (MAKE 2)
With crochet hook and MC, make a 6"/15cm long chain. Fasten off. Sew one end of chain to top of tassel, then sew opposite end of chain to corner of neck edge.

FRINGE
Cut 6"/15cm strands of CC. Using 3 strands for each fringe, attach fringe evenly spaced around edges of poncho. Trim ends evenly. ■

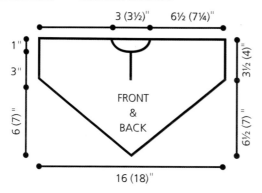

3 (3½)"   6½ (7¼)"

1"

3"

6 (7)"

3½ (4)"

6½ (7)"

FRONT
&
BACK

16 (18)"

Striped Ski Hat

This extra-warm cap is perfect for a winter's walk or playing in the snow.
Customize the colors to match a jacket or snowsuit.

DESIGNED BY NANCY CASSELS

Sizes
Instructions are written for newborn–3 months. Changes for size 6–12 months are in parentheses. (Shown in size 6–12 months.)

Knitted Measurements
Head circumference 14½ (16)"/37 (40.5)cm (stretched)
Depth 5½ (6)"/14 (15)cm (excluding cuff)

Materials
■ 1 1¾oz/50g hank (each approx 136yd/125m) of Cascade Yarns *220 Superwash Sport* (superwash merino wool) each in #1946 silver grey (MC) and #809 really red (CC)
■ One set (5) size 5 (3.75mm) double-pointed needles (dpns) *or size to obtain gauge*
■ Stitch marker
■ 2½"/5cm pompom maker

P1, K1 Rib
(over an even number of sts)
Rnd 1 (RS) *P1, k1; rep from * around.
Rep rnd 1 for p1, k1 rib.

Stripe Pattern
Working in p1, k1 rib, work *8 rnds CC, 8 rnds MC; rep from * (16 rnds) for stripe pat.

Hat
With MC, cast on 80 (88) sts, dividing sts evenly over 4 needles. Join and pm, taking care not to twist sts on needles. Work in p1, k1 rib for 3 (4)"/7.5 (10)cm. Beg stripe pat, AT THE SAME TIME, work even until piece measures 5½ (6½)"/14 (16.5)cm from beg.

CROWN SHAPING
Dec rnd 1 *K2tog, p2tog; rep from * around—40 (44) sts. Work even in rib until piece measures 7 (8)"/18 (20.5)cm from beg.

Dec rnd 2 *K2tog, p2tog; rep from * around—20 (22) sts. Work next rnd even in rib. Cut yarn, leaving an 8"/20.5cm tail, and thread through rem sts. Pull tog tightly and secure end.

POMPOM
Using MC and pompom maker, make a 2½"/6.5cm diameter pompom. Sew pompom to top of hat. Fold up bottom edge 1½ (2)"/4 (5)cm for cuff. ■

Gauge
37 sts and 32 rnds to 4"/10cm over p1, k1 rib using size 5 (3.75mm) dpns (unstretched).
Take time to check gauge.

23

Lace & Cables Cardigan

Beautiful lace edgings perfectly finish this gorgeous, and very girly, pink lacy cabled cardigan. A single button is all the adornment it needs.

DESIGNED BY GRACE AKHREM

Sizes

Instructions are written for size 3 months. Changes for 6 and 12 months are in parentheses. (Shown in size 3 months.)

Knitted Measurements

Chest (closed) 20 (22, 24)"/51 (56, 61)cm
Length 9¼ (10¼, 11¼)"/23.5 (26, 28.5)cm
Upper arm 7 (8, 9)"/18 (20.5, 23)cm

Materials

■ 2 (3, 4) 1¾oz/50g hanks (each approx 136yd/125m) of Cascade Yarns *220 Superwash Sport* (superwash merino wool) in #901 cotton candy

■ Size 6 (4mm) circular needle, 32"/81cm long, *or size to obtain gauge*

■ Size 3 (3.25mm) circular needle, 32"/81cm long

■ Scrap yarn

■ Stitch holders

■ One ¾"/19mm button

■ Size G/6 (4mm) crochet hook

■ Cable needle (cn)

Stitch Glossary

4-st RC Sl next 2 sts to cn and hold to back, k2, k2 from cn.
SK2P Sl 1, k2tog, pass sl st over k2tog.

Provisional Method Cast-on

Using scrap yarn and crochet hook, ch the number of sts to cast on plus a few extra. Cut a tail and pull the tail through the last chain. With knitting needle and yarn, pick up and knit the stated number of sts through the "purl bumps" on the back of the chain. To remove waste chain, when instructed, pull out the tail from the last crochet stitch. Gently and slowly pull on the tail to unravel the crochet stitches, carefully placing each released knit stitch on a needle.

Lace Edging

Row 1 (RS) With yarn held in front, sl 1, k2, k last st tog with 1 st from body. Turn.
Row 2 With yarn held in front, sl 1, k1, yo twice, k2tog. Turn.
Row 3 Yo RH needle, k1, [k1, p1] in double yo, k1, k last st tog with 1 st from body. Turn.
Row 4 With yarn held in front, sl 1, k5. Turn.
Row 5 With yarn held in front, skp, bind off the resulting st, k2, k last st tog with 1

st from body. Turn. Rep rows 2–5 for lace edging.

Cardigan

BODY
Using provisional method and larger needle, cast on 122 (133, 144) sts. Do not join. Purl 1 row on WS.

BEG CHART
Row 1 (RS) Work 11-st rep 11 (12, 13) times to last st, p1.
With 1 rev St st (purl on RS, knit on WS) at end of RS rows, work even foll lace chart until the 4-row rep has been worked 8 (8, 9) times and piece measures approx 4 (4, 5)"/10 (10, 12.5)cm from beg, end with a WS row.

BODICE
Next row (RS) Knit.
Next row K3 for front band, p to last 3 sts, k3 for front band. With first 3 sts and last 3 sts in garter st (knit every row), cont in St st (knit on RS, purl on WS) until piece measures 5 (5½, 6)"/12.5 (14, 15)cm from beg, end with a WS row.

Gauges

24 sts and 32 rows to 4"/10cm over lace chart pat using size 6 (4mm) needle.
24 sts and 32 rows to 4"/10cm over St st using size 6 (4mm) needle. *Take time to check gauges.*

Lace & Cables Cardigan

DIVIDE FOR ARMHOLES
Next row K30 (33, 35) sts for right front, place these sts on holder, k61 (66, 73) sts for back, place rem 31 (34, 36) sts on holder for left front.

BACK
Work even in St st until piece measures 8½ (9½, 10½)"/21.5 (24, 26.5)cm from beg. Bind off.

LEFT FRONT
Rejoin yarn to work RS row, k 30 (33, 35) sts. With last 3 sts in garter st, cont in St st until piece measures 6 (6, 7)"/15 (15, 18)cm from beg, end with a RS row.

NECK SHAPING
Bind off 4 (5, 6) sts at beg next 2 WS rows—22 (23, 23) sts. Dec 1 st at beg of WS rows 4 (5, 5) times—18 sts. Work even in St st until piece measures 8½ (9½, 10½)"/21.5 (24, 26.5)cm from beg. Bind off.

RIGHT FRONT
Rejoin yarn to work WS row, p27 (30, 32), k3. With first 3 sts in garter st, cont in St st until piece measures 6 (6, 7)"/15 (15, 18)cm from beg, end with a WS row.

NECK SHAPING
Bind off 4 (5, 6) sts at beg next 2 RS rows—22 (23, 23) sts. Dec 1 st at beg of RS rows 4 (5, 5) times—18 sts. Work even in St st until piece measures 8½ (9½, 10½)"/21.5 (24, 26.5)cm from beg. Bind off.

SLEEVES
Using provisional method and larger needle, cast on 45 (49, 56) sts. Purl 1 row on WS.

BEG CHART
Row 1 (RS) P0 (2, 0), work 11-st rep 4 (4, 5) times, p 1 (3, 1). With rev St sts at each end as established, work even foll lace chart until the 4-row rep has been worked 7 times, piece measures approx 3½"/9cm from beg.

UPPER SLEEVE
Next row (RS) With larger needle, knit. Work even in St st until piece measures 6 (6½, 7)"/15 (16.5, 18)cm. Bind off.

Finishing
Block pieces to measurements.

Sew shoulder seams.

LACE EDGING
Carefully remove scrap yarn from body sts, place these sts on smaller needle, ready for RS row. Cast on 4 sts to LH needle. Do not join. Work lace edging pat until all body sts have been used, end with RS row. Turn. Bind off on WS. Fasten off last st. Work lace edging on sleeves in same manner. Sew underarm seams, set sleeves into armholes. With crochet hook and RS facing, beg at lace edging of right front and work a row of sc to the beg of neck shaping, ch 6 for button loop, cont to sc around neck edge and left front. Sew button to left front opposite loop. ■

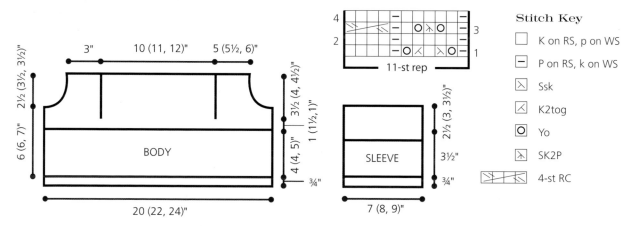

Stitch Key

☐	K on RS, p on WS
▬	P on RS, k on WS
◿	Ssk
◺	K2tog
○	Yo
⅄	SK2P
▱	4-st RC

11-st rep

BODY

SLEEVE

3" 10 (11, 12)" 5 (5½, 6)"

2½ (3½, 3½)" 6 (6, 7)"

3½ (4, 4½)" 1 (1½, 1)" 4 (4, 5)" ¾"

20 (22, 24)"

2½ (3, 3½)" 3½" ¾"

7 (8, 9)"

24

Bunny Blanket

Cuddly bunnies play hide and seek on this adorable blanket.
Hop to it and knit it for your little rabbit.

DESIGNED BY AMY BAHRT

Knitted Measurements
Approx 25¼" x 27¼"/64cm x 69cm

Materials
■ ·5 1¾oz/50g hanks (each approx 136yd/125m) of Cascade Yarns *220 Superwash Sport* (superwash merino wool) in #1914 alaska sky (A)
■ 1 hank each in #802 green apple (B), #826 tangerine (C), and #817 aran (D)
■ Size 5 (3.75mm) circular needle, 36"/91cm long, *or size to obtain gauge*
■ One pair size 5 (3.75mm) needles
■ Size G/6 (4mm) crochet hook
■ Bobbins
■ Two ⅜"/10mm 4-holed white buttons
■ Sewing needle and green sewing thread
■ Small amount of polyester fiberfill (for stuffing head)
■ 1½"/4cm pompom maker

Notes
1) Blanket is worked counting rows. Therefore, row gauge must be achieved for best results.
2) You must keep track of rows as you go. Using ruled paper, write down rows 1–226, using a separate line for each number. Check off each row as you work it.
3) Rows for chart pats are numbered (1–20 for chart 1, 1–54 for chart 2 and 1–21 for chart 3). These numbered rows are for following the charts only. They do not correspond to numbered rows for the blanket.
4) Work charts and borders using intarsia technique, using a separate bobbin of color for each color section.

Stitch Glossary
kf&b Inc 1 by knitting into the front and back of the next st.

Blanket
Note Bottom, top, and side borders are worked in garter st (knit every row); rem sts at worked in St st (knit on RS, purl on WS). With circular needle and A, cast on 153 sts.
Rows 1–4 With A, knit.
Rows 5–8 K3 with A, k147 with B, k3 with A.

BEG CHART PAT 1
Row 9 (RS) K3 with A, k3 with B, k21 with A, [work row 1 of chart 1 over 33 sts] 3 times, k21 with A, k3 with B, k3 with A.
Rows 10–28 Cont to work as established, working rows 2–20 of chart 1.
Row 29 (RS) K3 with A, k3 with B, k20 with A, k101 with B, k20 with A,

Gauge
24 sts and 33 rows to 4"/10cm over St st and chart pats using size 5 (3.75mm) circular needle (after blocking).
Take time to check gauge.

Bunny Blanket

CHART 1

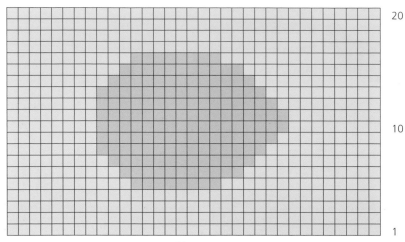

20

10

1

33 sts

Color Key

- ☐ Alaska Sky (A)
- ☐ Tangerine (C)
- ☐ Aran (D)

k3 with B, k3 with A.
Row 30 K3 with A, k3 with B, p20 with A, p101 with B, p20 with A, k3 with B, k3 with A.

BEG CHART PAT 2
Row 31 (RS) K3 with A, k3 with B, k20 with A, k2 with B, work row 1 of chart 2 over next 31 sts, k2 with B, k31 with A, k2 with B, work row 1 of chart 2 over next 31 sts, k2 with B, k20 with A, k3 with B, k3 with A.
Rows 32–46 Cont to work as established, working rows 2–16 of chart 2.

BEG CHART PAT 3/CONT CHART PAT 2
Row 47 (RS) K3 with A, k3 with B, work row 1 of chart 3 over next 20 sts, k2 with B, work row 17 of chart 2 over next 31 sts, k2 with B, k31 with A, k2 with B, work row 17 of chart 2 over next 31 sts, k2 with B, work row 1 of chart 3 over next 20 sts, k3 with B, k3 with A.
Rows 48–67 Cont to work as established, working rows 2–21 of chart 3 and rows 18–37 of chart 2.
Row 68 K3 with A, k3 with B, p20 with A, p2 with B, work row 38 of chart 2 over next 31 sts, p2 with B, p31 with A, p2 with B, work row 38 of chart 2 over next 31 sts, p2 with B, p20 with A, k3 with B, k3 with A.
Rows 69–84 Cont to work as established, working rows 39–54 of chart 2.
Rows 85 and 86 Rep rows 29 and 30.

BEG CHART PAT 2
Row 87 (RS) K3 with A, k3 with B, k20 with A, k2 with B, k31 with A, k2 with B, work row 1 of chart 2 over next 31 sts, k2 with B, k31 with A, k2 with B, k20 with

Bunny Blanket

A, k3 with B, k3 with A.
Rows 88–102 Cont to work as established, working rows 2–16 of chart 2.

BEG CHART PAT 3/CONT CHART PAT 2
Row 103 (RS) K3 with A, k3 with B, work row 1 of chart 3 over next 20 sts, k2 with B, k31 with A, k2 with B, work row 17 of chart 2 over next 31 sts, k2 with B, k31 with A, k2 with B, work row 1 of chart 3 over next 20 sts, k3 with B, k3 with A.
Rows 104–123 Cont to work as established, working rows 2–21 of chart 3 and rows 18–37 of chart 2.
Row 124 K3 with A, k3 with B, p20 with A, p2 with B, p31 with A, p2 with B, work row 38 of chart 2 over next 31 sts, p2 with B, p31 with A, p2 with B, p20 with A, k3 with B, k3 with A.
Rows 125–140 Cont to work as established, working rows 39–54 of chart 2.
Rows 141 and 142
Rep rows 29 and 30.

BEG CHART PATS 2 AND 3
Rows 143–196 Rep rows 31–84.
Rows 197 and 198 Rep rows 29 and 30.
Rows 199–218 Rep rows 9–28.
Rows 219–222 Rep rows 5–8.
Rows 223–226 Rep rows 1–4.
Bind off knitwise.

Head
With straight needles and D, cast on 2 sts.
Inc row 1 (RS) [Kf&b] twice—4 sts.
Inc row 2 P1, M1 p-st, p2, M1 p-st, p1—6 sts.
Inc row 3 (RS) K1, M1, k4, M1, k1—8 sts.
Inc row 4 P1, M1 p-st, p6, M1 p-st, p1—10 sts.

Cont in St st and work even for 10 rows, end with a WS row.
Dec row 1 (RS) K1, ssk, k4, k2tog, k1—8 sts.
Dec row 2 P1, p2tog, p2, p2tog tbl, p1—6 sts.
Bind off knitwise, leaving a 20"/51cm tail.

Ears (make 10)
With straight needles and D, cast on 3 sts.
Next (inc) row (RS) K1, M1, knit to last st, M1, k1—5 sts.
Purl next row. Rep last 2 rows once more—7 sts.
Cont in St st and work even for 14 rows.
Next (dec) row (RS) K1, ssk, k1, k2tog, k1—5 sts. Purl next row.
Next (dec) row (RS) Ssk, k1, k2tog—3 sts.
Purl next row. Cut yarn, leaving a 20"/51cm tail, and thread through rem sts. Pull tog tightly and secure end; this is bottom edge of ear. Do not cut yarn.

Finishing
Block piece lightly to measurements.

EARS
Using the tail, embroider a row of chain stitches following the outer edge. Set aside.

CENTER BUNNY
Using tail, embroider a row of chain stitches following the outer edge of the head. Using a double strand of green thread, sew on button eyes using cross stitches, as shown in photo. Sew head to center bunny, leaving a small opening. Stuff head lightly with fiberfill; sew opening closed. Using C, embroider a French knot nose, as shown. Sew bottom of each ear in place, then tack top of each ear in place.

CORNER BUNNIES
For each bunny, sew bottom of each ear in place, then tack top of each ear in place. Using D and pompom maker, make a 1½"/4cm in diameter pompom. Sew on pompom tail.

CARROT TOPS (make 24)
With crochet hook and B, make a 4"/10cm-long chain. Fasten off. Make an overhand knot at each end; trim yarn just beyond knots. For each carrot, sew the centers of 2 chains to center of last row of each carrot. ■

Color Key
☐ Alaska Sky (A)
☐ Tangerine (C)
☐ Aran (D)

Symbol Key
✕ Position of tail
● Position of ear

CHART 2

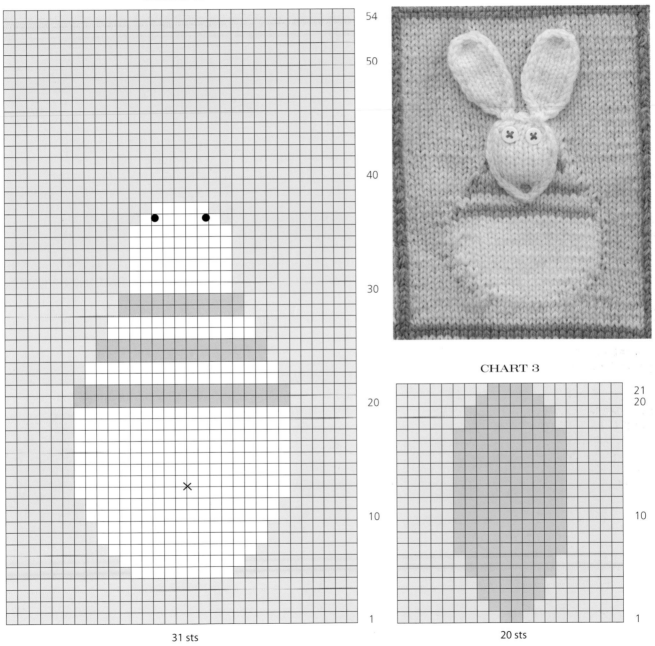

54

50

40

30

20

10

31 sts

CHART 3

21
20

10

1

20 sts

25

Octopus Beanie

A friendly sea creature with I-cord tentacles catches a ride on this simple striped hat.

DESIGNED BY AMY BAHRT

Size
Instructions are written for size 6–12 months.

Knitted Measurements
Head circumference 16"/40.5cm
Depth 5¾"/14.5cm (excluding octopus)

Materials
■ 1 1¾oz/50g hank (each approx 136yd/125m) of Cascade Yarns *220 Superwash Sport* (superwash merino wool) each in #813 blue velvet (A), #897 baby denim (B), and #821 daffodil (C)
■ One pair size 5 (3.75mm) needles *or size to obtain gauge*
■ Two size 5 (3.75mm) double-pointed needles (dpns)
■ Two ⅜"/10mm white buttons
■ Navy sewing thread

Stripe Pattern
Working in St st, work *2 rows B, 4 rows A; rep from * (6 rows) for stripe pat.

Beanie
With straight needles and A, cast on 82 sts.
Cont in St st for 10 rows, end with a WS row.

Next (inc) row (RS) K across, inc 8 sts evenly spaced—90 sts. Purl next row. Cont in stripe pat and work 6-row rep 5 times (30 rows), end with a WS row.

CROWN SHAPING
Dec row 1 (RS) With B, [k9, k2tog] 8 times, k2—82 sts. With B, purl next row.
Dec row 2 (RS) With A, [k8, k2tog] 8 times, k2—74 sts. With A, purl next row.
Dec row 3 (RS) With A, [k7, k2tog] 8 times, k2—66 sts. With A, purl next row.
Dec row 4 (RS) With B, [k6, k2tog] 8 times, k2—58 sts. With B, purl next row.
Dec row 5 (RS) With A, [k5, k2tog] 8 times, k2—50 sts. With A, purl next row.
Dec row 6 (RS) With A, [k4, k2tog] 8 times, k2—42 sts. With A, purl next row. Cut A and B.

OCTOPUS
With C only, cont crown shaping as foll:
Dec row 7 (RS) [K3, k2tog] 8 times, k2—34 sts. Purl next row.
Dec row 8 (RS) [K2, k2tog] 8 times, k2—26 sts. Purl next row.

BODY
Work even for 10 rows.

HEAD SHAPING
Dec row 1 (RS) [K4, k2tog] 4 times, k2—22 sts. Purl next row.
Dec row 2 (RS) [K3, k2tog] 4 times, k2—18 sts. Purl next row.
Dec row 3 (RS) [K2tog] 9 times—9 sts. Cut yarn, leaving an 8"/20.5cm tail, and thread through rem sts. Pull tog tightly and secure end.

Finishing
Sew back seam, using C for octopus and A for hat, and reversing seam over last 1"/2.5cm for rolled brim.

TENTACLES (MAKE 8)
With dpn and C, cast on 5 sts, leaving a long tail for sewing. Work in I-cord as foll:
***Next row (RS)** With 2nd dpn, k5, do not turn. Slide sts back to beg of needle to work next row from RS; rep from * until piece measures 2½"/6.5cm. Cut yarn, leaving an 8"/20.5cm tail. Thread this tail in tapestry needle, then thread through rem sts. Pull tog tightly, secure end, then weave in end. Thread beg tail in tapestry needle, then sew running stitches around top edge. Pull tog tightly to close opening, secure end, then use rem tail to sew tentacles evenly spaced around base of body. Using a double strand of navy thread, sew on button eyes using cross stitches, as shown in photo. ■

Gauge
22 sts and 32 rows to 4"/10cm over St st using size 5 (3.75mm) needles. *Take time to check gauge.*

Basic Baby Pants

Every baby needs a simple pair of pants to complete his wardrobe.
Belt loops and a faux fly give them the look of dungarees.

DESIGNED BY VERONICA MANNO

Sizes
Instructions are written for size 6 months. Changes for 12 and 18 months are in parentheses. (Shown in size 6 months.)

Knitted Measurements
Waist 20 (21, 22½)"/51 (53.5, 57)cm
Length 13½(15, 16½)"/34 (38, 42)cm
Inseam 6½ (7, 8)"/16.5 (18, 20.5)cm

Materials
■ 2 (3, 3) 1¾ oz/50g hanks (each approx 136yd/125m) of Cascade Yarns *220 Superwash Sport* (superwash merino wool) in #1944 westpoint blue heather

■ Size 6 (4mm) needles *or size to obtain gauge*

■ Stitch holders

K1, P1 Rib
(multiple of 2 sts)
Row 1 (RS) *K1, p1; rep from * to end.
Row 2 Rep row 1.
Rep rows 1 and 2 for k1, p1 rib.

K2, P2 Rib
(multiple of 4 sts)
Row 1 (RS) *K2, p2; rep from * to end.
Row 2 Rep row 1.
Rep rows 1 and 2 for k2, p2 rib.

Pants
FRONT LEGS
Cast on 28 (28, 30) sts. Work in k2, p2 rib for ¾"/2cm, end with a WS row. Work even in St st (knit on RS, purl on WS) until piece measures 6½ (7, 8)"/16.5 (18, 20.5)cm from beg, end with a WS row. Place sts on holder. Set leg aside, work second leg in same manner.

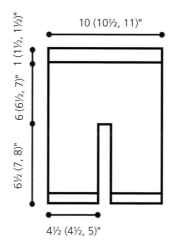

10 (10½, 11)"
1 (1½, 1½)"
6 (6½, 7)"
6½ (7, 8)"
4½ (4½, 5)"

JOIN LEGS
Next row (RS) Knit across 28 (28, 30) sts of one leg, cast on 5 (7, 7) sts, knit across 28 (28, 30) sts of second leg—61 (63, 67) sts. Work even until front measures 12½ (13½, 15)"/32 (34, 38)cm from beg. Work in k1, p1 rib for for 1 (1½, 1½)"/ 2.5 (4, 4) cm. Bind off.

BACK
Work in same manner as front.

RIBBED PANEL
Cast on 46 (48, 48) sts. Work in k2, p2 rib for ¾ (1, 1)"/2 (2.5, 2.5)cm. Bind off.

Finishing
Sew ribbed panel to center of front. Block pieces to measurements. Sew side seams and inseams.

BELT LOOPS (MAKE 3)
Cast on 4 sts. Work in St st for 2"/5cm. Bind off. Sew WS of belt loops to RS of waist ribbing, 1 loop at center of back, 1 loop evenly spaced on either side of ribbed panel. ■

Gauge
24 sts and 32 rows to 4"/10cm over St st using size 6 (4mm) needles.
Take time to check gauge.

27

Fabric Skirt Dress

Pretty enough for Sunday best, this charming dress combines a seed stitch bodice with a floral fabric skirt.

DESIGNED BY VERONICA MANNO

■■■□

Sizes

Instructions are written for size 6 months. Changes for 12 and 18 months are in parentheses. (Shown in size 18 months.)

Knitted Measurements

Chest 20 (22, 24)"/51 (56, 61)cm
Length (before hemming) 23½ (24½, 25½)"/59.5 (62, 64.5)cm

Materials

- 2 (2, 3) 1¾oz/50g hanks (each approx 136yd/125m) of Cascade Yarns *220 Superwash Sport* (superwash merino wool) in #836 pink ice
- One pair size 6 (4mm) needles *or size to obtain gauge*
- Size E/4 (3.5mm) crochet hook
- 1½ (1¾, 1¾)yd/1.5 (1.75, 1.75)m lightweight cotton fabric
- Three small snap fasteners
- Sewing needle and matching thread
- Sewing machine

K1, P1 Rib

(over a multiple of 2 sts plus 1)
Row 1 (RS) K1, *p1, k1; rep from * to end.
Row 2 P1, *k1, p1; rep from * to end.
Rep rows 1 and 2 for k1, p1 rib.

Seed Stitch

(over an even number of sts)
Row 1 (RS) *K1, p1; rep from * to end.
Row 2 K the purl sts and p the knit sts.
Rep row 2 for seed st.

Front Bodice

Cast on 61 (67, 73) sts. Work in k1, p1 rib for 4 rows, inc 1 st at end of last row—62 (68, 74) sts. Cont in seed st and work even until piece measures 2½ (3, 3½)"/6.5 (7.5, 9)cm from beg, end with a WS row.

ARMHOLE SHAPING

Bind off 3 (3, 4) sts at beg of next 2 rows, then 2 sts at beg of next 2 rows. Dec 1 st each side on next row, then every other row twice more—46 (52, 56) sts. Work even until armholes measure 1½ (2, 2½)"/ 4 (5, 6.5)cm, end with a WS row.

NECK SHAPING

Next row (RS) Work across first 19 (21, 23) sts, join a 2nd hank of yarn and bind off center 8 (10, 10) sts, work to end. Working both sides at once, bind off from each neck edge 3 sts twice, then 2 sts once. Dec 1 st from each neck edge every RS row twice—9 (11, 13) sts each side. Work even until armholes measure 3½ (4, 4½)"/9 (10, 11.5)cm, end with a WS row. Bind off each side for shoulders.

Right Back Bodice

Cast on 35 (39, 43) sts. Work in k1, p1 rib for 4 rows, inc 1 st at end of last row—36 (40, 44) sts. Cont in seed st and work even until piece measures 2½ (3, 3½)"/6.5 (7.5, 9)cm from beg, end with a WS row.

ARMHOLE SHAPING

At armhole edge, bind off 3 (3, 4) sts once, then 2 sts once. Dec 1 st from armhole edge every RS row 3 times—28 (32, 35) sts. Work even until armhole measures 1½ (2, 2½)"/4 (5, 6.5)cm, end with a RS row.

NECK SHAPING

At neck edge, bind off 9 (11, 12) sts once, 3 sts twice, then 2 sts once. Dec 1 st from each neck edge every RS row twice—9 (11, 13) sts. Work even until armhole measures 3½ (4, 4½)"/9 (10,

Gauge

24 sts and 44 rows to 4"/10cm over seed st using size 6 (4mm) needles.
Take time to check gauge.

11.5)cm, end with a WS row. Bind off for shoulder.

Left Back Bodice
Work as for right back bodice, reversing all shaping.

BOW
Cast on 22 sts. Work in seed st for 2"/5cm. Bind off in seed st.

LOOP
Cast on 5 sts. Work in St st (k on RS, p on WS) for 2½"/6.5cm. Bind off; cut yarn, leaving a long tail for sewing.

Finishing
Block pieces lightly to measurements. Sew shoulder and side seams.

NECK EDGING
With RS facing and crochet hook, join yarn with a sl st in side edge of first row of left back bodice.
Row 1 (RS) Ch 1, making sure that work lies flat, sc evenly along left back bodice opening, entire neck edge, then right back bodice opening, working 3 sc in each corner. Fasten off.

ARMHOLE EDGING
With RS facing and crochet hook, join yarn with a sl st in side seam.
Rnd 1 (RS) Ch 1, making sure that work lies flat, sc evenly around entire armhole edge, join rnd with a sl st in first st. Fasten off.

SKIRT
For front, cut a 26 (28, 30)"/66 (71, 76)cm wide by 18"/45.5cm long piece of fabric. For back cut two 13½ (14½, 15½)"/34 (37, 39.5)cm wide by 18"/45.5cm long pieces of fabric. For sash, cut a 47 (49, 51)"/119.5 (124.5, 129.5)cm long by 2½"/6.5cm wide strip of fabric; set aside. Place pieces tog RS facing and use a ½"/1.3cm seam allowance throughout. Sew back pieces tog along 18"/45.5cm length, sewing to within top 4"/10cm for back opening. Open seam; press flat. Topstitch around opening, ¼"/0.5cm from edge, stitching back and forth a few times across seam to reinforce bottom of opening; press. Sew front and back pieces tog; press seams open. Beginning and ending 1"/2.5cm from edge of back opening, hand-stitch two rows of running stitches, with the first ¼"/0.5cm from top edge and the second

¼"/0.5cm below first row of stitches. Turn bodice WS out. Place RS of skirt on WS of bodice, lapping skirt ½"/1.3cm over bottom edge of bodice. Pin top edge of skirt in place, matching side seams. Pull threads to gather in skirt to dimensions of bodice. Hand-stitch top edge of skirt to WS of bodice, taking care that stitches are not visible on RS. Remove bottom row of running stitches.
Place markers for top halves of 3 snaps on WS of right back bodice edge, with the first ¼"/0.5cm from lower edge, the last ¼"/0.5cm from neck edge and one more evenly spaced between. Sew on top halves of snaps. Sew on bottom halves along left back bodice edge. Hem to desired length.

SASH
With RS facing, fold fabric strip in half lengthwise. Sew seam. Open seam, then center along length; press seam open. Turn sash to RS; press. Turn each end ½"/1.3cm to WS; press. Slip open ends closed. Sew short edges of bow loop tog, allowing side edges to curl under to WS. Insert bow through loop, then center side to side. Using thread, sew bow to loop, then sew bow to center front of sash. ∎

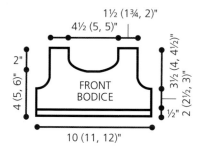

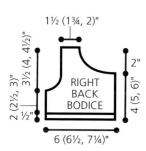

Hooded Sleep Sack

Your little one will always have sweet dreams when she snuggles into this cozy sack. Buttons down both sides make it easy to slip baby in and out.

DESIGNED BY JEANNIE CHIN

Sizes
Instructions are written for newborn. Changes for 3 months are in parentheses. (Shown in size newborn.)

Finished Measurements
Width (closed) 13½ (16)"/34 (40.5cm)
Length (from top of hood) 25 (31)"/63.5 (78.5)cm

Materials
■ 6 (9) 1¾oz/50g hanks (each approx 136yd/125m) of Cascade Yarns *220 Superwash Sport* (superwash merino wool) in #844 periwinkle

■ One pair size 6 (4mm) needles *or size to obtain gauge*

■ Size 6 (4mm) circular needle, 29"/74cm long

■ Stitch markers

■ 16 (20)¾"/19mm buttons

Note
Sleep sack is made in one piece from top edge of front to top edge of hood.

Stitch Glossary
RT (right twist) Skip next st on LH needle, k 2nd st in front of skipped st, then k skipped st, sl both sts from LH needle.
LT (left twist) With RH needle behind LH needle, skip next st on LH needle; knit 2nd st tbl, then knit skipped st in front lp, sl both sts from LH needle.

One-row buttonhole (over 3 sts) Sl 1 p-st wyif, *Sl 1 p-st wyib, pass first slipped stitch over; rep from * twice more. Slip last bound-off st purlwise back to LH needle; turn work. Cast on 4 sts using cable cast-on method; turn work. Slip first st wyib from LH needle and pass extra cast-on stitch over it to close buttonhole.

Slip Stitch Honeycomb Pattern
(over an odd number of sts)
Row 1 (RS) Knit.
Row 2 K1, *sl 1 wyib, k1; rep from * to end.
Row 3 Knit.
Row 4 K2, *sl 1 wyib, k1; rep from * to last st, end k1.
Rep rows 1–4 for sl st honeycomb pat.

Butterfly Pattern Stitch
(over a multiple of 8 sts plus 4)
Row 1 (RS) Knit.
Row 2 and all WS rows Purl.
Row 3 Knit.
Row 5 K2, *LT, RT, k4; rep from * to last 2 sts, end k2.
Row 7 K2, *RT, LT, k4; rep from * to last 2 sts, end k2.
Rows 9 and 11 Knit.
Row 13 K2, *k4, LT, RT;

Gauge
24 sts and 32 rows to 4"/10cm over butterfly pat st using size 6 (4mm) needles. *Take time to check gauge.*

Hooded Sleep Sack

rep from * to last 2 sts, end k2.
Row 15 K2, *k4, RT, LT; rep from * to last 2 sts, end k2.
Row 16 Purl.
Rep rows 1–16 for butterfly pat st.

Sleep Sack
FRONT
With straight needles, cast on 71 (87) sts. Work in sl st honeycomb pat for 16 rows, end with a WS row.
Next (dec) row (RS) K 17 (21), [k2tog, k16 (20)] 3 times—68 (84) sts. Beg with row 2, cont in butterfly pat st to row 16, then rep rows 1–16 six (eight) times more, then rows 1–4 once. Piece should measure approximately 15¾ (19¾)"/40 (50)cm from beg, end with a WS row.

BACK
Working rows 1 and 2 of butterfly pat st, cast on 8 sts at beg of next 2 rows—84 (100) sts. Work rows 3–16, then rep rows 1–16 until back measures 15¾ (19¾)"/40 (50)cm above cast-on row, end with a WS row. Place yarn markers at beg and end of last row for beg of hood.

HOOD
Cont to work even until piece measures 25 (31)"/63.5 (79)cm above cast-on row, end with a WS row. Knit next row. Bind off all sts purlwise. *Do not remove* yarn markers.

Finishing
Block piece lightly to measurements. Sew hood seam.

LEFT BUTTONBAND
With RS facing and straight needles, beg just below back cast-on sts and pick up and k 97 (121) sts evenly spaced along entire left side edge of front. Beg with row 2, cont in sl st honeycomb pat for 15 rows. Bind off all sts knitwise.

RIGHT BUTTONBAND
With RS facing and straight needles, beg at bottom edge and pick up and k 97 (121) sts evenly spaced along entire right side edge of front to just below back cast-on sts. Beg with row 2, cont in sl st honeycomb pat for 15 rows. Bind off all sts knitwise.

HOOD AND BUTTONBANDS
Row 1 (RS) With RS facing and circular needle, pick up and k 92 (116) sts evenly along side edge of right back to yarn marker, remove yarn marker, pm on needle; pick up and k 113 (139) sts evenly spaced around hood to 2nd yarn marker; remove yarn marker, pm on needle, then pick up and k 92 (116) sts evenly spaced along side edge of left back—297 (371) sts. Slipping markers every row, cont as foll:
Rows 2–8 Beg with row 2, work in sl st honeycomb pat.
Row (buttonhole) 9 (RS) K2, *work one-row buttonhole over next 3 sts, k9; rep from * 7 (9) times more, work one-row buttonhole over next 3 sts, k3, slip marker, knit to next marker, slip marker, k3, *work one-row buttonhole over next 3 sts, k9; rep from * 7 (9) times more, work one-row buttonhole over next 3 sts, k2. Beg with row 2, cont in sl st honeycomb pat for 7 rows more. Bind off sts knitwise. Sew side edges of buttonbands to cast-on edges of back. Sew on buttons. ∎

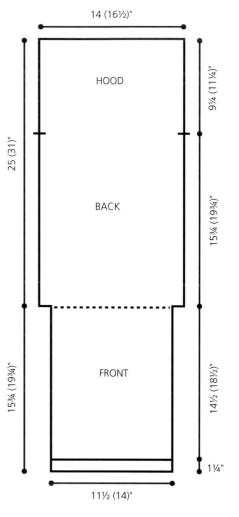

Apple Tree Sweater

This sunny yellow sweater features a knit-in ribbed tree and duplicate stitch birdhouse and apple motif. Embroidered apples and leaves complete the whimsical scene.

DESIGNED BY PAT OLSKI

Sizes
Instructions are written for size 12 months. Changes for 18 and 24 months are in parentheses. (Shown in size 12 months.)

Knitted Measurements
Chest 24 (25, 26)"/61 (63.5, 66)cm
Length 12 (12½, 13)"/30.5 (32, 33)cm
Upper arm 9 (10, 11)"/23 (25.5, 28)cm

Materials
■ 3 (4, 4) 1¾oz/50g hanks (each approx 136yd/125m) of Cascade Yarns *220 Superwash Sport* (superwash merino wool) in #878 lazy maize (MC)

■ 1 (2, 2) hanks in #802 green apple (A)

■ 1 hank each in #818 mocha (B) and #809 really red (C)

■ Size 5 (3.75mm) needles *or size to obtain gauge*

■ Size 3 (3.25mm) needles

■ Removable stitch markers

■ Three ½"/13mm buttons

Notes
1) Tree motif is a combination of intarsia knitting, duplicate st, and embroidery stitches. Apple motif is a combination of duplicate st and embroidery stitches.
2) Do not carry MC behind tree trunk, use 2 separate balls. When changing colors, pick up new color from under dropped color to prevent holes.

K1, P1 Rib
(worked over an odd number of sts)
Row 1 (RS) P1, *k1, p1; rep from * to end.
Row 2 K1, *p1, k1; rep from * to end.
Rep rows 1 and 2 for k1, p1 rib.

Sweater
BACK
With smaller needles and A, cast on 73 (75, 79) sts. Beg with row 2 on WS, work 9 rows in k1, p1 rib. Change to larger needles and MC, work even in St st until piece measures 11½ (12, 12½)"/29 (30.5, 32)cm, end with a WS row.

NECK SHAPING
Next row (RS) K26 for right shoulder, join second hank of MC, bind off 21 (23, 27) sts, knit to end for left shoulder. Working both sides at once,

work next row even on WS.
Next row K to last 3 sts of right shoulder, k2tog, k1; on left shoulder k1, ssk, k to end—25 sts each side. Work next row even on WS, mark beg of row for left shoulder.
Next row (RS) Bind off 25 sts for right shoulder; change to smaller needles, work left shoulder in k1, p1 rib. Work even in rib for ½"/13mm. Bind off in rib.

FRONT
With smaller needles and A, cast on 73 (75, 79) sts and rib 1 row on WS as for back.
Next row (RS) With A, p1, [k1, p1] 23 (23, 24) times; with B, [k1, p1] 4 times, k1; with A, p1, [k1, p1] 8 (9, 10) times.
Next row With A [k1, p1] 8 (9, 10) times, k1; with B, p1, [k1, p1] 4 times; with A, rib to end.
Work 6 rows even.
Change to larger needles.
Next row (RS) With MC, k 47 (47, 49) sts; with B, rib 9 sts as established; with MC, k to end.
Work even in St st (knit on RS, purl on

Gauge
24 sts and 33 rows to 4"/10cm over St st using size 5 (3.75mm) needles.
Take time to check gauge.

Apple Tree Sweater

WS) with MC and rib with B until piece measures 5¼ (5¾, 6¼)"/13.5 (14.5, 16.5)cm, end with a WS row.

BEG CHART
Row 1 (RS) K17 (19, 21), work sts 1–54 of tree chart, k to end.
Row 2 K2 (2, 4), work sts 54–1 of tree chart, k to end.
Work as established until piece measures 10½ (11, 11½)"/26.5 (28, 29)cm from beg, end with a WS row, AT THE SAME TIME, when 44 rows of chart have been worked, cont in MC only.

NECK SHAPING
Next row (RS) K29 for left shoulder, join a second ball of MC and bind off center 15 (17, 21) sts, work to end for right shoulder.
Working both sides at once, work 1 row even on WS.
Next (dec) row K to last 3 sts of left shoulder, k2tog, k1; on right shoulder k1, ssk, k to end—28 sts each side. Work next row even on WS. Rep last 2 rows 3 times more—25 sts each side.
Work even until piece measures 12 (12½, 13)"/30.5 (32, 33)cm from beg, end with a RS row.
Next row (WS) Bind off 25 sts for right shoulder; work even across left shoulder.
Next row (RS) Change to smaller needles and work left shoulder in k1, p1 rib. Mark this row for neckband. Work next row even on WS.
Next (buttonhole) row (RS) Rib 8 sts, k2tog, yo, rib 8 sts, yo, k2tog, rib 5 sts. Work even in rib until band measures

½"/13mm. Bind off in rib.

SLEEVES
With smaller needles and A, cast on 41 (43, 43) sts. Work in k1, p1 rib for 1"/2.5cm, end with a WS row. Change to larger needles and MC. Work 8 rows in St st.
Next (inc) row (RS) K1, M1, k to last st, M1, k1—43 (45, 45) sts. Rep inc row every 6th (4th, 4th) row 6 (8, 10) times more—55 (61, 65) sts. Work even until piece measures 7½ (8, 8½)"/19 (20.5, 21.5)cm from beg. Bind off.

EMBROIDERY
Following tree chart, work small branches, leaves, apples, and birdhouse. Work apple chart above front ribbing, using photo as guide for placement.

Finishing
Gently block piece to measurements. Sew right shoulder seam.

NECKBAND
With RS facing and A, beg at left front neck marker, pick up and k 63 (67, 77) sts evenly spaced around neck edge and back left shoulder band. Work next row even in k1, p1 rib.
Next (buttonhole) row (RS) Rib 2, yo, k2tog, rib to end. Work 2 rows even in rib. Bind off in rib. Set in right sleeve, sew right side and sleeve seams. Center left sleeve at shoulder marker. Sew in place, leaving front buttonhole band free. Sew left side and sleeve seams. Sew buttons opposite buttonholes. ∎

APPLE CHART

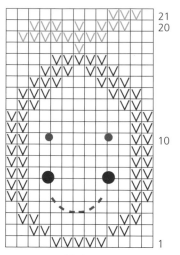

13 sts

Embroidery Key

V̲	Duplicate st with Green Apple (A)
V̅	Duplicate st with Really Red (C)
●	Large French knot Really Red (C)
●	Small French knot with Mocha (B)
–	Straight st with Mocha (B)

TREE CHART

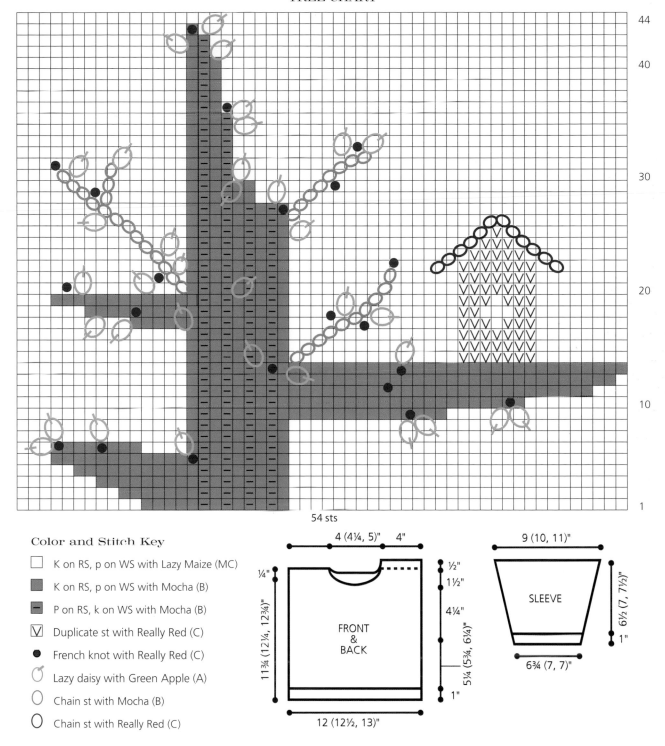

54 sts

Color and Stitch Key

- ☐ K on RS, p on WS with Lazy Maize (MC)
- ▨ K on RS, p on WS with Mocha (B)
- ▬ P on RS, k on WS with Mocha (B)
- Ⅴ Duplicate st with Really Red (C)
- ● French knot with Really Red (C)
- ♂ Lazy daisy with Green Apple (A)
- ○ Chain st with Mocha (B)
- ○ Chain st with Really Red (C)

FRONT & BACK

4 (4¼, 5)" 4"

¼"

½"

1½"

4¼"

5¼ (5¾, 6¼)"

1"

11¾ (12¼, 12¾)"

12 (12½, 13)"

SLEEVE

9 (10, 11)"

6½ (7, 7½)"

1"

6¾ (7, 7)"

Dot Pattern Blanket

Subtle points of pink and cream on a mocha background create a sophisticated palette that can go beyond the nursery.

DESIGNED BY LOIS S. YOUNG

Knitted Measurements
Approx 40" x 42"/101.5cm x 106.5cm

Materials
■ 10 1¾oz/50g hanks (each approx 136yd/125m) of Cascade Yarns *220 Superwash Sport* (superwash merino wool) in #873 extra creme cafe (MC)

■ 2 hanks each in #817 aran (A) and #1941 salmon (B)

■ Size 5 (3.75mm) circular needle, 36"/91cm long *or size to obtain gauge*

Seed Stitch
(over an odd number of sts)
Row 1 (RS) K1, *p1, k1; rep from * to end.
Rep row 1 for seed st.

Dot Pattern Stitch
Row 1 (RS) With MC, [k1, p1] twice, k1, *k1 with MC, k1 with A; rep from * to last 6 sts, end with MC, k1, [k1, p1] twice, k1.
Row 2 With MC, [k1, p1] twice, k1, *p1 with MC, k1 with A; rep from * to last 6 sts, end with MC, p1, [k1, p1] twice, k1.
Row 3 With MC, [k1, p1] twice, knit to last 5 sts, end [k1, p1] twice, k1.
Row 4 With MC, [k1, p1] twice, k1, purl to last 5 sts, end [k1, p1] twice, k1.

Row 5 With MC, [k1, p1] twice, k1, *k1 with MC, k1 with B; rep from * to last 6 sts, end with MC, k1, [k1, p1] twice, k1.
Row 6 With MC, [k1, p1] twice, k1, *p1 with MC, k1 with B; rep from * to last 6 sts, end with MC, p1, [k1, p1] twice, k1.
Row 7 With MC, [k1, p1] twice, knit to last 5 sts, end [k1, p1] twice, k1.
Row 8 With MC, [k1, p1] twice, k1, purl to last 5 sts, end [k1, p1] twice, k1.
Rep rows 1–8 for dot pat st.

Blanket
With MC, cast on 257 sts. Work in seed st for 7 rows, end with a RS row.
Next row (WS) Work row 8 of dot pat. Beg with row 1, cont in dot pat st and work even until piece measures approximately 41"/104cm from beg, end with row 4 or 8. Work in seed st for 7 rows. Bind off loosely in seed st.

Finishing
Block piece lightly to measurements. ■

Gauge
26 sts and 30 rows to 4"/10cm over dot pat st using size 5 (3.75mm) circular needle.
Take time to check gauge.

31
Dump Truck Cardigan

Any little guy (or gal) who's crazy for trucks will love this super-cute cardigan. Keep on truckin'!

DESIGNED BY SHEILA JOYNES

Size
Instructions are written for size 12 months.

Knitted Measurements
Chest 23½ "/59.5cm
Length 11"/28cm
Upper Arm 10"/25.5cm

Materials
■ 2 1¾oz/50g hanks (each approx 136yd/125m) of Cascade Yarns *220 Superwash Sport* (superwash merino wool) in #873 extra creme cafe (MC)

■ 1 hank each in #893 ruby (A), #841 moss (B), #813 blue velvet (C), #897 baby denim (D), and #854 navy (E)

■ One pair size 4 (3.5mm) needles *or size to obtain gauge*

■ Stitch holder

■ Six ½"/13mm buttons

Note
Work edge sts in St st (k on RS, p on WS) in same color as nearest st on chart.

Cardigan
BACK
With A, cast on 77 sts.
Rows 1–4 Knit.
Row 5 (RS) K9, M1, [k15, M1] 4 times, k8—82 sts.
Row 6 Purl.
Rows 7–13 Work edge st, work border chart 1 to last st, work edge st.
Row 14 With A, purl.
Row 15 K5, M1, [k8, M1] 9 times, k5—92 sts.
Row 16 Purl.
Rows 17–31 Work edge st, work dump truck chart to last st, work edge st.
Row 32 With A, purl.
Row 33 K5, k2tog, [k7, k2tog] 9 times, k4—82 sts.
Row 34 Purl.
Rows 35–41 Work edge st, work border chart 2 to last st, work edge st.
Row 42 With A, purl.
Row 43 K7, k2tog, k14, k2tog, k15, k2tog, k14, k2tog, k15, k2tog, k7—77 sts.

Row 44 With MC, purl.
With MC, work even in St st until piece measures 11"/28cm from beg, ending with a WS row.

NECK AND SHOULDER SHAPING
Next row (RS) Bind off 24 sts, k29 and place on holder for back neck, bind off to end.

LEFT FRONT
With A, cast on 38 sts.
Rows 1–4 Knit.
Row 5 (RS) K7, M1, [k12, M1] 2 times, k7—41 sts.
Row 6 Purl.
Rows 7–13 Work border chart 1, working first st on RS rows and last st on WS rows as edge st.
Row 14 With A, purl.
Row 15 K7, M1, [k8, M1] 3 times, k9, M1, k1—46 sts.
Row 16 Purl.
Rows 17–31 Work dump truck chart, working first st on RS rows and last st on WS rows as edge st.
Row 32 With A, purl.
Row 33 K4, k2tog, [k7, k2tog] 4 times, k4—41 sts.

Gauge
28 sts and 32 rows to 4"/10cm over dump truck pattern using size 4 (3.5mm) needles.
26 sts and 36 rows to 4"/10cm over St st using size 4 (3.5mm) needles.
Take time to check gauge.

Dump Truck Cardigan

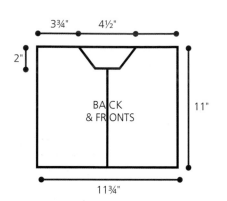

3¾" 4½"

2"

BACK & FRONTS

11"

11¾"

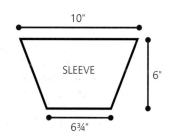

10"

SLEEVE

6"

6¾"

Row 34 Purl.
Rows 35–41 Work border chart 2, working first st on RS rows and last st on WS rows as edge st.
Row 42 With A, purl.
Row 43 K6, k2tog, [k11, k2tog] 2 times, k7—38 sts.
Row 44 With MC, purl.

With MC, work even in St st until piece measures 9"/23cm from beg, ending with a RS row.

NECK AND SHOULDER SHAPING
Next row (WS) Bind off 5 sts, work to end. Bind off 2 sts at neck edge every other row 3 times, then dec 1 st every other row 3 times—24 sts. Work even until piece measures same as back. Bind off.

RIGHT FRONT
Work as for left front, reversing all shaping.

SLEEVES
With A, cast on 44 sts.
Rows 1–4 Knit.
Row 5 (RS) K4, M1, [k5, M1] 7 times, k5—52 sts.
Row 6 Purl.
Rows 7–13 Work edge st, work border chart 1 to last st, work edge st.
Row 14 With A, purl.
Row 15 (inc row) K2, M1, knit to last 2 sts, M1, k2—54 sts.
Row 16 Purl.

With MC, work even in St st until piece measures 6"/15cm, working inc row every 4 rows 6 times more—66 sts. Bind off.

Finishing
Block pieces. Sew shoulder seams. Set in sleeves, sew side and sleeve seams.

NECKBAND
With RS facing and A, pick up and knit 21 sts from right front, 29 sts from holder, 21 sts from left front—71 sts. Knit 4 rows. Bind off purlwise.

BUTTONBAND
With RS facing and A, pick up and knit 60 sts along right front. Knit 4 rows. Bind off purlwise.

BUTTONHOLE BAND
With RS facing and A, pick up and knit 60 sts along left front. Knit 2 rows.
Next row K3, yo, k2tog, [k8, yo, k2tog] 5 times, yo, k2tog, k3. Knit 1 row. Bind off purlwise.

Weave in ends. Sew buttons opposite buttonholes. ∎

DUMP TRUCK CHART

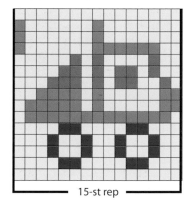

15-st rep

BORDER CHART 1

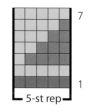

7

1

5-st rep

BORDER CHART 2

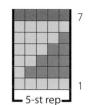

7

1

5-st rep

Color Key

- ■ Ruby (A)
- □ Moss (B)
- ■ Blue Velvet (C)
- □ Baby Denim (D)
- ■ Navy (E)

32

Parisian Cardigan

Ooh la la! Your little one will be *très chic* in this lovely cardigan with an Eiffel Tower motif worked in duplicate stitch.

DESIGNED BY PAT OLSKI

Sizes
Instructions are written for size 12 months. Changes for 18 and 24 months are in parentheses. (Shown in size 12 months.)

Knitted Measurements
Chest (closed) 21½ (23½, 25½)"/54.5 (59.5, 64.5)cm
Length 11½ (12½, 13½)"/29 (31.5, 34)cm
Upper arm 7½ (8½, 9½)"/19 (21.5, 24)cm

Materials
■ 3 (4, 5) 1¾oz/50g hanks (each approx 136yd/125m) of Cascade Yarns *220 Superwash Sport* (superwash merino wool) in #871 white (MC)

■ 1 hank in #854 navy (CC)

■ One pair each sizes 3 and 5 (3.25 and 3.75mm) needles *or size to obtain gauge*

■ Spare size 5 (3.75mm) needle (for 3-needle bind-off)

■ Stitch holders

■ Six ⁹⁄₁₆"/14mm buttons

Note
Chart pat is worked in duplicate st after knitting is completed.

K1, P1 Rib
(over a multiple of 2 sts plus 1)
Row 1 (WS) P1, *k1, p1; rep from * to end.
Row 2 K1, *p1, k1; rep from * to end.
Rep rows 1 and 2 for k1, p1 rib.

Back
With smaller needles and CC, cast on 75 (81, 87) sts. Work in k1, p1 rib for 1"/2.5cm, end with a WS row. Change to larger needles and MC. Cont in St st (knit on RS, purl on WS) until piece measures 2 (2½, 3)"/5 (6.5, 7.5)cm from beg, end with a WS row.

SIDE SHAPING
Next (dec) row (RS) K1, ssk, knit to last 3 sts, k2tog, k1. Rep dec row every 6th row 3 times more—67 (73, 79) sts. Work even until piece measures 7½ (8, 8½)"/19 (20.5, 21.5)cm from beg, end with a WS row.

ARMHOLE SHAPING
Bind off 3 (4, 5) sts at beg of next 2 rows.
Next (dec) row (RS) K1, ssk, knit to last 3 sts, k2tog, k1. Work next row even. Rep last 2 rows 6 times more—47 (51, 55) sts. Work even until armhole measures 3½ (4, 4½)"/9 (10, 11.5)cm, end with a WS row.

NECK SHAPING
Next row (RS) Work across first 16 (18, 19) sts, join a 2nd ball of MC and bind off center 15 (15, 17) sts, work to end. Working both sides at once, work next row even. Dec 1 st from each neck edge on next row, then every row once more. Place rem 14 (16, 17) sts each side on holders for shoulders.

Left Front
With smaller needles and CC, cast on 35 (39, 43) sts. Work in k1, p1 rib for 1"/2.5cm, dec 0 (0, 1) st at end of last row and end with a WS row—35 (39, 42)

Gauge
24 sts and 33 rows to 4"/10cm over St st using larger needles. *Take time to check gauge.*

Parisian Cardigan

sts. Change to larger needles and MC. Cont in St st until piece measures 2 (2½, 3)"/5 (6.5, 7.5)cm from beg, end with a WS row.

SIDE SHAPING
Next (dec) row (RS) K1, ssk, knit to end. Rep dec row every 6th row 3 times more—31 (35, 38) sts. Work even until piece measures same length as back to underarm, end with a WS row.

ARMHOLE SHAPING
Bind off 3 (4, 5) sts at beg of next row. Work next row even.
Next (dec) row (RS) K1, ssk, knit to end. Work next row even. Rep last 2 rows 6 times more—21 (24, 26) sts. Work even until armhole measures 2½ (3, 3½)"/6.5 (7.5, 9)cm, end with a RS row.

NECK SHAPING
Next row (WS) Bind off first 3 (4, 4) sts, work to end.
Next (dec) row (RS) Knit to last 3 sts,

k2tog, k1. Work next row even. Rep last 2 rows 3 (3, 4) times more. Work even on 14 (16, 17) sts until piece measures same length as back to shoulder, end with a WS row. Place sts on holder for shoulder.

Right Front
Work as left front to side shaping—35 (39, 42) sts.

SIDE SHAPING
Next (dec) row (RS) Knit to last 3 sts, k2tog, k1. Rep dec row every 6th row 3 times more—31 (35, 38) sts. Work even until piece measures same length as back to underarm, end with a RS row.

ARMHOLE SHAPING
Bind off 3 (4, 5) sts at beg of next row.
Next (dec) row (RS) Knit to last 3 sts, k2tog, k1. Work next row even. Rep last 2 rows 6 times more—21 (24, 26) sts. Work even until armhole measures 2½ (3, 3½)"/6.5 (7.5, 9)cm, end with a WS row.

NECK SHAPING
Next row (RS) Bind off first 3 (4, 4) sts, work to end. Work next row even.
Next (dec) row (RS) K1, ssk, knit to end. Work next row even. Rep last 2 rows 3 (3, 4) times more. Work even on 14 (16, 17) sts until piece measures same length as back to shoulder, end with a WS row. Place sts on holder for shoulder.

Sleeves
With smaller needles and CC, cast on 35 (37, 39) sts. Work in k1, p1 rib for 1"/2.5cm, end with a WS row. Change to larger needles and MC. Cont in St st and work even for 4 rows, end with a WS row.
Next (inc) row (RS) K1, M1, knit to last st, M1, k1. Rep inc row every 6th row 0 (6, 9) times more, then every 8th row 5 (1, 0) times more—47 (53, 59) sts. Work even until piece measures 7½ (8, 9)"/19 (20.5, 23)cm from beg, end with a WS row.

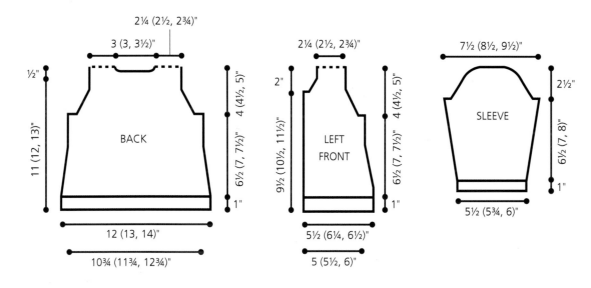

Parisian Cardigan

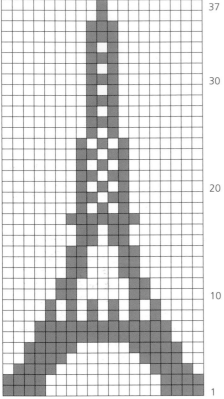

Color Key

☐ White (MC)

▨ Navy duplicate stitch (CC)

CAP SHAPING

Bind off 3 (4, 5) sts at beg of next 2 rows. **Next (dec) row (RS)** K1, ssk, knit to last 3 sts, k2tog, k1. Work next row even. Rep last 2 rows 6 times more—27 (31, 35) sts. Bind off 3 (4, 5) sts at beg of next 4 rows. Bind off rem 15 sts.

Finishing

Block pieces to measurements.

CHART PAT

On right front, count 4 (6, 8) MC rows up from bottom band, then count 7 (9, 11) sts in from front edge; mark next st with a pin for first st on chart. Working in duplicate st and using CC, beg chart with st 1 on row 1. Work to top of chart. Join shoulders using 3-needle bind-off.

BUTTONBAND

With RS facing, smaller needles, and CC, pick up and k 61 (67, 73) sts evenly spaced along left front edge. Beg with row 2, work in k1, p1 rib for 6 rows. Bind off loosely in rib. Place markers for 6 buttonholes on right front edge, with the first ½"/1.3cm from lower edge, the last 1"/2.5cm from neck edge, and 4 more evenly spaced between.

BUTTONHOLE BAND

With RS facing, smaller needles, and CC, pick up and k 61 (67, 73) sts evenly spaced along left front edge. Beg with row 2, work in k1, p1 rib for 1 row. **Next (buttonhole) row (RS)** *Work in rib to marker, yo, k2tog; rep from * 5 times more, work in rib to end. Cont in rib for 4 rows more. Bind off loosely in rib.

COLLAR

With RS facing, smaller needles, and CC, beg in center of top side edge of buttonhole band, pick up and k 3 sts along side edge of buttonhole band, 16 (17, 18) sts evenly spaced along right neck edge to shoulder, 23 (23, 25) sts along back neck edge to shoulder, 16 (17, 18) sts along left neck edge to buttonband, then 3 sts to center of top side edge of buttonband—61 (63, 67) sts. Beg with row 1 (RS of collar), cont in k1, p1 rib for 10 rows. Change to larger needles. Cont in rib until collar measures 2½ (2½, 2¾)"/6.5 (6.5, 7)cm from beg, end with a WS row. **Dec row 1 (RS)** K1, k2tog, work in rib to last 3 sts, ssk, k1. **Dec row 2** P1, p2tog tbl, work in rib to last 3 sts, p2tog, p1. Rep last 2 rows until collar measures 3 (3, 3¼)"/7.5 (7.5, 8)cm from beg, end with a WS row. Bind off loosely in rib. Set in sleeves. Sew side and sleeve seams. Sew on buttons. ■

Sailboat Blanket

Row, row, row your baby gently to sleep with this nautical blanket. Every budding sailor will love this unusual design featuring three-dimensional elements.

DESIGNED BY MARLA MUTCH

Knitted Measurements
Approx 45"/114.5cm wide (from bottom tip of right sail to bottom tip of left sail) x 29"/73.5cm high (from bottom edge to top of left sail)

Materials
■ 5 1¾oz/50g hanks (each approx 136yd/125m) of Cascade Yarns *220 Superwash Sport* (superwash merino wool) in #817 aran (A)

■ 2 hanks in #813 blue velvet (B)

■ 1 hank in #809 really red (C)

■ Two size 5 (3.75mm) circular needles, 36"/91cm long *or size to obtain gauge*

■ One pair size 5 (3.75mm) needles

■ Size H/8 (5mm) crochet hook

■ Stitch markers

Stitch Glossary
kf&b Inc 1 by knitting into the front and back of the next st.

Blanket
BOAT
With circular needle and B, cast on 150 sts.
Set-up row (RS) K1, kf&b, pm, k73, pm (center), k73, pm, kf&b, k1—152 sts. Knit next row.
Inc row (RS) K1, kf&b, knit to first marker, sl marker, knit to last marker, sl marker, knit to last 2 sts, kf&b, k1—154 sts. Knit next row.
Rep last 2 rows until there are 30 sts before first marker and 30 sts after last marker, end with a WS row—206 sts.
Cont to work last 2 rows, work in stripe pat as foll: 2 rows C, 2 rows B, 4 rows C, 2 rows B, and 6 rows C, end with a WS row—222 sts.

RIGHT SAIL
With RS facing, 2nd circular needle, and A, cable cast-on 16 sts, then k111 sts from boat needle to center marker (bottom of sail), pm for center, then cable cast-on 127 sts (left side edge of sail); leave rem sts on first needle for left sail—254 sts.
Knit next row.
Dec row (RS) K1, ssk, knit to 2 sts before center marker, ssk, sl marker, k2tog, knit to last 3 stitches, k2tog, k1—250 sts. Knit next row. Rep last 2 rows 61 times more, changing to straight needles when desired, end with a WS row—6 sts.
Next (dec) row (RS) [K2tog] 3 times—3 sts. Cut yarn, leaving an 8"/20.5cm tail, and thread through rem sts. Pull tog tightly, secure end, then weave in end.

LEFT SAIL
With RS facing, 2nd circular needle, and A, cable cast-on 10 sts (top of sail), then pick up and k 127 sts along left side edge of right sail, pm for center, knit rem 111 sts from boat needle, then cable cast-on 26 sts—274 sts. Knit next row.
Dec row (RS) K1, ssk, knit to 2 sts before center marker, ssk, sl marker, k2tog, knit to last 3 stitches, k2tog, k1—270 sts. Knit next row. Rep last 2 rows 66 times more, changing to straight needles when

Gauge
22 sts and 48 rows to 4"/10cm over garter st (knit every row) using size 5 (3.75mm) circular needle. *Take time to check gauge.*

Sailboat Blanket

desired, end with a WS row—6 sts.
Next (dec) row (RS) [K2tog] 3 times—3 sts. Cut yarn, leaving an 8"/20.5cm tail, and thread through rem sts. Pull tog tightly, secure end, then weave in end.

TOP RED FLAG
With RS facing, count 29 garter st loops down from top of left sail; place yarn marker in 30th loop. With RS facing, straight needles, and C, beg in loop after marked loop and pick up and k 1 st in each of next 29 loops. Knit next 3 rows, end with a WS row.
Dec row 1 (RS) K1, ssk, knit to last 3 sts, k2tog, k1—27 sts. Knit next 3 rows. Rep last 4 rows 11 times more—5 sts.
Dec row 2 (RS) Ssk, k1, k2tog—3 sts. Knit next 3 rows.
Dec row 3 (RS) SK2P—1 st. Fasten off.

CENTER BLUE FLAG
With RS facing, count 19 loops down from beg of top red flag foll the same row of loops; place yarn marker in next loop. With RS facing, straight needles, and B, beg in loop after marked loop and pick up and k 1 loop in each of next 29

loops; last 10 sts will share the same loops as top red flag. Knit next 3 rows, end with a WS row. Beg with dec row 1, cont to work as for top red flag.

BOTTOM RED FLAG
With RS facing, count 19 loops down from beg of center blue flag foll the same row of loops; place yarn marker in next loop. With RS facing, straight needles, and C, beg in loop after marked loop and pick up and k 1 st in each of next 29 loops; last 10 sts will share the same loops as center blue flag. Knit next 3 rows, end with a WS row. Beg with dec row 1, cont to work as for top red flag.

Life Preservers (make 2)
With crochet hook and 2 strands of C held tog, ch 20. Join ch with a sl st in first ch, forming a ring.
Rnd 1 (RS) Ch 5 (counts as 1 tr), work 39 tr in ring, join rnd with a sl st in 5th ch of ch-5.
Rnd 2 Ch 2 (counts as 1 sc), sc in each tr around, join rnd with a sl st in 2nd ch of ch-2. Fasten off.

ROPES
With RS facing and 2 strands of A held tog, join with a sl st in same place as joining last rnd.
Rnd 3 *Ch 15, sk next 9 sc, sc in next st, working between sts, tr into ring directly below sc just made, sc in same st as last sc; rep from * around 3 times more, end ch 15, join rnd with a sl st in same place as joining.

Finishing
Block piece lightly to measurements. Sew life preservers to boat, leaving ropes free. ∎

Cabled Cardi & Hat

This richly textured cardigan and hat ensemble will never go out of style.
A jaunty pompom keeps it from looking too grown-up.

DESIGNED BY JACQUELINE VAN DILLEN

Sizes

CARDIGAN
Instructions are written for size 6 months. Changes for 12 and 18 months are in parentheses. (Shown in size 6 months.)
HAT
Instructions are written for size 6 months. Changes for 12–18 months are in parentheses. (Shown in size 6 months.)

Knitted Measurements

CARDIGAN
Chest (closed) 21.5 (24.5, 26)"/54.5 (62, 66)cm
Length 9 (10½, 10½)"/23 (26.5, 26.5) cm
Upper arm 7 (8, 9)"/18 (20.5, 23)cm
HAT
Circumference (unstretched) 12 (15½)"/30.5 (39.5)cm
Depth 6½ (7)"/16.5 (18)cm

Materials

■ 4 (4, 5) 1¾oz/50g hanks (each approx 136yd/125m) of Cascade Yarns *220 Superwash Sport* (superwash merino wool) in #1946 silver grey
■ Size 5 (3.75mm) needles *or size to obtain gauge*
■ Size 4 (3.5mm) needles
■ Cable needle (cn)
■ Size F/5 (3.75mm) crochet hook
■ 5½"/1.3cm buttons
■ 3" pompom maker

Stitch Glossary

2-st RT K2tog leaving both sts on LH needle, k the first st again, drop both sts from needle.
3-st RPC Sl 1 st to cn and hold to *back,* k2, p1 from cn.
3-st LPC Sl 2 sts to cn and hold to *front,* p1, k2 from cn.
4-st RC Sl 2 sts to cn and hold to *back,* k2, k2 from cn.
4-st RPC Sl 2 sts to cn and hold to *back,* k2, p2 from cn.
4-st LPC Sl 2 sts to cn and hold to *front,* p2, k2 from cn.

K1, P1 Rib

(worked over an even number of sts)
Row 1 (RS) *K1, p1; rep from * to end.
Row 2 *P1, k1; rep from * to end.
Rep rows 1 and 2 for k1, p1 rib.

Moss Stitch

(worked over an odd number of sts)
Row 1 (RS) K1, *p1, k1; rep from * to end.
Row 2 P1, *k1, p1; rep from * to end.
Row 3 P1, *k1, p1; rep from * to end.
Row 4 K1, *p1, k1; rep from * to end.
Rep rows 1–4 for moss st.

Cardigan

BACK
With smaller needles, cast on 74 (82, 86) sts. Work in k1, p1 rib for 1½"/4cm, end with a RS row. Change to larger needles. Purl next row on WS.
Row 1 (RS) Work 9 (13, 15) sts in moss st, sts 1–56 of cardigan chart, 9 (13, 15) sts in moss st.
Row 2 Work 9 (13, 15) sts in moss st, sts 56–1 of cardigan chart, 9 (13, 15) sts in moss st.
Cont until 26-row repeat of cardigan chart has been worked once, then rep rows 3–26 1 (2, 2) time, then rep rows 3–14 1 (0, 0) time more, AT SAME TIME when piece measures 5½(6½, 6)"/14 (16.5, 15)cm from beg, end with a WS row and work as foll:

ARMHOLE SHAPING
Bind off 3 sts at beg of next 2 rows, 2 sts at beg of next 2 rows, dec 1 st both sides every other row 2 (3, 3) times—60 (66, 70) sts. Work even until all chart row repeats are complete, end with row 14

Gauges

CARDIGAN: 22 sts and 32 rows to 4"/10cm over moss st using size 5 (3.75mm) needles.
HAT: 36 sts and 32 rows to 4"/10cm over hat chart (unstretched) using size 5 (3.75mm) needles. *Take time to check gauges.*

Cabled Cardi & Hat

(26, 26)—piece measures approx 9 (10½, 10½)"/23 (26.5, 26.5)cm from beg. Bind off.

LEFT FRONT
With smaller needles, cast on 34 (38, 40) sts. Work in k1, p1 rib for 1½"/4cm, end with a RS row. Change to larger needles, purl next row on WS.
Row 1 (RS) Work 9 (13, 15) sts in moss st, sts 1–24 of cardigan chart, p1.
Row 2 K1, work sts 24–1 of cardigan chart, 9 (13, 15) sts in moss st.
Working chart row repeats as for back, cont as established, AT SAME TIME, when piece measures 5½ (6½, 6)"/14 (16.5, 15)cm from beg, end with a WS row and work as foll:

ARMHOLE SHAPING
Bind off at beg of RS rows—3 sts once, 2 sts once, then dec 1 st at same edge every other row 2 (3, 3) times—27 (30, 32) sts. Work even until piece measures 6½ (8, 8)"/16.5 (20.5, 20.5)cm from beg, end with a RS row.

NECK SHAPING
Next row (WS) Bind off 5 sts, work to end—22 (25, 27) sts.
At same edge, bind off 4 sts once, then dec 1 st 3 times—15 (18, 20) sts. Work even until same length as back, end with row 14 (26, 26). Bind off.

RIGHT FRONT
With smaller needles, cast on 34 (38, 40) sts. Work in k1, p1 rib for 1½"/4cm, end with a RS row. Change to larger needles, purl next row on WS.
Row 1 (RS) P1, work sts 33–56 of cable chart, 9 (13, 15) sts in moss st.
Row 2 (WS) Work 9 (13, 15) sts in moss

st, sts 56–33 of cable chart, k1.
Complete same as for left front, with armhole shaping at beg of WS rows and neck shaping at beg of RS rows.

SLEEVES
With smaller needles, cast on 46 (50, 54) sts. Work in k1, p1 rib for 1½ (1½, 2)"/4 (4, 5)cm, end with a RS row. Change to larger needles, purl next row on WS.
Row 1 (RS) Work 3 (5, 7) sts in moss st, sts 9–48 of cardigan chart, 3 (5, 7) sts in moss st.
Row 2 Work 3 (5, 7) sts in moss st, sts 48–9 of cardigan chart, 3 (5,7) sts in moss st.
Cont until 26-row repeat of cardigan chart has been worked once, then rep rows 3–26 1 time more, then rep rows 3–14 0 (1, 1) times more, AT SAME TIME, when 6 rows have been worked above rib, cont as foll:
Working new sts into moss st, inc 1 st each side on next row, then every 6th (6th, 4th) row 3 (5, 5) times more—54 (62, 66) sts. Work even and end with row 8 (16,12) of 2nd chart rep; piece

measures approx 5 (6¼, 6¼)"/12.5 (16, 16)cm from beg.

CAP SHAPING
Bind off 3 sts at beg of next 2 rows, 2 sts at beg of next 2 rows, then dec 1 st each side every other row 5 (7, 9) times—34 (38, 38) sts.
Bind off 3 (4, 4) sts at beg of next 2 rows, 4 (5, 5) sts at beg of next 2 rows, bind off rem 20 sts.

Finishing
Gently block pieces.

NECKBAND
With RS facing and larger needles, pick up 72 sts around neck edge. Work in k1, p1 rib for ½"/1.3cm. Change to smaller needles, cont in rib until neckband measures ¾"/2cm. Bind off.

BUTTONBAND
With RS facing and larger needles, pick up 50 (58, 58) sts along left front edge and neck band. Work in k1, p1 rib for ½"/1.3cm. Change to smaller needles, cont in rib until band measures 1"/2.5cm. Bind off.

BUTTONHOLE BAND
With RS facing and larger needles, pick up 50 (58, 62) sts along right front edge and neckband. Work in k1, p1 rib for ½"/1.3cm, end with a WS row.
Next (buttonhole) row (RS) Rib 4 sts, *k2tog, yo, rib 8 (10, 10) sts; rep from * 4 times more, end last rep rib 4 (4, 6) sts. Change to smaller needles, cont in rib until band measures 1"/2.5cm. Bind off. Sew shoulder seams. Set in sleeves. Sew side and sleeve seams. Sew buttons to buttonband opposite buttonholes.

CARDIGAN CHART

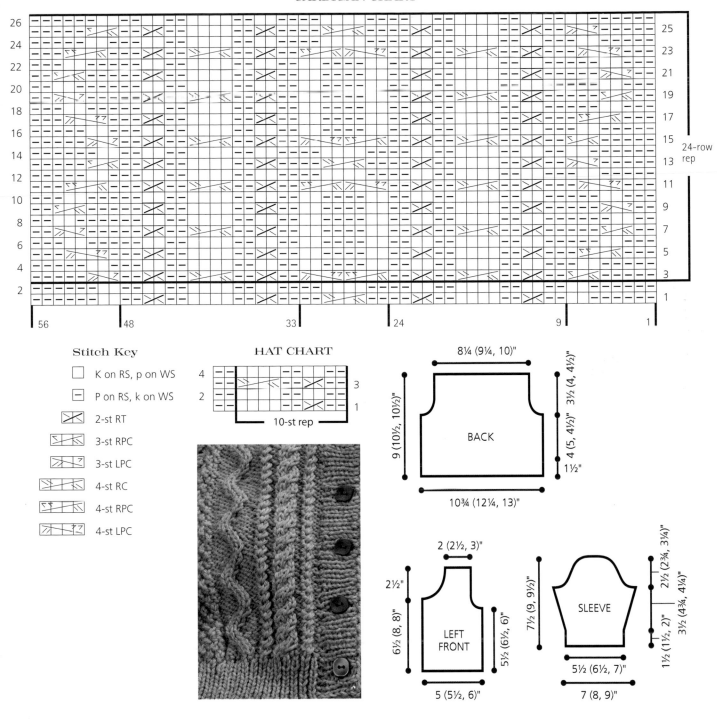

Stitch Key

- ☐ K on RS, p on WS
- − P on RS, k on WS
- ✕ 2-st RT
- 3-st RPC
- 3-st LPC
- 4-st RC
- 4-st RPC
- 4-st LPC

HAT CHART

10-st rep

BACK
8¼ (9¼, 10)"
9 (10½, 10½)"
3½ (4, 4½)"
4 (5, 4½)"
1½"
10¾ (12¼, 13)"

LEFT FRONT
2 (2½, 3)"
2½"
6½ (8, 8)"
5½ (6½, 6)"
5 (5½, 6)"

SLEEVE
7½ (9, 9½)"
2½ (2¾, 3¼)"
3½ (4¾, 4¼)"
1½ (1¾, 2)"
5½ (6½, 7)"
7 (8, 9)"

Cabled Cardi & Hat

Hat

With smaller needles, cast on 112 (142) sts. Work in k1, p1 rib for 1¼"/3cm, end with a RS row.
Next row (WS) Purl across, dec 1 st—112 (142) sts. Change to larger needles.

BEG HAT CHART
Row 1 (RS) Work 10-st rep of chart 11 (14) times across row, work last 2 sts of chart.
Row 2 Work last 2 sts of chart, work 10-st rep of chart from left to right 11 (14) times across row. Cont to work rows 1–4 of chart until hat measures 5 (5½)"/ 12.5 (14)cm from beg, end with a row 4.

CROWN SHAPING
Next (dec) row (RS) [P2, 2-st RT, p2tog, k4] 11 (14) times, p2—101 (128) sts.

Work 1 row even.
Next (dec) row (RS) [P2tog, 2-st RT, p1, 4-st RC] 11 (14) times, p2tog—89 (113) sts.
Work 1 row even.
Next (dec) row (RS) [P1, 2-st RT, p1, k1, k2tog, k1] 11 (14) times, p1—78 (99) sts.
Work 1 row even.
Next (dec) row (RS) [P1, 2-st RT, sl 2 sts to cn and hold to back, k2, k2tog from cn] 11 (14) times, p1—67 (85) sts.
Work 1 row even.
Next (dec) row (RS) P1, [2-st RT, k2, ssk] 10 (13) times, 2-st RT, k3, p1—57 (72) sts.
Work 1 row even.
Next (dec) row (RS) P1, [2-st RT, sl 1 st to cn and hold to back, k2tog, k1 from cn] 11 (14) times, p1—46 (58) sts.
Work 1 row even.
Next (dec) row (RS) P1, [k2tog] 22 (28) times, p1—24 (30) sts.
Work 1 row even.
Next (dec) row K2tog 12 (15) times—12 (15) sts. Work 1 row even.
Pull yarn end through rem sts.
Fasten off.

Finishing

Sew hat seam.

POMPOM
Wrap yarn densely around a 3"/7.5cm pompom maker. Finish pompom following package instructions.

CROCHETED CORD
With crochet hook, join yarn with a sl st to top of hat and ch for 4"/10cm. Join securely to pompom. Fasten off. ■

35

Skirted Onesie

Your little girl will be ready for a day at the beach when she dons this cheerful onesie.

DESIGNED BY DEVIN COLE

Sizes
Instructions are written for size 6 months. Changes for 12 and 18 months are in parentheses. (Shown in size 12 months.)

Knitted Measurements
Chest 18 (19, 20)"/45.5 (48, 51)cm
Length 15 (16, 17)"/38 (40.5, 43)cm

Materials
■ 3 (4, 4) 1¾oz/50g hanks (each approx 136yd/125m) of Cascade Yarns *220 Superwash Sport* (superwash merino wool) in #827 coral

■ One pair size 5 (3.75mm) needles *or size to obtain gauge*

■ Size 5 (3.75mm) circular needle, 16"/40cm long

■ Size E-4 (3.5mm) crochet hook

■ Two ½"/13mm snaps

■ Stitch markers

K2, P2 Rib
Row 1 (RS) *K2, p2; rep from * to last 1 (3, 3) sts, k1 (3, 3).
Row 2 P1 (3, 3), *k2, p2; rep from * across.
Rep rows 1 and 2 for k2, p2 rib.

Seed Stitch
Row 1 (RS) *K1, p1; rep from * across.
Row 2 Purl the knit sts and knit the purl sts as they appear.
Rep row 2 for seed st.

Onesie
BACK
With straight needles, cast on 13 sts.
Row 1 (RS) Knit, inc 1 st at beg of row.
Row 2 Purl, inc 1 st at beg of row.
Rows 3–24 (26, 30) Rep rows 1 and 2—37 (39, 43) sts.
Next row Knit, inc 2 sts at beg of row.
Next row Purl, inc 2 sts at beg of row.
Rep last 2 rows until there are 49 (51, 55) sts.
Work even in St st (k on RS, p on WS) until piece measures 6 (6¼, 6½)"/15 (16, 16.5)cm, ending with a WS row. Work in k2, p2 rib for 10 rows. Work in St st for 4 (4½, 5)"/10 (11.5, 12.5)cm from end of rib, ending with a WS row.

ARMHOLE SHAPING
Bind off 3 (3, 4) sts at beg of next 2 rows—43 (45, 47) sts. Bind off 2 sts at beg of foll 2 rows—39 (41, 43) sts. Bind off 1 st at beg of next 8 rows—31 (33, 35) sts.

Gauge
22 sts and 28 rows to 4"/10cm over St st using size 5 (3.75mm) needles.
Take time to check gauge.

Skirted Onesie

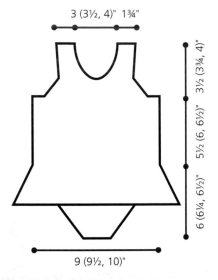

3 (3½, 4)" 1¾"

3½ (3¾, 4)"

5½ (6, 6½)"

6 (6¼, 6½)"

9 (9½, 10)"

NECK SHAPING
Next row (RS) Ssk, k11 (12, 13), join a second ball of yarn and bind off center 5 sts, k11 (12, 13), k2tog—12 (13, 14) sts per shoulder. Working both sides at the same time, bind off 1 st at each neck edge every other row 2 (3, 4) times—10 sts per shoulder. Work even until armhole measures 3½ (3¾, 4)"/9 (9.5, 10)cm. Bind off.

FRONT
With straight needles, cast on 13 sts.
Rows 1–6 Work in St st.
Cast on 1 st at beg of next 2 rows 2 (3, 5) times. Cast on 2 sts at beg of next 2 rows 3 times. Cast on 3 sts at beg of next 2 rows twice. Cast on 4 sts at beg of next 2 rows—49 (51, 55) sts.
Finish as for back.
Sew side and shoulder seams.

SKIRT
With circular needle and RS facing, pick up and knit 130 sts along lower edge of waist ribbing with garment turned upside down. Join, taking care not to twist sts on needle, pm every 26 sts, including beg of rnds. Purl next rnd.
Rnd 1 (RS) Knit, inc 1 st after each marker—135 sts.
Rnd 2 Knit, pm every 15 sts, removing old markers.
Rnd 3 Knit, inc 1 st each side of each marker—153 sts.
Rnd 4 Knit.
Rnds 5–14 Rep rnds 3 and 4—243 sts. Work even for 5 rnds. Bind off.

FIRST RUFFLE
Count down 15 rows from pick-up rnd of skirt. With straight needles and

RS facing, pick up and knit 68 (72, 76) sts across back of skirt. Pm every 17 (18, 19) sts.
Row 1 (RS) K1, inc 1, *knit to 1 st before marker, inc 1 st each side of marker; rep from * to last 2 sts, inc 1, k1—76 (80, 84) sts.
Row 2 Purl.
Rows 3–14 Rep rows 1 and 2—124 (128, 132) sts. Bind off.

SECOND RUFFLE
Count down 13 rows from pick-up row of first ruffle. With straight needles and RS facing, pick up and knit 48 (52, 56) sts across back of skirt. Pm every 12 (13, 14) sts.
Row 1 (RS) K1, inc 1, *knit to 1 st before marker, inc 1 st each side of marker; rep from * to last 2 sts, inc 1, k1—56 (60, 64) sts.
Row 2 Purl.
Rows 3–10 Rep rows 1 and 2—88 (92, 96) sts. Bind off.

Finishing
BOW
With straight needles, cast on 8 sts. Work in seed st for 53 rows. Bind off. For center piece, cast on 8 sts, work in seed st for 9 rows, bind off. Fold ends of longer piece toward center, wrap shorter piece around, sew in place. Sew to waistband on ribbing as shown.
With crochet hook, work 1 rnd of sc around neck, armholes, leg openings, and along the hem of the skirt and ruffles. Fasten off. Weave in ends. Attach snaps to crotch opening. ■

Heart Cardigan

This adorable cover-up features a Fair Isle heart motif and corrugated ribbing on the waistband and cuffs.

DESIGNED BY GRACE AKHREM

Sizes
Instructions are written for size 3 months. Changes for 6 and 12 months are in parentheses. (Shown in size 3 months.)

Knitted Measurements
Chest (closed) 20.5 (23, 25)"/ 52 (58.5, 63.5)cm
Length 8½ (9, 10½)"/ 21.5(23, 26.5)cm
Upper arm 7 (7, 8)"/18 (18, 20.5)cm

Materials
■ 2 (3, 4) 1¾ oz/50g hanks (each approx 136yd/125m) of Cascade Yarns *220 Superwash Sport* (superwash merino wool) in #849 dark aqua (MC)
■ 1 hank in #809 really red (CC)
■ One pair size 6 (4mm) needles *or size to obtain gauge*
■ One ¾"/19mm button
■ Size G/6 (4mm) crochet hook
■ Stitch holders

Corrugated Rib
(multiple of 4 sts plus 2)
Row 1 (RS) K2 MC, *k2 CC, k2 MC; rep from * to end.
Row 2 P2 MC, *k2 CC, p2 MC; rep from * to end.
Row 3 K2 MC, *p2 CC, k2 MC; rep from * to end.
Row 4 P2 MC, *k2 CC, p2 MC; rep from * to end.
Rows 5–8 Rep rows 3 and 4.

Cardigan
BACK
With MC, cast on 62 (70, 74) sts.
Purl 1 row on WS.
Join CC and work in corrugated rib for 8 rows. Set aside on stitch holder.

FRONTS
With MC, cast on 34 (38, 42) sts.
Purl 1 row on WS.
Join CC and work in corrugated rib for 8 rows. Set aside on stitch holder, make second front in same manner.

BODY
Next row (RS) With MC knit 34 (38, 42) front sts, 62 (70, 74) back sts, 34 (38, 42) front sts—130 (146, 158) sts. Work in St st (knit on RS, purl on WS) for 1 row.

BEG CHART PATTERN
Row 1 (RS) Join CC and work 10-st rep 13 (14, 15) times, work to st 0 (6, 8) of chart.
Row 2 Beg with st 0 (6, 8), work from left to right to st 0 (1, 1), work 10-st rep from left to right 13 (14, 15) times. Work even until row 15 of chart is finished, cont in MC only until piece measures 5 (5½, 6)"/ 12.5 (14, 15)cm from beg, end with WS row.

DIVIDE FOR ARMHOLES
BACK
Next row K 34 (38, 42) sts for right front, place these sts on holder, k 62 (70, 74) sts for back, place rem 34 (38, 42) sts on holder for left front.

BACK
Work even in St st until piece measures 8½ (9, 10½)"/21.5 (23, 26.5)cm from beg. Bind off.

LEFT FRONT
Rejoin MC to work RS row. Cont in St st until piece measures 6 (6, 7)"/15 (15, 18)cm from beg, end with a RS row.

Gauge
24 sts and 32 rows to 4"/10cm over St st using size 6 (4mm) needles. *Take time to check gauge.*

Heart Cardigan

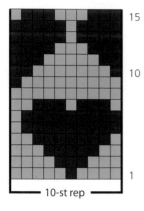

15

10

1

10-st rep

Color Key

■ Dark Aqua (MC)

■ Really Red (CC)

NECK SHAPING
Bind off 4 (5, 6) sts at the beg of next 2 WS rows—26 (28, 30) sts.
Purl 1 row.
Next (dec) row (RS) K to last 4 sts, k2tog, k2—25 (27, 29) sts.
Purl 1 row. Rep last 2 rows 3 (5, 7) times more—22 sts. Work even until piece measures 8½ (9, 10½)"/21.5 (23, 26.5)cm from beg. Bind off.

RIGHT FRONT
Rejoin MC to work RS row. Cont in St st until piece measures 6 (6, 7)"/15 (15, 18)cm from beg, end with a WS row.

NECK SHAPING
Bind off 4 (5, 6) sts at the beg of next 2 RS rows—26 (28, 30) sts. Purl 1 row.
Next (dec) row (RS) K2, ssk, k to end—25 (27, 29) sts.
Purl 1 row. Rep last 2 rows 3 (5, 7) times more—22 sts. Work even until piece measures 8½ (9, 10½)"/21.5 (23, 26.5)cm from beg. Bind off.

SLEEVES
With MC, cast on 42 (42, 52) sts. Purl 1 row on WS.
Row 1 (RS) Join CC, k0 (0, 1) MC, work in corrugated rib over 42 (42, 50) sts, k0 (0, 1) MC. Work even until row 8 of corrugated rib is finished.

With MC, work in St st for 2 rows.

BEG CHART PATTERN
Row 1 (RS) K1 MC (selvage st), work 10-st rep 4 (4, 5) times, k1 MC (selvage st).
Work through row 15 of chart, working St st selvages in MC. Cont in MC only until piece measures 6¾ (7¼, 7¾)"/17 (18.5, 19.5)cm from beg. Bind off.

Finishing
Block piece to measurements. Sew shoulder seams.

NECK EDGING
With RS facing and MC, pick up and knit 21 (26, 31) sts along right front neck, 21 (25, 29) sts along back neck, 21 (26, 31) sts along left front neck—63 (77, 91) sts. Knit 1 row. Bind off knitwise.

LEFT FRONT EDGING
With RS facing and MC, pick up and k 36 (36, 42) sts evenly spaced along left front edge. Knit 1 row. Bind off knitwise.

RIGHT FRONT EDGING
Pick up and knit same as left front band. Bind off to last 6 sts, with crochet hook ch 5 sts for button loop, bind off rem sts. Sew sleeve seams, leaving ½"/12mm open above cast-on edge. Set in sleeves. Sew button to left front opposite loop. ■

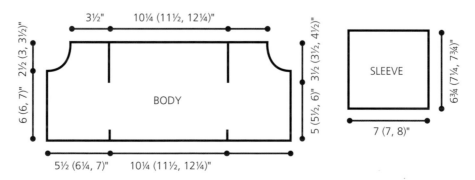

37

Bear Hat

Bring out your child's wild side with this cuddly topper.
The garter stitch ties will keep it from escaping!

DESIGNED BY JACQUELINE VAN DILLEN

Size
Instructions are written for
size 6–12 months.

Knitted Measurements
Head circumference 16½"/42cm
Depth 5¾"/14.5cm (excluding ties)

Materials
■ 1 1¾oz/50g hank (each approx
136yd/125m) of Cascade Yarns *220
Superwash Sport* (superwash merino
wool) each in #811 como blue (A),
#819 chocolate (B), #873 extra creme
cafe (C), and #818 mocha (D)

■ One pair size 5 (3.75mm) needles *or
size to obtain gauge*

■ Size E/4 (3.5mm) crochet hook

■ Contrasting sewing thread

Note
Hat is made in 2 pieces.

Back
With A, cast on 50 sts. Work in garter st
(knit every row) for 6 rows, end with a
WS row. Cont in St st (knit on RS, purl on
WS) and work even until piece measures
2¼"/5.5cm from beg, end with a WS
row. Change to B. Knit next 2 rows.
Change to C. Cont in St st until piece

measures 4¾"/12cm from beg, end
with a WS row.

CROWN SHAPING
Dec row 1 (RS) *K2tog, k3; rep from * to
end—40 sts. Purl next row.
Dec row 2 (RS) *K2tog, k2; rep from * to
end—30 sts. Purl next row.
Dec row 3 (RS) *K2tog, k1; rep from * to
end—20 sts. Purl next row.
Dec row 4 (RS) [K2tog] 10 times—10 sts.
Cut yarn, leaving an 8"/20.5cm tail and
thread through rem sts. Pull tog tightly
and secure end.

Front
Work as for back.

Finishing
On hat front, measure and mark
center with a pin. Using a double strand
of sewing thread, sew a vertical row of
running stitches up center of hat as a
guideline.

EYES
On hat front, measure ½"/1.3cm up from
top edge of B garter st ridge. Using a
double strand of sewing thread, sew a

Gauge
24 sts and 30 rows to 4"/10cm over St st using size 5 (3.75mm) needles.
Take time to check gauge.

Bear Hat

horizontal row of running stitches ½"/1.3cm up from top edge of B garter st ridge. Using B, embroider two ½"/1.3cm diameter horizontal straight stitch eyes, spaced 1"/2.5cm from either side of center vertical guideline and so bottom edges are ½"/1.3cm from top edge of B garter st ridge.

MOUTH

Measure 1¼"/3cm up from bottom edge of hat. Using a double strand of sewing thread, sew a horizontal row of running stitches 1¼"/3cm up from bottom edge of hat. Using B, embroider a 2½"/6.5cm long horizontal row of chain stitches, centering the length on center vertical guideline.

Using B, embroider ¾"/2cm-wide straight stitch lips above and below chain stitch mouth, and centered on vertical guideline.

NOSE

With crochet hook and B, make a 2"/5cm long chain. Fasten off, leaving a long tail for sewing. Sew each end of chain just below B garter st ridge, centering it over vertical guideline and leaving it a little slack. Remove all sewing thread guidelines. Sew hat seams.

EARS

Along left side seam, measure and mark 1¾"/4.5cm up from top edge of B garter st ridge. With RS facing and D, pick up and k 13 sts evenly spaced between ridge and marker. Work in garter st for 7 rows, end with a WS row.

Dec row 1 K6, k2tog, k5—12 sts. Knit next row.

Dec row 2 K4, [k2tog] twice, k4—10 sts. Knit next row.

Dec row 3 K3, [k2tog] twice, k3—8 sts. Knit next row.

Dec row 4 K2, [k2tog] twice, k2—6 sts.

Dec row 5 K1, [k2tog] twice, k1—4 sts. Bind off knitwise. Rep on opposite side of hat.

TIES

With RS facing and bottom edge of hat at top, use D to pick up and k 4 sts before side seam and 4 sts after side seam—8 sts. Cont in garter st for 8"/20.5cm. Bind off knitwise. Rep on opposite side of hat. ∎

✳Pattern for Boatneck Pullover is on page 14.

38

Lace Sleep Sack

Sweet dreams will be easy to achieve in this lovely lace bunting with delicate picot edgings.

DESIGNED BY JACQUELINE VAN DILLEN

Sizes
Instructions are written for size 3 months. Changes for 6 months are in parentheses. (Shown in size 3 months.)

Knitted Measurements
Chest 21 (25½)"/53 (65)cm
Length (buttoned) 19 (23)"/48 (58.5)cm

Materials
■ 4 (5) 1¾oz/50g hanks (each approx 136yd/125m) of Cascade Yarns *220 Superwash Sport* (superwash merino wool) in #1967 wisteria (MC)

■ 1 hank in #850 lime sherbet for I-cord tie (CC)

■ Size 5 (3.75mm) needles *or size to obtain gauge*

■ Two size 5 (3.75mm) double-pointed needles (dpns) for I-cord

■ Size F/5 (3.75mm) crochet hook

■ Stitch markers

■ Two ⅜"/10mm buttons

Stitch Glossary
SK2P Slip next st, k2tog, pass slipped st over k2tog.

Picot Edging
Sc in first st, *ch 3, join with sl st to second ch, skip 2 sts, sc in next st; rep from * to end, join with sl st to first sc.

Sleep Sack
BACK
With MC and straight needles, cast on 75 (93) sts. Knit 1 row on WS.

BEG CHART
Row 1 (RS) Work first 10 sts of chart, work 18-st rep 3 (4) times, work last 11 sts of chart. **Row 2** Beg with last st of chart, work to repeat line, work 18-st rep 3 (4) times, work to first st of chart.
Cont to foll chart in this way until row 36 has been worked, then rep rows 1–36 for 2 (3) times more. Piece measures approximately 14 (18)"/35.5 (45.5)cm. **Next (dec) row (RS)** [K2, k2tog] 18 (23) times, k 3 (1)—57 (70) sts. Purl 1 row on WS. **Next (eyelet) row (RS)** K6, [yo, k2tog, k4 (6)] 8 times, k3 (0). Work even in St st until piece measures 2 (1½)"/5 (4)cm above eyelet row, end with a WS row.

ARMHOLE SHAPING
Bind off 3 sts at beg of next 2 rows, 2 sts at beg of next 2 (4) rows—47 (56) sts. Dec 1 st both sides 6 times—35 (44) sts. Work

in St st until piece measures 5"/12.5cm above eyelet row, end with WS row.

NECK SHAPING
Mark center 11 (14) sts for back neck.
Next row Work to marker, join second ball of yarn and bind off marked sts, work to end—12 (15) sts each side. Working both sides at once, bind off 3 sts at neck edge once (twice)—9 sts each side. Work even until piece measures 20½ (24½)"/52 (62)cm from beg, end with a WS row.
Work each side separately as foll:
Next (buttonhole) row (RS) K3, k2tog, yo, k4. Work 1 row on WS. **Next (dec) row** K2tog, k to last 2 sts, k2tog—7 sts. Work 1 row on WS. Bind off.

FRONT
Work same as back until piece measures 2 (1½)"/5 (4)cm above eyelet row, end with a WS row.

ARMHOLE SHAPING
Bind off 3 sts at beg of next 2 rows, 2 sts at beg of next 0 (2) rows—51 (60) sts. Dec 1 st both sides 8 times—35 (44) sts. AT THE SAME TIME, when piece measures 3½"/9cm above eyelet row, end with a WS row and work as foll:

Gauges
22 sts and 34 rows to 4"/10cm over St st using size 5 (3.75mm) needles. One 6-row chart rep measures approx 4½"/11.5cm using size 5 (3.75mm) needles. One 18-st rep measures approx 3"/7.5cm using size 5 (3.75mm) needles. *Take time to check gauges.*

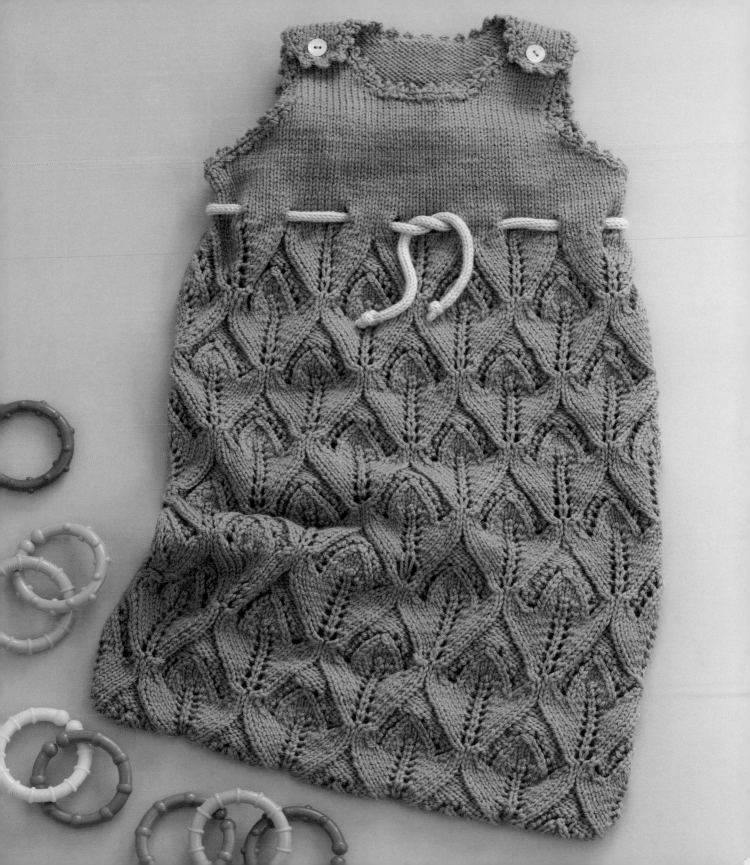

38
Lace Sleep Sack

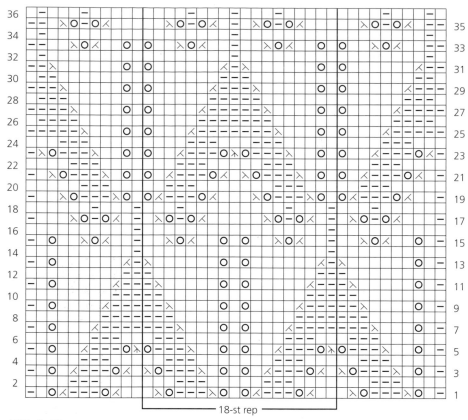

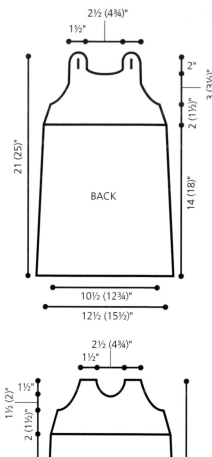

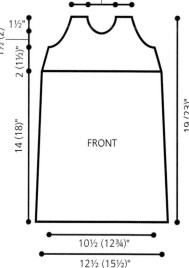

Stitch Key

☐ K on RS, p on WS ◻️Yo ◻️K2tog

– P on RS, k on WS ◻️Ssk ◻️SK2P

NECK SHAPING

Mark center 5 (8) sts for front neck.
Next row (RS) Work to marker, join
second ball of yarn and bind off marked
sts, work to end—15 (18) sts each side.
Working both sides at once, bind off 2
sts at each neck edge once (twice), then
dec 1 st at same edge 4 (5) times—9 sts
each side. Work even until piece
measures 19 (23)"/48 (58.5)cm from beg,
end with a WS row. Bind off.

Finishing

Block piece to measurements.
Sew side seams. Sew cast-on edges
together. Sew buttons to front, opposite
buttonholes.

CROCHET EDGING

With MC and crochet hook,
beg at right side seam and work picot
edging all around both armhole
and neck edges.

4-ST I-CORD

With CC, cast 4 sts onto 1 dpn. *Knit 4,
do not turn. Slide sts back to other end of
dpn, pull yarn snug across WS; rep from *
until piece measures 35"/90cm long. Bind
off. Beg at center front of sleep sack,
thread I-cord in and out of eyelet holes.
Knot each end. ■

39

Asian Inspiration Jacket

A striking color combination and elegant frog closures make for a sophisticated cover-up worthy of a little emperor or empress.

DESIGNED BY ERSSIE MAJOR

Sizes
Instructions are written for size 6 months. Changes for 12 and 18 months are in parentheses. (Shown in size 12 months.)

Knitted Measurements
Chest (closed) 20 (22, 24)"/51 (56, 61)cm
Length 9 (10, 11)"/23 (25.5, 28)cm
Upper arm 7½ (8½ , 9½)"/19 (21.5, 24)cm

Materials
- 2 (3, 3) 1¾oz/50g hanks (each approx 136yd/125m) of Cascade Yarns 220 *Superwash Sport* (superwash merino wool) in #809 really red (MC)
- 2 hanks in #815 black (CC)
- One pair size 6 (4mm) needles *or size to obtain gauge*
- Spare size 6 (4mm) needle (for 3-needle bind-off)
- Stitch holders
- Stitch markers
- Three ¾" x 2⅝"/19mm x 66mm black satin frog closures
- Black sewing thread

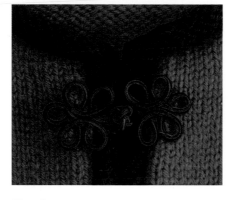

Back
With MC, cast on 58 (64, 70) sts. Work even in St st (knit on RS, purl on WS) until piece measures 9 (10, 11)"/23 (25.5, 28)cm from beg, end with a RS row.

NECK AND SHOULDER SHAPING
Next row (WS) P17 (20, 22), bind off center 24 (24, 26) sts, p17 (20, 22). Place 17 (20, 22) sts each side on holders for shoulders.

Left Front
With MC, cast on 26 (29, 32) sts. Work even in St st until piece measures 7½ (8½ , 9½)"/19 (21.5, 24)cm from beg, end with a RS row.

NECK SHAPING
At neck edge, bind off 3 (3, 4) sts once, then 3 sts twice—17 (20, 22) sts. Work even until piece measures same length as back to shoulder, end with a WS row. Place 17 (20, 22) sts on holder for shoulder.

RIGHT FRONT
Work as for left front, reversing all shaping. Join shoulders using 3-needle bind-off. Place markers 3¾ (4¼, 4¾)"/9.5 (11, 12)cm down from shoulders on back and fronts.

Sleeves
With RS facing and MC, pick up and k 44 (50, 56) sts evenly spaced between markers. Beg with a purl row, cont in St st for 3 rows, end with a WS row. Dec 1 st each side on next row, then every 6th row 5 (3, 5) times more, then every 4th row 0 (4, 3) times—32 (34, 38) sts. Work even until piece measures 4½ (5, 6)"/11.5 (12.5, 15)cm from beg, end with a WS row.

Gauge
29 sts to 5"/12.5cm and 31 rows to 4"/10cm over St st using size 6 (4mm) needles.
Take time to check gauge.

Asian Inspiration Jacket

CUFF

Change to CC. Cont in St st for 1½"/4cm, end with a WS row. Beg with a purl row, cont in reverse St st (purl on RS, knit on WS) for 1½"/4cm, end with a WS row. Cont in garter st (knit every row) for 4 rows. Bind off loosely knitwise.

Finishing

Block piece lightly to measurements. Sew side and sleeve seams (reversing seam for cuff fold-back).

FRONT BANDS

With RS facing and CC, pick up and k 44 (50, 56) sts evenly spaced along front edges. Beg with a purl row, cont in St st for 7 rows. Bind off loosely knitwise.

NECKBAND

With RS facing and CC, pick up and k 4 sts across top side edge of right front band, 12 (12, 13) sts along right neck edge to shoulder, 24 (24, 26) sts across back neck edge to shoulder, 12 (12, 13) sts along left neck edge, then 4 sts across top side edge of left front band—56 (56, 60) sts. Beg with a purl row, cont in St st for 7 rows. Bind off loosely knitwise.

LOWER BAND

With RS facing and CC, pick up and k 4 sts across lower side edge of left front band, 26 (29, 32) sts across left front lower edge, 58 (64, 70) sts across back lower edge, 26 (29, 32) sts across right front lower edge, then 4 sts across lower side edge of right front band—118 (130, 142) sts. Beg with a purl row, cont in St st for 9 rows. Bind off loosely knitwise. Tack side edges of neck and bottom bands in place. Sew on frogs using black thread. Fold up cuffs along turning ridge. ■

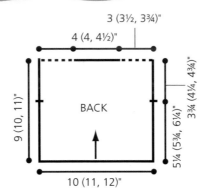

BACK

3 (3½, 3¾)"
4 (4, 4½)"
9 (10, 11)"
3¾ (4¼, 4¾)"
5¼ (5¾, 6¼)"
10 (11, 12)"

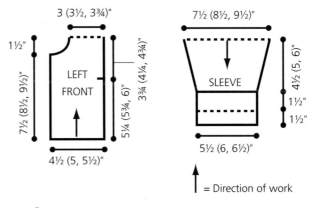

LEFT FRONT

3 (3½, 3¾)"
1½"
7½ (8½, 9½)"
3¾ (4¼, 4¾)"
5¼ (5¾, 6)"
4½ (5, 5½)"

SLEEVE

7½ (8½, 9½)"
4½ (5, 6)"
1½"
1½"
5½ (6, 6½)"

↑ = Direction of work

Quick Tip

When giving a handknit gift, it's helpful to include the yarn label for fiber content and care information.

Sailor Dress

Knit in patriotic red, white, and blue, this nautical-style dress is perfect for a boat ride or watching fireworks.

DESIGNED BY JOAN FORGIONE

Sizes
Instructions are written for size 6 months. Changes for 12 and 18 months are in parentheses. (Shown in size 12 months.)

Knitted Measurements
Chest 20 (22, 24)"/51 (56, 61)cm
Length 13 (14, 15)"/33 (35.5, 38)cm
Upper arm 7½ (8½, 9½)"/19 (21.5, 24)cm

Materials
- 3 (3, 4) 1¾oz/50g hanks (each approx 136yd/125m) of Cascade Yarns *220 Superwash Sport* (superwash merino wool) in #845 denim (MC)
- 1 hank each in #808 sunset orange (A) and #871 white (B)
- Size 5 (3.75mm) circular needles, 16"/40cm and 24"/61cm long *or size to obtain gauge*
- One pair size 5 (3.75mm) needles
- Size E/4 (3.5mm) crochet hook
- Stitch markers
- Two 7/16"/11mm buttons
- Sewing needle and red sewing thread

Note
Skirt is made in one piece to underarms.

Dress
SKIRT
With longer circular needle and A, cast on 152 (164, 176) sts. Join and pm, taking care not to twist sts on needle. Work around in St st (knit every rnd) for 4 rnds.
Next (picot) rnd *K2tog, yo; rep from * around. Cont in St st for 3 rnds. Cont in stripe pat as foll: 2 rnds B, 2 rnds A, and 2 rnds B. Change to MC. Knit one rnd, purl one rnd for garter st ridge.
Next rnd K76 (82, 88), pm for side marker, knit to end of rnd. Knit next rnd.

SIDE SHAPING
Dec rnd K1, ssk, knit to 3 sts before side marker, k2tog, k1, sl marker, k1, ssk, knit to 3 sts before rnd marker, k2tog, k1—148 (160, 172) sts. Rep dec rnd every 9th (10th, 11th) rnd 7 times more—120 (132, 144) sts. AT THE SAME TIME, change to shorter circular needle when there are too few sts on needle to work comfortably. Work even until piece measures 9 (9½, 10)"/23 (24, 25.5)cm above picot rnd.

DIVIDE FOR BACK AND FRONT
BACK
Change to straight needles and cont in St st as foll:

Next row (RS) Bind off first 2 sts, knit to side marker, turn; leave rem 60 (66, 72) sts on circular needle for front. Cont armhole shaping as foll:

ARMHOLE SHAPING
Bind off 2 sts at beg of next 3 rows, then dec 1 st each side on next RS row once—50 (56, 62) sts. Work even until armhole measures 2¼ (2¾, 3¼)"/5.5 (7, 8)cm, end with a WS row.

NECK OPENING
Next row (RS) K21 (24, 27), p1, k3 for right back; with a 2nd hank of MC, cast on 4 sts for buttonhole band, then p1, k24 (27, 30) for left back—25 (28, 31) sts for right back and 29 (32, 35) sts for left back. Working both sides at once, work even as established for ½"/1.3cm, end with a WS row.
Next (buttonhole) row (RS) With first hank of yarn, work across right back sts; with 2nd hank, k2, yo, k2tog, p1, work to end. Work even for 5 rows. Rep buttonhole row. Cont to work even until armhole measures 4 (4½, 5)"/10 (11.5, 12.5)cm, end with a WS row. Bind off each side.

FRONT
Change to straight needles and cont in St st as foll:

Gauge
24 sts and 34 rnds to 4"/10cm over St st using size 5 (3.75mm) circular needle. *Take time to check gauge.*

Sailor Dress

ARMHOLE SHAPING

Bind off 2 sts at beg of next 4 rows, then dec 1 st each side on next RS row once—50 (56, 62) sts. Work even until armhole measures 1 (1½, 2)"/2.5 (4, 5)cm, end with a WS row.

NECK SHAPING

Next row (RS) K24 (27, 30), join a 2nd ball of MC and bind off center 2 sts, knit to end. Working both sides at once, purl next row. Dec 1 st from each neck edge on next row, then every other 11 (12, 12) times more—12 (14, 17) sts each side. Work even until piece measures same length as back to shoulder, end with a WS row. Bind off each side.

SLEEVES

With straight needles and A, cast on 46 (50, 56) sts. Work in St st for 4 rows.
Next (picot) row (RS) K1, *k2tog, yo; rep from *, end k1. Beg with a purl row, cont in St st for 3 rows. Cont in stripe pat as foll: 2 rows B, 2 rows A, and 2 rows B. Change to MC. Knit next 2 rows for garter st ridge. Cont in St st until piece measures 2"/5cm from picot row, end with a WS row.

CAP SHAPING

Bind off 2 sts at beg of next 4 rows. Dec 1 st each side on next row, then every other row 1 (2, 4) times more, end with a WS row—34 (36, 38) sts. Bind off 2 sts at beg of next 6 rows, then 3 sts at beg of next 4 rows. Bind off rem 10 (12, 14) sts.

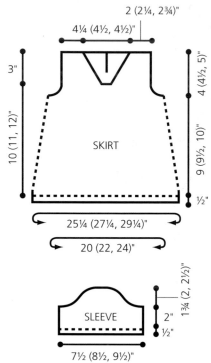

2 (2¼, 2¾)"
4¼ (4½, 4½)"
3"
10 (11, 12)"
4 (4½, 5)"
SKIRT
9 (9½, 10)"
½"
25¼ (27¼, 29¼)"
20 (22, 24)"

1¾ (2, 2½)"
SLEEVE
2"
½"
7½ (8½, 9½)"

Neck Insert

With straight needles and A, cast on 18 (20, 20) sts.
Rows 1–4 Knit.
Row (dec) 5 (RS) With A, k1, ssk, knit to last 3 sts, k2tog, k1—16 (18, 18) sts.
Row 6 With A, purl.
Row (dec) 7 With B, k1, ssk, knit to last 3 sts, k2tog, k1—14 (16, 16) sts.
Row 8 With B, purl. Rep last 4 rows twice more, then rows 5 and 6 once—4 (6, 6) sts. Bind off.

Bow

With straight needles and A, cast on 12 sts.
Row 1 (RS) Knit.

Row 2 K1, p10, k1.
Rows 3 and 4 Rep rows 1 and 2.
Row (picot) 5 K1, *k2tog, yo; rep from *, end k1.
Row 6 Rep row 2. Rep rows 1 and 2 until piece measures 2½ (3, 3)"/6.5 (7.5, 7.5)cm from picot row, end with a WS row. Rep row 5 for picot row. Beg with row 2, work even for 3 rows. Bind off.

LOOP

With straight needles and A, cast on 6 sts. Work even in St st for 2"/5cm. Bind off.

Finishing

Block pieces to measurements. Sew shoulder seams.

NECK AND BUTTONHOLE BAND EDGING

With RS facing and crochet hook, join MC with a sl st in bottom side edge of right back opening.
Rnd 1 (RS) Ch 1, working from left to right, and working 2 sc in each corner, sc evenly around entire edge, including bottom edge of buttonhole band. Fasten off.

Turn bottom hem to WS along picot rnd and sew in place. Sew neck insert to WS of front neck. Sew sleeve seams. Set in sleeves. Turn sleeve hems to WS along picot row and sew in place. Fold side edges of bow to WS along picot row and hem in place. Sew short edges of bow loop tog, allowing side edges to curl under to WS. Insert bow through loop, then center side to side. Using thread, sew bow to loop, then sew bow to front of dress as shown in photo. Sew on buttons. ■

126

Mittens & Booties Set

Little hands and feet will be warm *and* coordinated with these matching mitts and booties. And with a crocheted cord linking them together, there won't be any lost mittens!

DESIGNED BY JACQUELINE VAN DILLEN

Size
Instructions are written for size newborn–3 months.

Knitted Measurements
MITTENS
Hand circumference 5"/12.5cm
Length of cuff Approx ⅝"/1.5cm (folded back)

BOOTIES
Foot circumference 4½"/11.5cm
Foot length 3¼"/8cm

Materials
- 1 1¾oz/50g hank (each approx 136yd/125m) of Cascade Yarns *220 Superwash Sport* (superwash merino wool) in #841 moss
- One pair size 3 (3.25mm) needles *or size to obtain gauge*
- Size E/4 (3.5mm) crochet hook
- Three size 3 (3.25mm) double-pointed needles (dpns)
- Large safety pins
- Stitch markers

Mittens (Make 2)
CUFF
With straight needles, cast on 31 sts.
Row 1 (RS) K1, *p1, k1; rep from * to end.
Row 2 P1, *k1, p1; rep from * to end.
Rep rows 1 and 2 four times more, end with a WS row.

HAND
Cont in garter st (knit every row) for 14 rows, end with a WS row.

THUMB GUSSET
Inc row 1 (RS) K15, pm, M1, k1, M1, pm, k15—33 sts. Knit next row.
Inc row 2 (RS) K15, sl marker, M1, k3, M1, sl marker, k15—35 sts. Knit next row.
Inc row 3 (RS) K15, sl marker, M1, k5, M1, sl marker, k15—37 sts. Knit next row.
Inc row 4 (RS) K15, sl marker, M1, k7, M1, sl marker, k15—39 sts. Knit next row.
Next row (RS) K15, cast on 2 sts, drop marker, place next 9 sts on holder for thumb, drop marker, k15—32 sts. Work even until piece measures 3½"/9cm from beg, end with a WS row.

TOP SHAPING
Dec row 1 (RS) K1, k2tog, k10, k2tog, k2, k2tog, k10, k2tog, k1—28 sts. Knit next row.
Dec row 2 (RS) K1, k2tog, k8, k2tog, k2, k2tog, k8, k2tog, k1—24 sts. Knit next row.
Dec row 3 (RS) K1, k2tog, k6, k2tog, k2, k2tog, k6, k2tog, k1—20 sts. Knit next row.

Gauges
29 sts to 5"/12.5cm and 52 rows to 4"/10cm over garter st using size 3 (3.25mm) needles.
27 sts and 36 rows to 4"/10cm over St st using size 3 (3.25mm) needles.
Take time to check gauges.

Dec row 4 (RS) K1, k2tog, k4, k2tog, k2, k2tog, k4, k2tog, k1—16 sts. Cut yarn, leaving a 10"/25.5cm tail and thread through rem sts. Pull tog tightly and secure end. Do not cut rem tail.

THUMB

With RS facing and first dpn, pick up and k 1 st in first cast-on st at base of thumb, then k 5 sts from thumb holder; with 2nd dpn, k 4 rem sts on holder, then pick up and k 1 st in 2nd cast-on st at base of thumb—11 sts. Using 3rd dpn, work back and forth in garter st for 5 rows, end with a WS row.

TOP SHAPING

Dec row (RS) K1, [k2tog] 5 times—6 sts. Cut yarn, leaving an 8"/20.5cm tail, and thread through rem sts. Pull tog tightly and secure end. Sew thumb seam.

Finishing

Sew each mitt seam using rem tail from top of hand, reversing seam over cuff.

CORD

With crochet hook, make a 27"/68.5cm long chain. Fasten off, leaving a long tail for sewing. Sew each end of chain to inside seam of mitts, just below cuff. Fold back cuffs.

Booties (Make 2)

CUFF

With straight needles, cast on 36 sts.
Row 1 (RS) *K1, p1; rep from * to end. Rep this row 9 times more. Cont in St st (knit on RS, purl on WS) for 12 rows, end with a WS row.
Next row (RS) K12, place these sts on safety pin for back of heel, k12, place rem 12 sts on safety pin for back of heel—12 sts.

INSTEP

Beg with a purl row, cont in St st for 3 rows.
Dec row 1 (RS) Ssk, k8, k2tog—10 sts. Work even for 3 rows.
Dec row 2 (RS) Ssk, k6, k2tog—8 sts. Work even for 3 rows.
Dec row 3 (RS) Ssk, k4, k2tog—6 sts. Work next row even. Place rem 6 sts on safety pin for toe. Cut yarn.

FOOT

Next row (RS) K12 sts from first back-of-heel holder, pick up and k 10 sts evenly spaced along instep to toe sts, k 6 sts from toe holder, pick up and k 10 sts evenly spaced along opposite side of instep, to back-of-heel holder, k 12 sts from 2nd back-of-heel holder—50 sts. Cont in garter st for 7 rows, end with a WS row.

SOLE

Dec row 1 (RS) K4, k2tog, k14, k2tog, k6, k2tog, k14, k2tog, k4—46 sts. Knit next row.
Dec row 2 (RS) K4, k2tog, k12, k2tog, k6, k2tog, k12, k2tog, k4—42 sts. Knit next row.
Dec row 3 (RS) K3, k2tog, k12, k2tog, k4, k2tog, k12, k2tog, k3—38 sts. Knit next row.
Dec row 4 (RS) K3, k2tog, k10, k2tog, k4, k2tog, k10, k2tog, k3—34 sts. Knit next row.
Dec row 5 (RS) K2, k2tog, k10, k2tog, k2, k2tog, k10, k2tog, k2—30 sts. Knit next row.
Dec row 6 (RS) K2, k2tog, k9, [k2tog] twice, k9, k2tog, k2—26 sts. Bind off knitwise. Sew each sole and back heel seam, reversing seam over cuff. Fold back cuffs. ∎

12

Slip Stitch Cardigan

Knit in soft Easter-egg shades, this textured cardi is the perfect springtime cover-up.

DESIGNED BY E. J. SLAYTON

Sizes

Instructions are written for size 6 months. Changes for 12 and 18 months are in parentheses. (Shown in size 12 months.)

Knitted Measurements

Chest (closed) 20 (22, 24)"/51 (56, 61)cm
Length 10½ (11½, 12½)"/26.5 (29, 31.5)cm
Upper arm 9 (10, 11)"/23 (25.5, 28)cm

Materials

■ 2 (3, 3) 1¾oz/50g hanks (each approx 136yd/125m) of Cascade Yarns *220 Superwash Sport* (superwash merino wool) in #1967 wisteria (A)

■ 1 hank each in #836 pink ice (B) and #850 lime sherbet (C)

■ Two size 4 (3.5mm) circular needles, 24"/61cm long, *or size to obtain gauge*

■ One size 3 (3.25mm) circular needle, 24"/61cm long

■ Cable needle (cn)

■ Stitch holder

■ Stitch markers

■ Four ⁹⁄₁₆"/14mm buttons

✳Pattern for Picot Edge Cap is on page 4.

Stitch Glossary

T2R Sl next st to cn and hold to *back,* sl next st purlwise, k1 from cn.
T2L Sl next st to cn and hold to *front,* k1, sl st purlwise from cn.
Slide sts Slide all sts to opposite end of needle.

K1, P1 Rib

(over a multiple of 2 sts plus 1)
Row 1 (RS) K1, *p1, k1; rep from * to end.
Row 2 P1, *k1, p1; rep from * to end.
Rep rows 1 and 2 for k1, p1 rib.

Slip Stitch Pattern

(over a multiple of 9 sts plus 3)
Row 1 (RS) With B, *[k1, p1] twice, k4, p1; rep from* to last 3 sts, end k1, p1, k1.
Row 2 With C, purl.
Row 3 With A, k4, *T2R, T2L, k5; rep from * across, end last rep k4 instead of k5.
Row 4 With A, purl.
Row 5 With A, knit.
Row 6 (WS) With A, purl across; slide sts.
Row 7 (WS) With B, *[p1, k1] twice, p4, k1; rep from * to last 3 sts, end p1, k1, p1.
Row 8 (RS) With C, knit across; slide sts.
Row 9 (RS) With A, rep row 3.
Rows 10 and 11 With A, rep rows 4 and 5.
Row 12 With A, purl.
Rep rows 1–12 for slip st pat.

Back

With smaller circular needle and A, cast on 55 (63, 69) sts. Work back and forth in k1, p1 rib for 6 rows, end with a WS row. Change to larger circular needles.
Next (inc) row (RS) Knit across, inc 6 (5, 5) sts evenly spaced—61 (68, 74) sts.
Next row (WS) P2 (1, 4), pm, p57 (66, 66), pm, p2 (1, 4). Keeping 2 (1, 4) sts each side in St st (knit on RS, purl on WS), work rem sts in slip st pat using 2 needles.

Gauge

24 sts and 32 rows to 4"/10cm over slip st pat using larger circular needle. *Take time to check gauge.*

Slip Stitch Cardigan

Work even until piece measures 6 (6½, 7)"/15 (16.5, 18)cm from beg, end with row 4 or 10.

ARMHOLE SHAPING
With A, bind off 6 sts at beg of next 2 rows—49 (56, 62) sts. Work even in slip st pat as established until armhole measures 4½ (5, 5½)"/11.5 (12.5, 14)cm, end with row 4 or 10.

NECK SHAPING
Next row (RS) With A, bind off 12 (15, 17) sts knitwise, knit until there are 25 (26, 28) sts on needle, place these sts on holder for back neck, bind off rem 12 (15, 17) sts.

Left Front
With smaller circular needle and A, cast on 29 (31, 35) sts. Work back and forth in k1, p1 rib for 6 rows, end with a WS row. Change to larger circular needles.
Next (inc) row (RS) Knit across, inc 2 (3, 2) sts evenly spaced—31 (34, 37) sts.

FOR SIZE 6 MONTHS ONLY
Next row (WS) P30, pm, p1. Keeping 1 st at side edge in St st, work rem sts in slip st pat using 2 needles.

FOR SIZES 12 AND 18 MONTHS ONLY
Next row (WS) P2 (3), pm, p30, pm, p2 (4). Keeping 2 (3) sts at front edge and 2 (4) sts at side edge in St st, work rem sts in slip st pat using 2 needles.

FOR ALL SIZES
Work even until piece measures same length as back to underarm, end with row 4 or 10.

ARMHOLE SHAPING
With A, bind off first 6 sts—25 (28, 31) sts. Work even in slip st pat as established until armhole measures 3 (3½, 4)"/7.5 (9, 10)cm, end with row 5 or 11.

NECK SHAPING
Next row (WS) With A, bind off first 9 (9, 10) sts, work to end—16 (19, 21) sts. Dec 1 st from neck edge on next row, then every other row 3 times more—12 (15, 17) sts. Work even until piece measures same length as back to shoulder, end with a WS row. With A, bind off all sts knitwise for shoulder.

Right Front
With smaller circular needle and A, cast on 29 (31, 35) sts. Work back and forth in k1, p1 rib for 6 rows, end with a WS row. Change to larger circular needles.
Next (inc) row (RS) Knit across, inc 2 (3, 2) sts evenly spaced—31 (34, 37) sts.

FOR SIZE 6 MONTHS ONLY
Next row (WS) P1, pm, p30. Keeping 1 st at side edge in St st, work rem sts in slip st pat using 2 needles.

FOR SIZES 12 AND 18 MONTHS ONLY
Next row (WS) P2 (4), pm, p30, pm, p2 (3). Keeping 2 (3) sts at front edge and 2 (4) sts at side edge in St st, work rem sts in slip st pat using 2 needles.

FOR ALL SIZES
Work even until piece measures same length as back to underarm, end with row 5 or 11.

ARMHOLE SHAPING
With A, bind off first 6 sts—25 (28, 31) sts. Work even in slip st pat as established until armhole measures 3 (3½, 4)"/7.5 (9, 10)cm, end with row 4 or 10.

NECK SHAPING
Next row (RS) With A, bind off first 9 (9, 10) sts, work to end—16 (19, 21) sts. Work next row even. Dec 1 st from neck edge on next row, then every other row 3 times more—12 (15, 17) sts. Work even until piece measures same length as back to shoulder, end with a WS row. With A, bind off all sts knitwise for shoulder.

Sleeves
With smaller circular needle and A, cast on 41 (43, 45) sts. Work back and forth in k1, p1 rib for 8 rows, end with a WS row. Change to larger circular needles.
Next (inc) row (RS) Knit across, inc 7 sts evenly spaced—48 (50, 52) sts.

FOR SIZE 6 MONTHS ONLY
Next row (WS) Purl. Work in slip st pat using 2 needles for 1"/2.5cm, end with a WS row.

FOR SIZES 12 AND 18 MONTHS ONLY
Next row (WS) P1 (2), pm, p48, pm, p1 (2). Keeping 1 (2) sts each side in St st, work rem sts in slip st pat using 2 needles for 1"/2.5cm, end with a WS row.

FOR ALL SIZES
Working inc in St st, inc 1 st each side on next row, then every 12th (8th, 6th) row 2 (4, 6) times more—54 (60, 66) sts. Work even until piece measures 5½ (6, 7)"/14 (15, 18)cm from beg, end with a WS row. Mark beg and end of last row

for sleeve cap. Work even for 1"/2.5cm, end with row 4, 5, 10, or 11. With A, bind off knitwise on a RS row, or purlwise on a WS row

Finishing
Block pieces lightly to measurements. Sew shoulder seams. Place markers for 4 buttonholes on right front edge, with the first 4½ (5, 5½)"/11.5 (12.5, 14)cm from lower edge, the last at neck edge and 2 more evenly spaced between.

OUTER BAND
With RS facing, smaller circular needle, and A, pick up and k 52 (57, 62) sts evenly spaced along right front edge, pm, pick up and k 8 (8, 9) sts in bound-off sts of neck, pm, pick up and k 8 sts along right neck edge to shoulder seam, k 25 (26, 28) sts from back neck holder dec 3 sts evenly spaced, pick up and k 8 sts along left neck edge, pm, pick up and k 8 (8, 9) sts in bound-off sts of neck, pm, pick up and k 52 (57, 62) sts evenly spaced along left front edge—158 (169, 183) sts.
Row 1 and all WS rows Sl 1, knit to end.
Row 2 Sl 1, knit to first marker, M1, sl marker, k1, M1, knit to 1 st before 2nd marker, S2KP, knit to 3rd marker, S2KP, knit to last marker, M1, sl marker, k1, M1, knit to end.
Row 4 (buttonhole) row Rep row 2, working (yo, k2tog) at each buttonhole marker.
Rows 5–7 Rep rows 1 and 2 once more, then row 1. Bind off loosely purlwise. Set in sleeves, sewing last 1"/2.5cm marked at top of sleeve to bound-off armhole sts. Sew side and sleeve seams. Sew on buttons. ∎

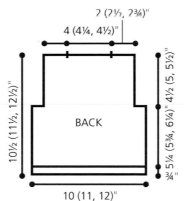

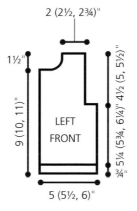

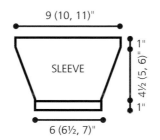

Staggered Rib Blanket

This sumptuous blanket knit in a beautiful heather shade of blue is easy to make but will please even the most discriminating gift recipient.

DESIGNED BY KENNITA TULLY

Knitted Measurements
Approx 30" x 33"/76cm x 84cm

Materials
■ 8 1¾oz/50g hanks (each approx 136yd/125m) of Cascade Yarns *220 Superwash Sport* (superwash merino wool) in #1910 summer sky heather

■ Size 6 (4mm) circular needle, 36"/91cm long *or size to obtain gauge*

■ Size E/4 (3.5mm) crochet hook

Staggered Rib Stitch
(over a multiple of 3 sts plus 2)
Rows 1 and 3 (RS) K1, *p2, k1; rep from *, end k1.
Rows 2 and 4 P1, *p1, k2; rep from *, end p1.
Row 5 Knit.
Row 6 Purl.
Rows 7 and 9 K1, *k1, p2; rep from *, end k1.
Rows 8 and 10 P1, *k2, p1; rep from *, end p1.
Row 11 Knit.
Row 12 Purl.
Rows 13 and 15 K1, *p1, k1, p1; rep from *, end k1.
Rows 14 and 16 P1, *k1, p1, k1; rep from *, end p1.
Row 17 Knit.
Row 18 Purl.
Rep rows 1–18 for staggered rib st.

Blanket
Cast on 176 sts. Work even in staggered rib st until piece measures 32"/81cm from beg, end with row 4, 10, or 16. Bind off all sts loosely knitwise.

Finishing
Block piece lightly to measurements.

EDGING
With RS facing and crochet hook, join yarn with a sl st in any corner.
Rnd 1 (RS) Ch1, making sure that work lies flat, sc evenly around entire edge, working 3 sc in each corner, join rnd with a sl st in first sc.
Rnd 2 (RS) Ch1, working from left to right, reverse sc in each st around, join rnd with a sl st in first sc. Fasten off. ■

Gauge
24 sts and 33 rows to 4"/10cm over staggered rib st using size 6 (4mm) circular needle.
Take time to check gauge.

Asymmetrical Stripes Cardigan

Graphic stripes, bold edgings, and an asymmetrical color pattern come together to create a little piece of modern art.

DESIGNED BY KENNITA TULLY

Sizes

Instructions are written for size 6 months. Changes for 12 and 18 months are in parentheses. (Shown in size 12 months.)

Knitted Measurements

Chest (closed) 22 (24, 26)"/56 (61, 66)cm
Length 11 (12½, 13½)"/28 (31.5, 34)cm
Upper arm 10 (11,12)"/25.5 (28, 30.5)cm

Materials

■ 1 1¾oz/50g hank (each approx 136yd/125m) of Cascade Yarns *220 Superwash Sport* (superwash merino wool) each in #1913 jet (A), #900 charcoal (C), and #1946 silver grey (D)

■ 1 (1, 2) hanks in #1910 summer sky heather (B)

■ One size 6 (4mm) circular needle, 24"/61cm long, *or size to obtain gauge*

■ One pair size 6 (4mm) needles

■ Stitch holder

■ Bobbins

■ Two ¹¹⁄₁₆"/17mm buttons

Notes

1) Body is made in one piece to the underarms.
2) Body, back, fronts, and sleeves are worked counting rows. Therefore, row gauge must be achieved for best results.
3) Do not carry colors across. Use a separate bobbin of color for each color section.

Stripe Pattern

Working in garter st (knit every row), *work 12 rows C, 12 rows D; rep from * (24 rows) for stripe pat.

Body

With circular needle and A, cast on 112 (124, 132) sts. Work back and forth in garter st (knit every row) for 10 rows, end with a WS row.
Row 1 K6 with A, k47 (53, 57) with B, k6 with A, k47 (53, 57) with C, k6 with A.
Rows 2–12 Knit in colors as established.
Rows 13 K6 with A, k47 (53, 57) with B, k6 with A, k47 (53, 57) with D, k6 with A.
Rows 14–24 Knit in colors as established. Rep rows 1–24 for colorblock and stripe pat. Work even until 4 (4, 5) stripes have been completed, end with a WS row. Cont to work even for 0 (8, 0) rows; piece should measure approximately 6 (7, 7½)"/15 (18, 19)cm from beg, end with a WS row.

DIVIDE FOR BACK AND FRONTS
Change to straight needles.
Next row (RS) Work across first 28 (31, 33) sts, place these sts on holder for right front, work across next 56 (62, 66) sts for back, leave rem 28 (31, 33) sts on circular needle for left front.

BACK
Work even until 8 (9, 10) stripes have been completed from beg, end with a WS row; piece should measure 11 (12½, 13½)"/28

Asymmetrical Stripes Cardigan

(31.5, 34)cm from beg. Bind off knitwise, changing colors as you go.

LEFT FRONT
Change to straight needles.
Next row (RS) Keeping to color pat as established, join color in progress, k 28 (31, 33) sts. Work even until 6 (7, 8) stripes have been completed, end with a WS row. Cont to work even for 3 (5, 3) rows more; piece should measure approximately 9 (10½ ,11½)"/23 (26.5, 29)cm from beg, end with a RS row.

NECK SHAPING
Next row (WS) Bind off first 6 sts. Dec 1 st from neck edge on next RS row, then every other row 7 times more—14 (17, 19) sts. Work even until 8 (9, 10) stripes have been completed from beg, end with a WS row. Bind off knitwise.

RIGHT FRONT
Change to straight needles.
Next row (WS) Keeping to color pat as

established, join color in progress, k 28 (31, 33) sts. Work even until piece measures 6½ (8, 9)"/16.5 (20.5, 23)cm from beg, end with a WS row.
Next (buttonhole) row (RS) With A, k2, bind off next 2 sts, work to end in established colors.
Next row (WS) Knit across, casting on 2 sts over bound-off sts. Work even until piece measures same length as left front

✳ Pattern for Bobble Hat is on page 52.

to neck shaping, end with a WS row. Shape neck as for left front—14 (17, 19) sts. Work even until piece measures same length as back to shoulder, end with a WS row. Bind off knitwise.

Right Sleeve
With straight needles and A, cast on 32 (34, 36) sts. Work in garter st for 10 rows, end with a WS row. Change to C. Cont in stripe pat. AT THE SAME TIME, work even for 2 rows. **Inc 1 st each side on next row, then every 4th row 7 (7, 6) times more, then every 6th row 2 (4, 6) times—52 (58, 62) sts.** Work even until 4 (5, 6) stripes have been completed, end with a WS row. Bind off knitwise.

Left Sleeve
With straight needles and A, cast on 32 (34, 36) sts. Work in garter st for 10 rows, end with a WS row. Change to B. Work even for 2 rows. Rep from ** to ** as for right sleeve—52 (58, 62) sts. Work even until piece measures same length as right sleeve, end with a WS row. Bind off knitwise.

Finishing
Sew shoulder seams.

NECKBAND
With RS facing, straight needles, and A, pick up and k 2 sts over first 6 sts of right front, cable cast-on 2 sts for 2nd buttonhole, skip next 2 sts, cont to pick up and k 18 sts along right neck edge to shoulder, 28 sts across back neck edge to shoulder, then 22 sts along left neck edge—72 sts. Cont in garter st for 9 rows. Bind off knitwise. Sew sleeve seams. Set in sleeves. Sew on buttons. ■

SLEEVE
10 (11, 12)"
5 (6¼, 7½)"
1"
6 (6½, 6¾)"

BODY
5½"
2¾ (3½, 3¾)"
LEFT FRONT
BACK
RIGHT FRONT
BODY
5 (5½, 6)"
6 (7, 7½)"
2"
2½"
6½ (8, 9)"
22 (24, 26)"

45 Daisy Stitch Cardigan

Crocheted edgings and buttons and a vintage stitch pattern give this classy cardigan old-fashioned appeal.

DESIGNED BY ISABEL SANCHEZ

Sizes
Instructions are written for size 6 months. Changes for 12 and 18 months are in parentheses. (Shown in size 6 months.)

Knitted Measurements
Chest (closed) 19¾ (22, 24½)"/50 (56, 62.5)cm
Length 9 (10½, 12)"/23 (26.5, 30.5)cm
Upper arm 7 (8¼, 9½)"/18 (21, 24)cm

Materials
- 2 (3, 4) hanks (each approx 136yd/125m) of Cascade Yarns *220 Superwash Sport* (superwash merino wool) in #894 strawberry cream (MC)
- 1 hank each in #827 coral (A) and #802 green apple (B)
- Size 6 (4mm) circular needle, 32"/81cm long, *or size to obtain gauge*
- Size D/3 (3.25mm) crochet hook
- Stitch holders
- Stitch markers

Note
Body is worked in one piece to the underarms.

Daisy Stitch
(multiple of 4 sts plus 3)
Row 1 (RS) *[K3tog tbl, leaving st on LH needle, yo, k these 3 sts tog tbl once more], k1; rep from *, end [k3tog tbl, leaving st on LH needle, yo, k these 3 sts tog tbl once more].
Rows 2 and 4 Purl.
Row 3 K1, *k1, [k3tog tbl, leaving st on LH needle, yo, k these 3 sts tog tbl once more]; rep from *, end k2.
Work rows 1–4 for daisy st.

K1, P1 Rib
(over an odd number of sts)
Row 1 (RS) *K1, p1; rep from *, k1.
Row 2 *P1, k1; rep from *, p1.
Work rows 1 and 2 for k1, p1 rib.

Cardigan
SLEEVES
With MC, cast on 49 (57, 65) sts. Work in k1, p1 rib for ¾"/2cm, end with a WS row.

BEG DAISY ST
Next row (RS) K1, work row 1 to last st, k1.
Next row P1, work row 2 to last st, p1.
Next row (RS) K1, work row 3 to last st, k1.
Next row P1, work row 4 to last st, p1.
Work even until piece measures 5 (6, 7)"/ 12.5(15, 17.5)cm from beg, end with a row 2. Change to A, work even for 3 rows. Change to MC.
Next row (WS) Bind off 2 sts, work row 2 across to last 4 sts, bind off 2 sts at end of row—45 (53, 61) sts. Place sleeve sts on holders.

BODY
With circular needle and MC, cast on 139 (155, 171) sts. Do not join. Work back and forth in rows in k1, p1 rib for 1"/2.5cm, end with a WS row.

BEG DAISY ST
Next row (RS) Work first 6 sts in rib as established, pm, work row 1 of pattern to last 6 sts, pm, work to end in rib.

Gauge
27 sts and 32 rows to 4"/10cm over daisy st using size 6 (4mm) needle. *Take time to check gauge.*

Daisy Stitch Cardigan

Slip markers every row, work even in daisy st, keeping first 6 sts and last 6 sts in rib, until body measures 6½ (7½, 8½)"/16.5 (19, 21.5)cm from beg, end with a row 1.

DIVIDE FOR FRONTS AND BACK
Next row (WS) Work 35 (39, 43) sts, bind off 5 st for left armhole, p until there are 59 (67, 75) sts on RH needle after bind-off, bind off next 5 sts for right armhole, work to end of row.

YOKE
Next row (RS) Rib 6, work row 3 of daisy pattern as foll: 29 (33, 37) sts for right front, 45 (53, 61) sts from sleeve holder, 59 (67, 75) sts for back, 45 (53, 61) sts from sleeve holder, 29 (33, 37) sts for left front, rib 6—219 (251, 283) sts.
Work even over all sts for 9 rows, end with a row 4.
Change to B, work even for 3 rows.

Change to MC, work even until piece measures 9 (10½, 12)"/23 (26.5, 30.5)cm from beg, end with a row 4.

NECKBAND
Next (dec) row (RS) Rib 6, [k3tog tbl, p1] 51 (59, 67) times, k3tog tbl, rib 6—115 (131, 147) sts. Work 1 row in rib as established on WS.
Next (dec) row Rib 18 (20, 22), k3tog tbl, rib 21 (25, 29), k3tog tbl, rib 25 (29, 33), k3tog tbl, rib 21 (25, 29), k3tog tbl, rib 18 (20, 22)—107 (123, 139) sts. Work 1 row even on WS.
Next (dec) row Rib 17 (19, 21), p3tog tbl, rib 19 (23, 27), p3tog tbl, rib 23 (27, 31), p3tog tbl, rib 19 (23, 27), p3tog tbl, rib 17 (19, 21)—99 (115, 131) sts. Work 1 row even on WS.
Next (dec) row Rib 16 (18, 20), k3tog tbl, rib 17 (21, 25), k3tog tbl, rib 21 (25, 29), k3tog tbl, rib 17 (21, 25), k3tog tbl, rib 16 (18, 20)—91 (107, 123) sts. Work 1 row even on WS. Bind off in pat.

Finishing
Sew sleeve seams. Sew underarm seams.

CROCHETED EDGING
With RS facing, crochet hook, and B, beg at center of back neck, [sc in next st, ch 2, sk 2 sts] around entire edge, working [sc in next st, ch 2, sc in same st, ch 2, sc in same st, ch 2, sk 2] in corners. Fasten off.

BUTTONS (MAKE 2)
With crochet hook and A, make a slipknot, leaving a 12"/30.5cm tail.
Next rnd Ch 2 (counts as 1 sc), work 7 sc into slipknot, do not turn.
Next rnd Work 2 sc in each sc around—14 sts. Join with sl st to first sc. Fasten off. Weave in end, use tail to sew buttons onto garment, centering above B stripe on yoke. Use ch-2 sp opposite buttons as buttonholes. ∎

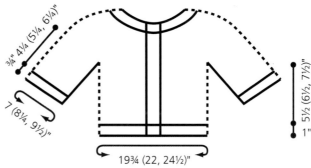

46

Argyle Vest

A subtle combination of several shades of green and yellow makes the stranded argyle band on this preppy little vest look more complex than it actually is.

DESIGNED BY PAT OLSKI

Sizes

Instructions are written for size 12 months. Changes for 18 months are in parentheses. (Shown in size 12 months.)

Knitted Measurements

Chest 22 (24)"/56 (61)cm
Length 12½ (13½)"/31.5 (34)cm

Materials

■ 2 (3) 1¾oz/50g balls (each approx 136yd/125m) of Cascade Yarns *220 Superwash Sport* (superwash merino wool) in #841 moss (MC)

■ 1 hank each in #850 lime sherbet (A), #801 army green (B), and #821 daffodil (C)

■ Sizes 3 and 5 (3.25 and 3.75mm) circular needles, 24"/61cm long, *or size to obtain gauge*

■ Size 3 (3.25mm) circular needle, 16"/41cm long

■ One pair size 5 (3.75mm) needles

■ One set (5) size 3 (3.25mm) double-pointed needles (dpns)

■ Safety pin

■ Stitch markers

Notes

1) Body is worked in one piece to the underarms.
2) To work in the rnd, always read chart from right to left.

K1, P1 Rib

(over a multiple of 2 sts)
Rnd 1 (RS) *K1, p1; rep from * around.
Rep rnd 1 for k1, p1 rib.

Body

With longer, smaller circular needle and MC, cast on 134 (146) sts. Join and pm for beg of rnds. Work around in k1, p1 rib for 1¼"/3cm. Change to larger circular needle.
Next rnd K 67 (73), pm for side, knit to end of rnd. Cont in St st (knit every rnd) until piece measures 2½ (2¾)"/6.5 (7)cm from beg.

BEG CHART PAT

Rnd 1 *Beg chart where indicated for size being made and work to rep line, work 16-st rep 4 times, then end chart where indicated for size being made; rep from * once more. Cont to foll chart in this way to rnd 29. With MC only, cont to work even until piece measures 7½ (8)"/19 (20.5)cm from beg.

BACK

Change to straight needles.

ARMHOLE SHAPING

Next row (RS) Bind off first 3 sts, knit to side marker; turn, dropping marker.
Next row (WS) Bind off first 3 sts, purl to end—61 (67) sts. Leave rem 67 (73) sts on needle for front. Cont armhole shaping as foll:
Bind off 2 sts at beg of next 2 rows.
Next (dec) row (RS) K2, k2tog, knit to last 4 sts, ssk, k2. Purl next row. Rep last 2 rows 6 times more—43 (49) sts. Work even until armhole measures 4 1/2 (5)"/11.5 (12.5)cm, end with a WS row.

NECK SHAPING

Next row (RS) K 10 (12), join a 2nd ball of MC and bind off center 23 (25) sts, knit to end. Working both sides at once, cont as foll:
Dec row 1 (WS) With first ball of MC, purl to last 3 sts, p2tog, p1; with 2nd ball of MC, p1, p2tog tbl, purl to end.
Dec row 2 (RS) With first ball of MC, knit to last 3 sts, k2tog, k1; with 2nd ball of MC, k1, ssk, knit to end. Rep dec row 1 once more. Bind off rem 7 (9) sts each side knitwise for shoulders.

Gauge

24 sts and 30 rnds to 4"/10cm over St st and chart pat using larger circular needle.
Take time to check gauge.

Argyle Vest

Color Key

- Moss (MC)
- Lime Sherbet (A)
- Army Green (B)
- Daffodil (C)

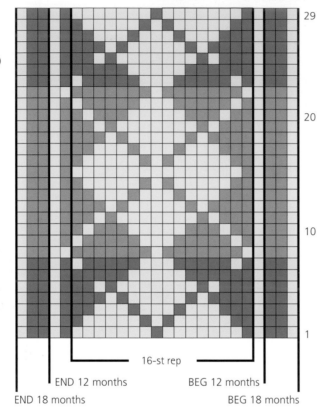

29

20

10

1

16-st rep

END 12 months

BEG 12 months

END 18 months

BEG 18 months

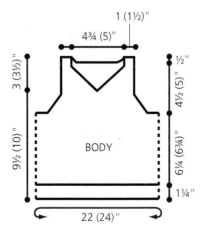

1 (1½)"

4¾ (5)"

3 (3½)"

½"

4½ (5)"

9½ (10)"

6¼ (6¾)"

BODY

1¼"

22 (24)"

of MC, p1, p2tog tbl, purl to end.

Dec row 2 (RS) With first ball of MC, knit to last 3 sts, k2tog, k1; with 2nd ball of MC, k1, ssk, knit to end. Rep last 2 rows 5 (6) times more, then dec row 1 one (0) time more—7 (9) sts each side. Work even until piece measures same length as back to shoulder, end with a WS row. Bind off each side for shoulders.

Finishing

Block piece lightly to measurements. Sew shoulder seams.

NECKBAND

With RS facing, shorter, smaller circular needle, and C, beg at left shoulder seam and pick up and k 25 (29) sts evenly spaced along left neck edge to center st, k1 st from safety pin (replace safety pin to indicate center st), pick up and k 25 (29) sts along right neck edge to right shoulder seam, pick up and k 33 (35) sts along back neck edge—84 (94) sts. Join and pm for beg of rnds.

Rnd 1 P1, *k1, p1; rep from * to center st, k1 st from safety pin (replace safety pin), *p1, k1; rep from * to end.

Rnd (dec) 2 Work in rib to 1 st before center st, remove safety pin, S2KP, replace safety pin, work in rib to end. Rep last 2 rnds once more. Bind off loosely in rib, working one more S2KP as you bind off.

ARMBANDS

With RS facing, dpn, and B, pick up and k 64 (72) sts evenly spaced around armhole, dividing sts evenly between 4 needles. Join and pm for beg of rnds. Work around in k1, p1 rib for 5 rnds. Bind off loosely in rib. ■

FRONT

Change to straight needles. Shape armholes same as back—43 (49) sts. Work even until armhole measures 2"/5cm, end with a WS row.

NECK SHAPING

Next (dec) row (RS) K 18 (21), k2tog, k1, place center st on safety pin, join a 2nd ball of MC, k1, ssk, knit to end. Working both sides at once, cont as foll:

Dec row 1 (WS) With first ball of MC, purl to last 3 sts, p2tog, p1; with 2nd ball

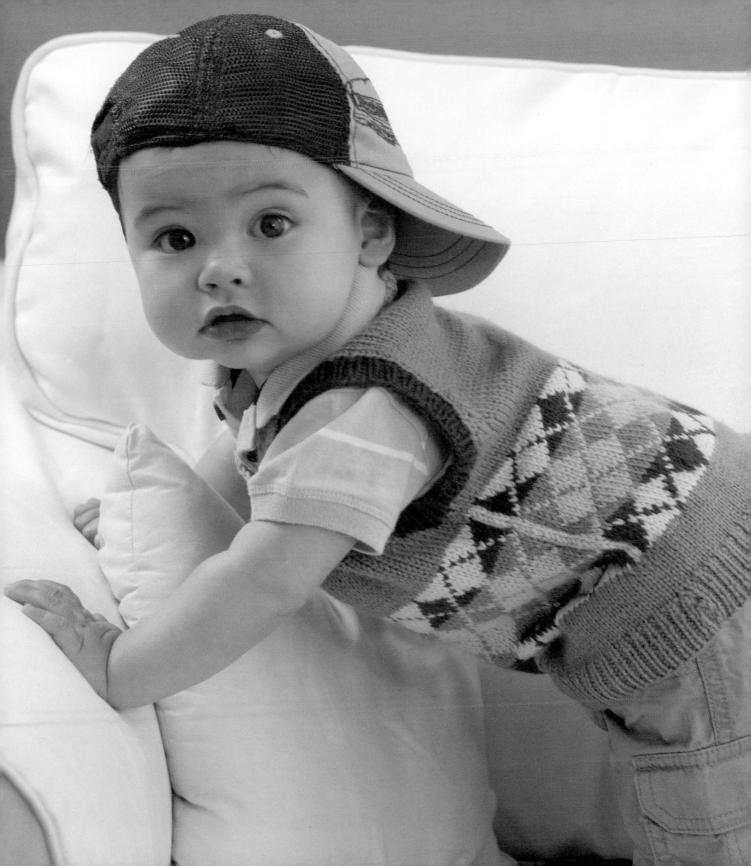

Trinity Stitch Hat

Alternating bands of trinity stitch and bobbles create a gorgeously textured autumn topper for your little pumpkin.

DESIGNED BY NICHOLE REESE

Size
Instructions are written for size 6 months.

Knitted Measurements
Head circumference 15½"/39.5cm
Depth 6½"/16.5cm

Materials
■ 1 1¾oz/50g hank (approx 136yd/125m) of Cascade Yarns *220 Superwash Sport* (superwash merino wool) in #822 pumpkin

■ Size 5 (3.75mm) circular needle, 16"/40cm long, *or size to obtain gauge*

■ One set (5) size 5 (3.75mm) double-pointed needles (dpns)

■ Stitch marker

Stitch Glossary
MB (make bobble) [K1, p1] twice in next st, making 4 sts from one; turn. SKP, k2tog, turn. SKP—1 st.

K2, P2 Rib
(over a multiple of 4 sts)
Rnd 1 (RS) *K2, p2; rep from * around.
Rep rnd 1 for k2, p2 rib.

Bobble Pattern
(over a multiple of 4 sts)
Rnds 1 and 2 Knit.
Rnd 3 *K3, MB; rep from * around.
Rnd 4 and 5 Knit.
Work rnds 1–5 for bobble pat.

Trinity Stitch
(over a multiple of 4 sts)
Rnd 1 Purl.
Rnd 2 *(P1, k1, p1) in next st, p3tog; rep from * around.
Rnd 3 Purl.
Rnd 4 *P3tog, (p1, k1, p1) in next st; rep from * around.
Rep rnds 1–4 for trinity st.

Hat
With circular needle, cast on 96 sts. Join and pm, taking care not to twist sts on needles. Work around in k2, p2 rib for 4 rnds. Cont in pat sts as foll:
*Work rnds 1–5 of bobble pat, [work rnds 1–4 of trinity st] twice, knit 1 rnd; rep from * twice more. Piece should measure approximately 5"/12.5cm from beg.

CROWN SHAPING
Change to dpns (dividing sts evenly between 4 needles).
Dec rnd 1 *K6, k2tog; rep from * around—84 sts. Knit next rnd.
Dec rnd 2 *K5, k2tog; rep from * around—72 sts. Knit next rnd.
Dec rnd 3 *K4, k2tog; rep from * around—60 sts. Knit next rnd.
Dec rnd 4 *K3, k2tog; rep from * around—48 sts. Knit next rnd.
Dec rnd 5 *K2, k2tog; rep from * around—36 sts. Knit next rnd.
Dec rnd 6 *K1, k2tog; rep from * around—24 sts. Knit next rnd.
Dec rnd 7 [K2tog] 12 times—12 sts.
Cut yarn leaving an 8"/20.5cm tail, and thread through rem sts. Pull tog tightly and secure end. ■

Gauge
24 sts and 28 rnds to 4"/10cm over St st using size 5 (3.75mm) circular needle.
Take time to check gauge.

48

Barnyard Play Mat

Your little farmer will love counting sheep (and tucking them in at night) with this colorful blanket complete with finger puppets.

DESIGNED BY HELEN FIRING

Knitted Measurements
PLAY MAT
Approx 23½" x 22¾"/59.5cm x 58cm
SHEEP FINGER PUPPETS
Approx 3"/7.5cm tall

Materials
■ 2 1¾oz/50g hanks (each approx 136yd/125m) of Cascade Yarns *220 Superwash Sport* (superwash merino wool) each in #808 sunset orange (A) and #849 dark aqua (E)

■ 1 hank each in #841 moss (B), #864 christmas green (C), #821 daffodil (D), and #871 white (F)

■ Size 5 (3.75mm) circular needle, 36"/91cm long, *or size to obtain gauge*

■ One pair size 5 (3.75mm) needles

■ Two size 5 (3.75mm) double-pointed needles (dpns) for I-cords

■ Bobbins

■ One ¾"/19mm white button

■ Sewing needle and white sewing thread

Note
Use a separate bobbin of color for each color section.

Seed Stitch
(over an even number of sts)
Row 1 (RS) *K1, p1; rep from * to end.
Row 2 K the purl sts and p the knit sts. Rep row 2 for seed st.

Play Mat
BOTTOM BORDER
With circular needle and A, cast on 120 sts. Work in seed st for 1¾"/4.5cm. Cont in St st (k on RS, p on WS) as foll:

BEG CHART PAT 1
Row 1 (RS) K24 with B, k24 with C, k24 with D, work chart over last 48 sts.
Row 2 Work chart over first 48 sts, p24 with D, p24 with C, p24 with B.
Rows 3–32 Rep rows 1 and 2.
Row 33 (RS) K24 with D, k24 with B, k24 with C, work chart over last 48 sts.
Row 34 Work chart over first 48 sts, p24 with C, p24 with B, p24 with D.
Rows 35–64 Rep rows 33 and 34.
Row 65 (RS) K24 with C, k24 with D, k24 with B, k24 with C, k24 with D.
Row 66 P24 with D, p24 with C, p24 with B, p24 with D, p24 with C.
Rows 67–96 Rep rows 65 and 66.

Row 97 (RS) With E, knit.
Row 98 With E, purl.
Rows 99–106 Rep rows 97 and 98.

BEG CHART PAT 2
Row 107 (RS) K76 with E, work row 1 of chart over next 16 sts, k28 with E.
Row 108 P28 with E, work row 2 of chart over next 16 sts, p76 with E. Cont to foll chart in this way to row 19. AT THE SAME TIME, work through row 114.
Row 115 (RS) K46 with E, work row 1 of chart over next 16 sts, work to end as established. Cont to foll chart in this way to row 19. AT THE SAME TIME, work through row 122.
Row 123 (RS) K16 with E, work row 1 of chart over next 16 sts, work to end as established. Cont to foll chart in this way to row 19. AT THE SAME TIME, work through row 130.
Row 131 (RS) Work across first 94 sts as established, work row 1 of chart over next 16 sts, k10 with E. Cont to foll chart in this way to row 19.
Row 150 (WS) With E, purl.
Rows 151–160 Rep rows 97 and 98.

TOP BORDER
Change to A. Work in seed st for 1¾"/4.5cm. Bind off in seed st.

Gauge
28 sts and 41 rows to 5"/12.5cm over St st and chart pats using size 5 (3.75mm) circular needle (after blocking).
Take time to check gauge.

Barnyard Play Mat

SIDE BORDERS
With RS facing, circular needle, and A, pick up and k 136 sts evenly spaced along side edge. Work in seed st for 1¾"/4.5cm. Bind off in seed st.

Left Barn Door
With straight needles and A, cast on 24 sts.

BEG CHART PAT 3
Row 1 (RS) Work 24 sts of chart.
Cont to foll chart in this way to row 42. Bind off.

Right Barn Door
With straight needles and A, cast on 18 sts.

BEG CHART PAT 4
Row 1 (RS) Work 18 sts of chart. Cont to foll chart in this way to row 42. Bind off.

Finishing
Block pieces lightly to measurements.

BUTTON LOOP
With dpn and F, cast on 3 sts, leaving a long tail for sewing. Work in I-cord as foll:
*Next row (RS) With 2nd dpn, k3, do not turn. Slide sts back to beg of needle to work next row from RS; rep from * for 1"/2.5cm. Cut yarn, leaving an 8"/20.5cm tail. Thread this tail in tapestry needle, then thread through rem sts. Pull tog tightly,

secure end; do not cut rem tail. To close opposite end of I-cord, sew running stitches around edge, then pull tog tightly to close opening and secure end; do not cut rem tail. Using tails, sew button loop to LH edge of right barn door. Using sewing needle and thread, sew button to left barn door where indicated on chart. Place left barn door on top of barn, matching A edges at bottom and LH edges. Using A, sew bottom edge, LH edge, and top edge in place. Place right barn door on top of barn, matching A edges at bottom and RH edges; front edge of right door will overlap front edge of left door. Using A, sew bottom edge, RH edge, and top edge in place, working through all layers where doors overlap.

Sheep Puppets (make 3)
BODY
With straight needles and F, cast on 20 sts.
Row 1 (RS) Purl.
Row 2 *Work (k1, p1, k1) in next st, p3tog; rep from * to end.
Row 3 Purl.
Row 4 *P3tog, work (k1, p1, k1) in next st; rep from * to end.
Rep rows 1–4 three times more.

HEAD
Beg with a knit row, cont in St st for 4 rows, end with a WS row.
Next row (RS) K6, sl 1 knitwise; turn.

Next (dec) row P2tog, purl to end.
Rep last 2 rows 3 times more—16 sts.
Next row (RS) Knit.
Next row P6, sl 1 purlwise; turn.
Next (dec) row (RS) K2tog, knit to end.
Rep last 2 rows 3 times more—12 sts.
Next (dec) row [P2tog] 6 times—6 sts.
Next (dec) row [K2tog] 3 times—3 sts.
Cut yarn, leaving an 8"/20.5cm tail.
Thread tail in tapestry needle, then thread through rem sts. Pull tog tightly, secure end, then sew head and body seam.

EYES
Embroider one duplicate st each side of head, using E.

EARS
With dpn and F, cast on 3 sts, leaving a long tail for sewing. Work in I-cord as foll:
*Next row (RS) With 2nd dpn, k3, do not turn. Slide sts back to beg of needle to work next row from RS; rep from * for 2¼"/5.5cm. Cut yarn, leaving an 8"/20.5cm tail. Thread this tail in tapestry needle, then thread through rem sts. Pull tog tightly, secure end, then weave in end. Thread beg tail in tapestry needle. Pull I-cord through head approximately 3/4"/2cm from tip of nose, then center side to side. To close this end of I-cord, sew running stitches around edge, then pull tog tightly to close opening. Secure end, then weave in end. On seam side of head, tack ears to seam, using sewing needle and thread.

ARMS
Work I-cord as for ears until piece measures 3"/7.5cm. Pull I-cord through body approximately 1½"/4cm from bottom edge, then center side to side. Close end of I-cord as for ears. On seam side of body, tack arms to back using sewing needle and thread. ∎

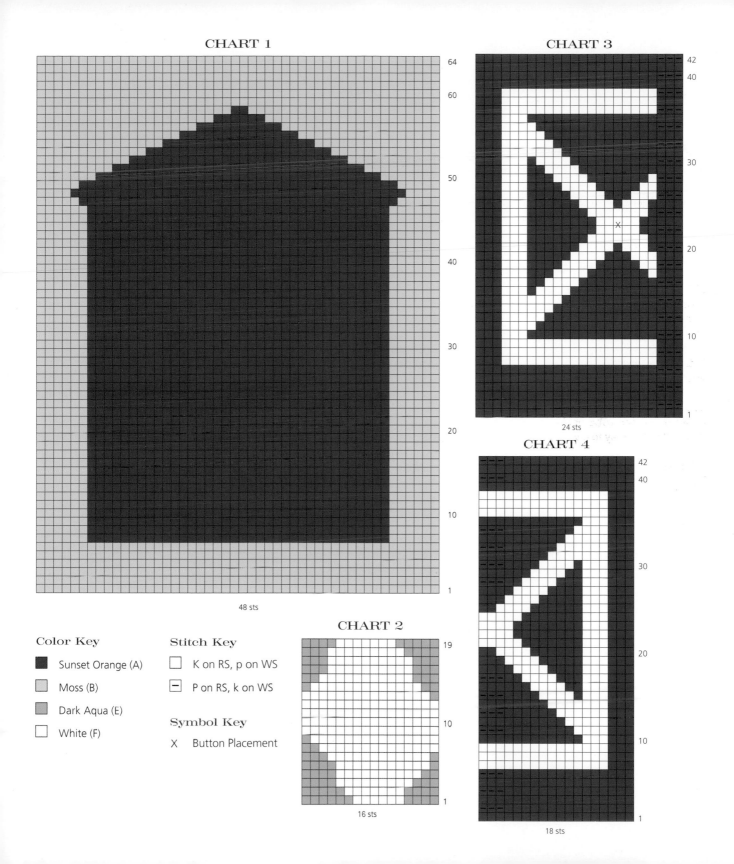

CHART 1

64
60
50
40
30
20
1

48 sts

CHART 3

42
40
30
20
10
1

24 sts

CHART 4

42
40
30
20
10
1

18 sts

CHART 2

19
10
1

16 sts

Color Key

■ Sunset Orange (A)

▨ Moss (B)

▨ Dark Aqua (E)

□ White (F)

Stitch Key

□ K on RS, p on WS

▬ P on RS, k on WS

Symbol Key

X Button Placement

Garter Stitch Booties

Basic booties play dress-up with gingham ribbon threaded through eyelets.
Try purchased cord or make your own I-cord for a different look.

DESIGNED BY JACQUELINE VAN DILLEN

Size
Instructions are written for size newborn–3 months.

Knitted Measurements
Length of sole 3½"/9cm
Width of foot 1¾"/4.5cm

Materials
- 1 1¾oz/50g hank (approx 136yd/125m) of Cascade Yarns *220 Superwash Sport* (superwash merino wool) in #1944 westpoint blue heather
- One set (4) size 4 (3.5mm) double-pointed needles (dpns) *or size to obtain gauge*
- Size D/3 (3.25mm) crochet hook
- 32"/81cm length of ¼"/6mm wide grosgrain ribbon
- Stitch markers

Stitch Glossary
kf&b Inc 1 by knitting into the front and back of the next st.

Booties (make 2)
SOLE
Beg at heel, cast on 8 sts. Using yarn marker, pm between 4th and 5th sts. Working back and forth using 2 dpns, work in garter st (knit every row) as foll:
Next (inc) row Knit to last st, kf&b—9 sts. Rep last row 3 times more—12 sts. Work even for 40 rows.
Next (dec) row K2tog, knit to end—11 sts. Rep last row once more—10 sts. Using yarn markers, mark beg and end of last row for beg of instep.

INSTEP
Work even for 30 rows.
Next (eyelet) row [K2tog, yo] twice, k2, [yo, k2tog] twice. Knit next 3 rows. Bind off.

SIDES
With RS facing and first dpn, beg at instep marker and pick up and k 19 sts evenly spaced along side edge of sole to 4 sts before heel marker, with 2nd dpn, pick up and k 8 sts along heel sts (remove heel marker), with 3rd dpn, pick up and k 19 sts evenly spaced along opposite side edge of sole to 2nd instep marker—46 sts. Working back and forth using 4th dpn, knit next 4 rows.
Next (dec) row K17, k2tog, k8, k2tog, k17—44 sts. Knit next 3 rows.
Next (dec) row K16, k2tog, k8, k2tog, k16—42 sts.
Next (eyelet) row Bind off first 9 sts, k1, [k2tog, yo] 5 times, k2, [yo, k2tog] 5 times, k10—33 sts.
Next row Bind off first 9 sts, knit to end—24 sts. Bind off 4 sts at beg of next 6 rows.

Finishing
Sew sides to side edges of instep, matching up eyelet rows.

EDGING
With RS facing and crochet hook, join yarn with a sl st in center top of heel.
Rnd 1 (RS) Ch1, working from left to right, sc evenly around top edge, join rnd with a sl st in first st. Fasten off. Cut ribbon in half, then trim ends at an angle. Beg and ending at center front, weave ribbon through eyelets. ■

Gauge
22 sts and 44 rows to 4"/10cm over garter st using size 4 (3.5mm) dpns.
Take time to check gauge.

Double-Breasted Jacket

This sweetly sophisticated cardigan looks especially demure with its matching buttons.
Use contrasting ones for more pop.

DESIGNED BY HOLLI YEOH

Sizes
Instructions are written for size 6 months. Changes for 12 and 18 months are in parentheses. (Shown in size 18 months.)

Knitted Measurements
Chest (closed) 20 (22, 24)"/51 (56, 61)cm
Length 10 (11, 12)"/25.5 (28, 30.5)cm
Upper arm 9 (10, 11)"/23 (25.5, 28)cm

Materials
■ 3 (3, 4) 1¾oz/50g hanks (each approx 136yd/125m) of Cascade Yarns *220 Superwash Sport* (superwash merino wool) in #813 blue velvet

■ One pair each sizes 5 and 6 (3.75 and 4mm) needles *or size to obtain gauge*

■ Sizes 5 and 6 (3.75 and 4mm) circular needles, 29"/74cm long

■ Stitch holder

■ Stitch markers

■ 10 (12, 12) ½"/13mm buttons

Note
Fronts are made separately from the lower edge up to the shoulder. Back is added on and worked from the shoulders down to the lower edge.

Stitch Glossary
ssp (slip, slip, purl) Sl first st knitwise, then sl next st knitwise. Slip these 2 sts back to LH needle, then purl them tog tbl.
k2tog bind-off *K2tog, place st on RH needle back on LH needle; rep from * as many times as stated in instructions.

Right Front
With smaller needles, cast on 39 (42, 45) sts. Work in garter st (knit every row) for 2½"/6.5cm, end with a WS row.
Next row (RS) K16, pm, k23 (26, 29). Change to larger needles. **Next row** P23 (26, 29), sl marker, k16. Keeping 16 sts at front edge in garter st and rem sts in St st (k on RS, p on WS), work even until piece measures 5½ (6, 6½)"/14 (15, 16.5)cm from beg (measured over St st section), end with a WS row.

SLEEVE SHAPING
Inc row 1 (RS) Knit to last 2 sts, M1, k2.
Inc row 2 (WS) P2, M1 p-st, work to end. Rep last 2 rows twice more—45 (48, 51) sts. **Next row (RS)** Work to end of row, cast on 26 (29, 35) sts—71 (77, 86) sts.
Next row (WS) K16, pm, purl to next marker, sl marker, k16. Keeping 16 sts each side in garter st and sts between markers in St st, work even until sleeve measures 1½ (2, 2½)"/4 (5, 6.5)cm from

cast-on edge (measured over St st section), end with a WS row. Change to smaller needles.

NECKBAND
Work in garter st over all sts for 6 rows, dropping markers on first row. Cont in garter st as foll:

NECK SHAPING
Row (dec) 1 (RS) Using k2tog bind-off, bind off first 16 sts, knit to end—55 (61, 70) sts. **Row 2** Knit to last st, bring yarn to the front; turn. **Row (dec) 3** Sl 1 purlwise, pass first st over slipped st to bind off; using k2tog bind-off, bind off next 2 sts, knit to end—52 (58, 67) sts. **Row 4** Knit to last st, bring yarn to the front; turn. **Row (dec) 5** Sl 1 purlwise, pass first st over slipped st to bind off; using k2tog bind-off, bind off 1 st, knit to end—50 (56, 65) sts. **Row 6** Knit to last st, bring yarn to the front; turn. **Row 7** Sl 1 purlwise, pass first st over slipped st to bind off, knit to end—49 (55, 64) sts. Work even in garter st until sleeve measures 3½ (4, 4½)"/9 (10, 11.5)cm from cast-on row, end with a WS row. Place sts on holder. Place markers for 5 (6, 6) buttonholes on right front edge, with the first 2½"/6.5cm from lower edge, the last 3 garter st ridges from neck

Gauges
24 sts and 32 rows to 4"/10cm over St st using larger needles. 24 sts and 48 rows to 4"/10cm over garter st using larger needles. *Take time to check gauges.*

Double-Breasted Jacket

edge, and 3 (4, 4) more evenly spaced between.

Left Front

With smaller needles, cast on 39 (42, 45) sts. Work in garter st for 2½"/6.5cm, end with a WS row.

Next row (RS) K23 (26, 29), pm, k16. Change to larger needles. **Next row** K16, sl marker, p23 (26, 29). Keeping 16 sts at front edge in garter st and rem sts in St st, work even until piece measures 5½ (6, 6½)"/14 (15, 16.5)cm from beg (measured over St st section), end with a WS row. AT THE SAME TIME, beg to work 5 (6, 6) pairs of buttonholes opposite markers as foll:

Buttonhole row (RS) Work to last 16 sts, sl marker, k2, bind off next 2 sts, k5, bind off next 2 sts, knit to end.

Next row Work across, casting on 2 sts over bound-off sts.

SLEEVE SHAPING

Inc row 1 (RS) K2, M1, knit to end.
Inc row 2 (WS) Work to last 2 sts, M1 p-st, p2. Rep last 2 rows twice more—45 (48, 51) sts. **Next row (RS)** Cast on 26 (29, 35) sts, work to end of row—71 (77, 86) sts. **Next row (WS)** K16, sl marker, purl to last 16 sts, pm, k16. Keeping 16 sts each side in garter st

and sts between markers in St st, work even until sleeve measures 1½ (2, 2½)"/4 (5, 6.5)cm from cast-on edge (measured over St st section), end with a RS row. Change to smaller needles.

NECKBAND

Work in garter st over all sts for 6 rows; dropping markers on first row. Cont in garter st as foll:

NECK SHAPING

Row (dec) 1 (WS) Using k2tog bind-off, bind off first 16 sts, knit to end—55 (61, 70) sts. **Row 2** Knit to last st, bring yarn to the front; turn. **Row (dec) 3** Sl 1 purlwise, pass first st over slipped st to bind off; using k2tog bind-off, bind off next 2 sts, knit to end—52 (58, 67) sts. **Row 4** Knit to last st, bring yarn to the front; turn. **Row (dec) 5** Sl 1 purlwise, pass first st over slipped st to bind off; using k2tog bind-off, bind off 1 st, knit to end—50 (56, 65) sts. **Row 6** Knit to last st, bring yarn to the front; turn. **Row 7** Sl 1 purlwise, pass first st over slipped st to bind off, knit to end—49 (55, 64) sts. Work even in garter st until sleeve measures 3½ (4, 4½)"/9 (10, 11.5)cm from cast-on row, end with a WS row. Do not cut yarn.

Back

With smaller circular needle, k 49 (55, 64) sts of left front, cable cast-on 28 sts for back neck, k 49 (55, 64) sts from right front holder—126 (138, 156) sts. Mark beg and end of last row. Knit next 11 rows. Change to larger circular needle.

Next row (RS) K16, pm, knit to last 16 sts, pm, k16. Keeping 16 sts each side in garter st and sts between markers in St st, work even until sleeve measures 3½ (4, 4½)"/9 (10, 11.5)cm above marked row, end with a WS row, dropping markers.

SLEEVES

Bind off 26 (29, 35) sts at beg of next 2 rows—74 (80, 86) sts. Cont in St st as foll:

Dec row 1 (RS) K2, k2tog, knit to last 4 sts, ssk, k2. **Dec row 2 (WS)** P2, ssp, purl to last 4 sts, p2tog, p2. Rep last 2 rows twice more—62 (68, 74) sts. Work even until piece measures 7½ (8½, 9½)"/19 (21.5, 24)cm above marked row, end with a WS row. Change to smaller needles. Work in garter st for 2½"/6.5cm, end with a WS row. Bind off using k2tog bind-off.

Finishing

Block piece to measurements. Sew side and sleeve seams. Sew on buttons opposite buttonholes. ∎

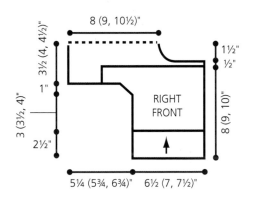

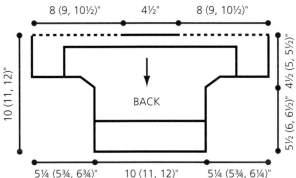

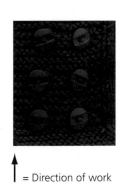

= Direction of work

Pinwheel Blanket

Take this freewheeling blanket to the park for a summer picnic on the grass. The four squares are created separately, then joined and finished with a picot edging.

DESIGNED BY GINGER LUTERS

Knitted Measurements

Approx 33½" x 33½"/85cm x 85cm

Materials

- 4 1¾oz/50g hanks (each approx 136yd/125m) of Cascade Yarns *220 Superwash Sport* (superwash merino wool) in #820 lemon (A)

- 3 hanks in #802 green apple (B)

- 4 hanks in #845 denim (C)

- Two size 5 (3.75mm) circular needles, 36"/91cm long, *or size to obtain gauge*

- Spare size 5 (3.75mm) needle (for 3-needle bind-off)

- Size 4 (3.5mm) circular needle, 36"/91cm long

- Safety pin

Squares (make 4)

TRIANGLE 1

With larger circular needle and A, cast on 35 sts.

Row 1 (WS) P1, knit to last st, p1.

Row 2 K1, ssk, knit to last 3 sts, k2tog, k1. Rep rows 1 and 2 until 5 sts rem.

Next (dec) row (RS) Ssk, k1, k2tog—3 sts.

Next row P1, k1, p1.

Next (dec) row S2KP. Fasten off last st.

TRIANGLE 2

Refer to diagram for square.

With RS facing, larger circular needle, and B, pick up and k 25 sts along left edge of triangle 1.

Row 1 (WS) P1, knit to last st, p1.

Row 2 Knit to last 3 sts, k2tog, k1. Rep rows 1 and 2 until 3 sts rem.

Next (dec) row (RS) K2tog, k1—2 sts.

Next row P1, k1.

Next (dec) row K2tog. Fasten off last st.

TRIANGLE 3

Refer to diagram for square.

With RS facing, larger circular needle, and C, pick up and k 49 sts along right edges of triangles 1 and 2.

Row 1 (WS) P1, knit to last st, p1.

Row 2 K1, ssk, knit to last 3 sts, k2tog, k1. Rep rows 1 and 2 until 5 sts rem.

Next (dec) row (RS) Ssk, k1, k2tog—3 sts.

Next row P1, k1, p1.

Next (dec) row S2KP. Fasten off last st.

TRIANGLE 4

Refer to diagram for square.

With RS facing, larger circular needle, and A, pick up and k 35 sts along right edge of triangle 3.

Row 1 (WS) P1, knit to last st, p1.

Row 2 K1, ssk, knit to last 3 sts, k2tog, k1. Rep rows 1 and 2 until 5 sts rem.

Next (dec) row (RS) Ssk, k1, k2tog—3 sts.

Next row P1, k1, p1.

Next (dec) row S2KP. Fasten off last st.

Cont to add triangles per diagram for square until last triangle 3 is completed. Sew side edge of last triangle 3 to cast-on edge of triangle 1.

Gauge

20 sts and 40 rows to 4"/10cm over garter st using larger circular needle.
Each square measures 15½" x 15½"/39.5cm x 39.5cm (after blocking). *Take time to check gauge.*

Pinwheel Blanket

SQUARE

TOP EDGE

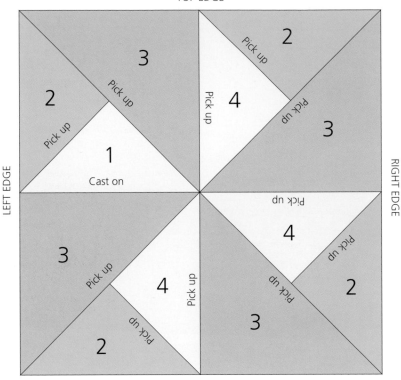

LEFT EDGE

RIGHT EDGE

BOTTOM EDGE

Color Key

☐ Lemon (A)

▨ Green Apple (B)

▨ Denim (C)

spaced across side edge of band 2, then pick up and k 70 sts evenly spaced across edge of square—75 sts.
Work in garter st for 9 rows. Bind off all but last st knitwise.

BAND 4
With RS facing, turn square so left edge is at top, then pick up and k 4 sts evenly spaced across side edge of band 3, then pick up and k 70 sts evenly spaced across edge of square, then pick up and k 5 sts evenly spaced across side edge of band 1—80 sts. Work in garter st for 9 rows. Bind off all sts knitwise.

Finishing
Block squares lightly to measurements.

JOINING SQUARES
Refer to diagram for square and assembly diagram to see where bands are picked up and joined.

BANDS 5 AND 6
With RS facing, first larger circular needle, and B, turn square so bottom edge is at top, then pick up and k 80 sts evenly spaced across edge. Work in garter st for 3 rows. Leave sts on needle. With RS facing, 2nd larger circular needle, and B, turn a 2nd square so top edge is at top, then pick up and k 80 sts evenly spaced across edge. Work in garter st for 3 rows. Leave sts on needle. With WS tog, use spare needle to join squares using a 3-needle bind-off. Rep for rem 2 squares.

BORDER BANDS
Refer to diagram for square to see where bands are picked up.

BAND 1
With RS facing, larger circular needle, and A, turn square so bottom edge is at top, then pick up and k 70 sts evenly spaced across edge. Work in garter st (knit every row) for 9 rows. Bind off all but last st knitwise. Last st on needle counts as first st of next band.

BAND 2
With RS facing, turn square so right edge is at top, then pick up and k 4 sts evenly spaced across side edge of band 1, then pick up and k 70 sts evenly spaced across edge of square—75 sts. Work in garter st for 9 rows. Bind off all but last st knitwise.

BAND 3
With RS facing, turn square so top edge is at top, then pick up and k 4 sts evenly

51

Pinwheel Blanket

ASSEMBLY DIAGRAM

TOP EDGE

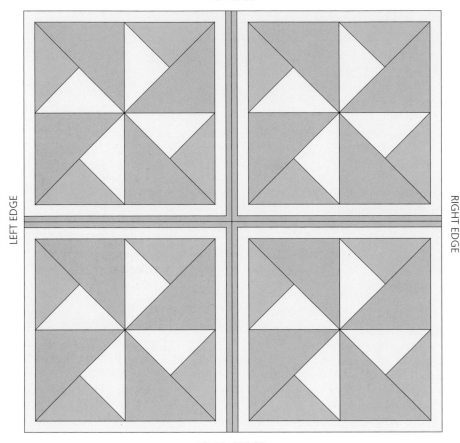

LEFT EDGE

RIGHT EDGE

BOTTOM EDGE

Color Key

☐ Lemon (A)

◼ Green Apple (B)

◼ Denim (C)

across edge. Work in garter st for 5 rows. Change to C and cont in garter st for 2 rows. Change to small circular needle. Work picot bind-off as foll: Bind off first st, *place last st on RH needle to LH needle, cast on 4 sts to LH needle, bind off 4 sts on LH needle, bind off next 3 sts; rep from *. Place rem st on safety pin.

BAND 10

With RS facing, larger circular needle, and B, turn blanket so right edge is at top, then pick up and k 167 sts evenly spaced across edge. Work in garter st for 5 rows. Place C st on safety pin onto working needle, then pick up and k 2 sts across side edge of B band. Cont in garter st for 2 rows. Change to small circular needle. Work picot bind-off as for band 9. Place rem st on safety pin.

BAND 11

With RS facing, larger circular needle, and B, turn blanket so top edge is at top, then pick up and k 167 sts evenly spaced across edge. Cont to work as for band 10.

BAND 12

With RS facing, larger circular needle, and B, turn blanket so left edge is at top, then pick up and k 170 sts evenly spaced across edge. Cont to work as for band 10, binding off last picot bind-off st. Sew side edges of picot bind-off rows where they meet in last corner. Block piece lightly to measurements. ◼

BANDS 7 AND 8

With RS facing, first larger circular needle, and B, turn a pair of joined squares so right edge is at top, then pick up and k 164 sts evenly spaced across edge. Work in garter st for 3 rows. Leave sts on needle. With RS facing, 2nd larger circular needle and B, turn the rem pair of joined squares so left edge is at top, then pick up and k 164 sts evenly spaced

across edge. Work in garter st for 3 rows. Leave sts on needle. With WS tog, use spare needle to join strips using a 3-needle bind-off.

OUTER BORDER BANDS
BAND 9

With RS facing, larger circular needle, and B, turn blanket so bottom edge is at top, then pick up and k 164 sts evenly spaced

Ruffled Cardigan

This lovely cardigan with ruffled edgings is a little girl's dream. The smaller stripes on the upper body and sleeves enhance the A-line shape.

DESIGNED BY CHERYL MURRAY

Sizes
Instructions are written for size 6 months. Changes for 12 and 18 months are in parentheses. (Shown in size 12 months.)

Knitted Measurements
Chest (closed) 20 (22, 24)"/51 (56, 61)cm
Length 12½ (13, 13½)"/31.5 (33, 34)cm
Upper arm 7 (8, 9)"/18 (20.5, 23)cm

Materials
■ 2 (3, 3) 1¾oz/50g hanks (each approx 136yd/125m) of Cascade Yarns *220 Superwash Sport* (superwash merino wool) each in #807 raspberry (A) and #803 royal purple (B)

■ Size 6 (4mm) circular needles, 24"/61cm and 36"/91cm long, *or size to obtain gauge*

■ Size 5 (3.75mm) circular needle, 24"/61cm long

■ One pair size 6 (4mm) needles

■ Stitch holder

■ Three ¾"/18mm buttons

Note
Body is made in one piece to underarms.

Ruffle
(over an even number of sts)
Row 1 (RS) Purl. **Rows 2 and 3** Knit.
Row 4 Purl. **Row 5** Knit. **Row 6** Purl.
Row 7 *K2tog; rep from * to end.
Work rows 1–7 for ruffle.

Body
RUFFLE
With longer, larger circular needle and A, cast on 280 (304, 328) sts.
Work rows 1–7 of ruffle—140 (152, 164) sts. Cut yarn; leave sts on needle.
Cont body as foll:
With shorter, larger circular needle and B, cast on 140 (152, 164) sts.

Next (joining) row (RS) With RS of cast-on sts facing, place ruffle sts in back of cast-on sts, so RS of ruffle is facing. Insert straight needle knitwise into first st of each needle and wrap yarn around each needle as if to knit. Knit these 2 sts tog and sl them off the needles. *Knit the next 2 sts tog in the same manner; rep from * to end—140 (152, 164) sts.
Next row (WS) P35 (38, 41), pm, p70 (76, 82), pm, p35 (38, 41). Cont in St st (k on RS, p on WS) and work even for 8 rows more. Cont in stripe pat as foll: [12 rows A, 10 rows B] twice. AT THE SAME TIME, shape sides as foll:

SIDE SHAPING
Dec row (RS) *Knit to next marker, ssk, sl marker, k2tog; rep from * once more, knit to end—136 (148, 160) sts. Rep dec row every 10th row 4 times more—120 (132, 144) sts. Work even until stripe pat has been completed, end with a WS row. Work 4 rows A, then 2 rows B. Piece should measure approximately 7½"/19cm from beg (excluding ruffle).

DIVIDE FOR FRONTS AND BACK
Cont with B as foll:
Next row (RS) K 25 (28, 30) sts (right front), bind off next 10 (10, 12) sts, knit until there are 50 (56, 60) sts on RH

Ruffled Cardigan

needle (back), bind off next 10 (10, 12) sts, knit until there are 25 (28, 30) sts on RH needle (left front).

LEFT FRONT

Change to straight needles.
Next row (WS) Purl. Change to A. Working in a stripe pat of 4 rows A and 4 rows B, cont as foll: **Dec row 1 (RS)** K1, ssk, knit to last 3 sts, k2tog, k1.
Dec row 2 (WS) P1, p2tog tbl, purl to end. Rep last 2 rows 3 times more. **Dec row 3 (RS)** Knit to last 3 sts, k2tog, k1. Purl next row. Rep last 2 rows 2 (3, 3) times more—10 (12, 14) sts. Work even until armhole measures 4 (4½, 5)"/10 (11.5, 12.5)cm, end with a WS row. Bind off.

BACK

Change to straight needles.
Next row (RS) Join B, p 50 (56, 60) sts; leave rem 25 (28, 30) sts on needle for right front. Change to A. Working in a stripe pat of 4 rows A and 4 rows B, cont as foll: **Dec row (RS)** K1, ssk, knit to last 3 sts, k2tog, k1. Purl next row. Rep last 2 rows 3 times more—42 (48, 52) sts. Work even until armhole measures 3½ (4, 4½)"/9 (10, 11.5)cm, end with a WS row.

NECK SHAPING

Next row (RS) K 11 (13, 15) sts, join a 2nd hank of color in progress and bind off center 20 (22, 22) sts, knit to end. Working both sides at once, purl next row.
Next (dec) row (RS) With first hank of yarn, k to last 3 sts, k2tog, k1; with 2nd hank of yarn, k1, ssk, knit to end—10 (12, 14) sts each side. Work even until piece measures same length as left front to shoulder, end with a WS row. Bind off.

RIGHT FRONT

Change to straight needles.
Next row (WS) Purl. Change to A. Working in a stripe pat of 4 rows A and 4 rows B, cont as foll:
Dec row 1 (RS) K1, ssk, knit to last 3 sts, k2tog, k1. **Dec row 2 (WS)** Purl to last 3 sts, p2tog, p1. Rep last 2 rows 3 times more. **Dec row 3 (RS)** K1, ssk, knit to end. Purl next row. Rep last 2 rows 2 (3, 3) times more—10 (12, 14) sts. Work even until armhole measures 4 (4½ ,5)"/10 (11.5, 12.5)cm, end with a WS row. Bind off.

Sleeves

RUFFLE

With shorter, larger circular needle and A, cast on 76 (88, 100) sts. Work rows 1–7 of ruffle—38 (44, 50) sts. Cut yarn; leave

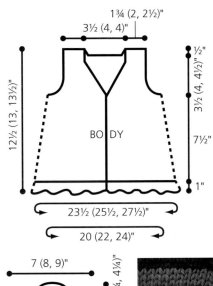

1¾ (2, 2½)"
3½ (4, 4)"
½"
3½ (4, 4½)"
12½ (13, 13½)"
BODY
7½"
1"
23½ (25½, 27½)"
20 (22, 24)"

7 (8, 9)"
3¼ (3¾, 4¼)"
SLEEVE
1"
1"
6½ (7½, 8½)"

sts on needle. Cont sleeve as foll:
With straight needles and B, cast on 38 (44, 50) sts.
Next (joining) row (RS) Work as for body ruffle—38 (44, 50) sts. Purl next row.
Next (inc) row (RS) K1, M1, knit to last st, M1, k1—40 (46, 52) sts. Purl next row. Change to A. Work next 2 rows even.
Next (inc) row (RS) K1, M1, knit to last st, M1, k1—42 (48, 54) sts. Purl next row. Change to B. Work next 2 rows even.

CAP SHAPING

Bind off 4 (4, 5) sts at beg of next 2 rows. Change to A. Working in a stripe pat of 4 rows A and 4 rows B, cont as foll:
Next (dec) row (RS) K1, ssk, knit to last 3 sts, k2tog, k1. Purl next row. Rep last 2 rows 10 (12, 14) times more—12 (14, 14) sts. Bind off 1 st at beg of next 4 rows. Bind off rem 8 (10, 10) sts.

Finishing

Block pieces to measurements. Sew shoulder seams.

OUTER BAND

Row 1 (RS) With RS facing, smaller circular needle, and B, skip side edge of ruffle edge, pick up and k 66 (69, 72) sts evenly spaced along right front edge to shoulder, 26 (28, 28) sts across back neck edge to shoulder, then 66 (69, 72) sts along left front edge to ruffle—158 (166, 172) sts. On right front, place yarn marker at beg of neck shaping. **Row 2** Knit. Change to A. **Row 3** Knit.
Row (buttonhole) 4 (WS) Knit to 2 sts before yarn marker, [k2tog, yo, k3] 3 times, knit to end. **Rows 5 and 6** Knit. Change to B. **Row 7** Knit. Bind off loosely knitwise. Sew sleeve seams. Set in sleeves. Sew on buttons. ∎

Pocket Vest

Everyone needs a place to store small treasures. Simple crocheted edges, side buttons, and a striped pocket add detail to this cute and practical design.

DESIGNED BY VERONICA MANNO

Sizes
Instructions are written for size 3 months. Changes for 6 and 12 months are in parentheses. (Shown in size 6 months.)

Knitted Measurements
Chest 19 (21, 23)"/48.5 (53.5, 58.5)cm
Length 10 (11, 12)"/ 25.5 (28, 30.5)cm

Materials
■ 2 (3, 3) 1¾oz/50g hanks (each approx 136yd/125m) of Cascade Yarns *220 Superwash Sport* (superwash merino wool) in #1946 silver grey (MC)

■ 1 hank in #900 charcoal (CC)

■ Size 6 (4mm) needles *or size to obtain gauge*

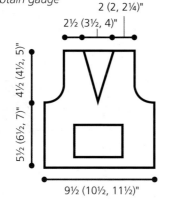

2 (2, 2¼)"
2½ (3½, 4)"
4½ (4½, 5)"
5½ (6½, 7)"
9½ (10½, 11½)"

■ Size E/4 (3.5mm) crochet hook

■ Six ½"/13mm buttons

Vest
BACK
With MC, cast on 59 (65, 71) sts. Knit 2 rows. Work in St st (knit on RS, purl on WS) until piece measures 5½ (6½ ,7)"/14 (16.5, 18) cm from beg, end with a WS row.

ARMHOLE SHAPING
Bind off from each side 3 sts twice, 2 sts once, 1 st twice—39 (45, 51) sts. Work even in St st until armholes measure 4½ (4½ , 5)"/11.5 (11.5, 12.5)cm. Bind off.

FRONT
Cast on and work same as back for ½" (13mm), end with a WS row.
Next (buttonhole) row (RS) K3, bind off 2 sts, k to last 5 sts, bind off 2 sts, k to end.
Next row P3, cast on 2 sts, p to second buttonhole, cast on 2 sts, p to end. Cont in St st and work buttonhole row at 3 (3½ , 3½)"/7.5 (9, 9)cm from beg, then once more at 5 (6, 6½)"/12.5 (15, 16.5)cm from beg. When piece measures 5½ (6½, 7)"/14 (16.5, 18)cm, work armhole shaping same as for back—39 (45, 51) sts, end with a WS row. AT THE SAME TIME, work neck shaping as follows:

NECK SHAPING
Mark center st of front.
Next row (RS) K to marked st, join second ball in MC and k2tog, k to end—19 (22, 25) sts each side of neck. Working both sides, work 1 row even. Dec 1 st from each neck edge on next row, then every other row 6 (9, 10) times more—12 (12, 14) sts. Work even until armholes measure 4½ (4½, 5)"/11.5 (11.5, 12.5)cm. Bind off.

Finishing
FRONT POCKET
With CC, cast on 24 (30, 30) sts. Knit 1 row on WS. Work in St st as foll: [4 rows CC, 4 rows MC] 2 (3, 3) times, 3 rows CC. With CC, knit 1 row on WS. Bind off knitwise. Sew pocket to front. Using photo as a guide, place pocket in center of front approx 1"/2.5cm above cast-on row. Sew sides and bottom of pocket to front, leaving bound-off edge as opening. Block pieces to measurements. Sew shoulder seams.

CROCHETED EDGES
With crochet hook and CC, work 1 rnd of sc around neck edge. Work 1 row sc along side edges and armholes. Sew buttons to sides of back opposite buttonholes. ■

Gauge
24 sts and 32 rows to 4"/10cm over St st using size 6 (4mm) needles. *Take time to check gauge.*

54

Checks & Buttons Hat

Check it out! This cozy beanie is cute as a button and easy to customize by changing the colors and buttons.

DESIGNED BY LINDA MEDINA

Size
Instructions are written for size 6 months.

Knitted Measurements
Head circumference 16"/40.5cm
Depth 7¼"/18.5cm

Materials
■ 1 1¾oz/50g hank (each approx 136yd/125m) of Cascade Yarns *220 Superwash Sport* (superwash merino wool) each in #873 extra creme cafe (MC), #818 mocha (A), and #849 dark aqua (B)

■ Size 6 (4mm) circular needle, 16"/40cm long, *or size to obtain gauge*

■ One set (5) size 6 (4mm) double-pointed needles (dpns)

■ Stitch marker

■ Seven ⅝"/16mm buttons each in turquoise and dark brown

Pattern Stitch
(over a multiple of 14 sts)
Rnd 1 *K7 with A, k7 with MC; rep from * around.
Rnd 2 *P7 with A, k7 with MC; rep from * around.
Rnd 3 Rep rnd 1.
Rnd 4 Rep rnd 2.
Rnd 5 *K7 with B, k7 with MC; rep from * around.
Rnd 6 *P7 with B, k7 with MC: rep from * around.
Rnd 7 *K7 with MC, k7 with A; rep from * around.
Rnd 8 *K7 with MC, p7 with A; rep from * around.
Rnd 9 Rep rnd 7.
Rnd 10 Rep rnd 8.
Rnd 11 *K7 with MC, k7 with B; rep from * around.
Rnd 12 * K7 with MC, p7 with B; rep from * around.
Rep rnds 1–12 for pat st.

K1, P1 Rib
(over a multiple of 2 sts)
Rnd 1 (RS) *K1, p1; rep from * around.
Rep rnd 1 for k1, p1 rib.

Hat
With circular needle and B, cast on 98 sts. Join and pm for beg of rnds. Work around in k1, p1 rib for 9 rnds. Cont in pat st, rep rnds 1–12 twice, then rnds 1–7 once.

CROWN SHAPING
Change to dpns, (dividing sts evenly between 4 needles).
Dec rnd 1 *With MC, k2, k2tog, k3, with A, p7; rep from * around—91 sts.

Dec rnd 2 *With MC, k2, k2tog, k2, with A, k7; rep from * around—84 sts.
Dec rnd 3 *With MC, k1, k2tog, k2, with A, p7; rep from * around—77 sts.
Dec rnd 4 *With MC, k1, k2tog, k1, with B, k7; rep from * around—70 sts.
Dec rnd 5 *With MC, k2tog, k1, with B, p7; rep from * around—63 sts.
Next rnd *With A, k2, with MC, k7; rep from * around.
Dec rnd 6 *With A, p2, with MC, k2, k2tog, k3; rep from * around—56 sts.
Dec rnd 7 *With A, k2, with MC, k2, k2tog, k2; rep from * around—49 sts.
Dec rnd 8 *With A, p2, with MC, k1, k2tog, k2; rep from * around—42 sts.
Dec rnd 9 *With B, k2, with MC, k1, k2tog, k1; rep from * around—35 sts.
Dec rnd 10 *With B, p2, with MC, k2tog, k1; rep from * around—28 sts.
Dec rnd 11 *With B, k2tog, with MC, k2tog; rep from * around—14 sts.
Cut yarn, leaving an 8"/20.5cm tail. Thread tail in tapestry needle, then thread through rem sts. Pull tog tightly and secure end.

Finishing
Sew turquoise buttons to centers of MC squares of first stripe, then sew brown buttons to centers of MC squares of second stripe. ■

Gauge
24 sts and 28 rnds to 4"/10cm over pat st using size 6 (4mm) circular needle. *Take time to check gauge.*

Mary Jane Booties

Tiny feet get the sweet treatment in these seed stitch booties that are reminiscent of the classic little girls' shoes but so much softer.

DESIGNED BY JEANNIE CHIN

Size
Instructions are written for size 3–6 months.

Knitted Measurements
Length of sole 3¾"/9.5cm
Width of foot 2"/5cm

Materials
■ 1 1¾oz/50g hank (each approx 136yd/125m) of Cascade Yarns *220 Superwash Sport* (superwash merino wool) in #901 cotton candy
■ One pair size 5 (3.75mm) needles *or size to obtain gauge*
■ Stitch markers
■ Two ⅜"/9mm white pearl buttons

Stitch Glossary
kf&b Inc 1 by knitting into the front and back of the next st.
pf&b Inc 1 by purling into the front and back of the next st.
ssp (slip, slip, purl) Sl first st knitwise, then sl next st knitwise. Slip these 2 sts back to LH needle, then purl them tog tbl.

Seed Stitch
(over an odd number of sts)
Row 1 (RS) K1, *p1, k1; rep from * to end. **Row 2** K the purl sts and p the knit sts. Rep row 2 for seed st.

Booties (make 2)
SOLE
Beg at heel, cast on 7 sts. Cont in seed st as foll: **Row 1 (RS)** K1, *p1, k1; rep from * to **Row 2** K the purl sts and p the knit sts. **Row (inc) 3** Pf&b in first st, work in seed st to last st, kf&b—9 sts. **Rows 4–10** Rep row 2. **Row (inc) 11** Kf&b in first st, work in seed st to last st, pf&b—11 sts. **Rows 12–18** Rep row 2. **Row 19** Rep row 3—13 sts. **Rows 20–26** Rep row 2. **Row 27** Rep row 11—15 sts. **Rows 28–38** Rep row 2. **Row (dec) 39** P2tog, work in seed st to last 2 sts, p2tog—13 sts. **Row (dec) 40** K2tog, work in seed st to last 2 sts, k2tog—11 sts. **Row 41** Rep row 39—9 sts (this is the toe). Bind off in seed st.

SIDES
Cast on 63 sts. Work in seed st until piece measures ¾"/2cm from beg. Bind off in seed st.

INSTEP AND T-STRAP LOOP
Beg at bottom edge of instep, cast on 9 sts. Cont in seed st as foll: **Row 1 (RS)** K1, *p1, k1; rep from * to end. **Row 2** K the purl sts and p the knit sts. **Row (inc) 3** Pf&b in first st, work in seed st to last st, kf&b—11 sts. **Rows 4–10** Rep row 2. **Row (dec) 11** K2tog tbl, work in seed st to last 2 sts, k2tog—9 sts. **Row (dec) 12** P2tog tbl, work in seed st to last 2 sts, ssp—7 sts. **Row 13** Rep row 11—5 sts **Row 14** Rep row 12—3 sts. **Rows 15 to 36** Rep row 2. Bind off in seed st.

STRAP
Cast on 3 sts. Cont in seed st as foll: **Rows 1–3** K1, p1, k1. **Row (buttonhole) 4** K1, yo, p2tog. **Rows 5 to 31** Rep row 1. Bind off in seed st.

Finishing
Fold sides in half lengthwise. Mark fold as center front of foot. Sew short side edges of sides tog; seam is center back of heel. Sew sole to sides, centering seam on heel and center front on toe. Mark center bottom edge of instep/T-strap. Sew bottom edge of instep to top edge of sides, centering bottom edge with center front of foot. Fold T-strap loop in half to WS and sew end in place. For right bootie, position bootie so heel is facing you. Sew bound-off edge of strap to left top edge of sides. Thread strap through loop, then sew button to right edge of sides. For left bootie, reverse position of strap. ■

Gauge
24 sts and 40 rows to 4"/10cm over seed st using size 5 (3.75mm) needles. *Take time to check gauge.*

Garter Ridge Hat

The contrasting ridges in this textured cap really stand out, and it's easy to change the colors to create a hat for a little boy.

DESIGNED BY TERRI KRUSE

Sizes
Instructions are written for size 12–18 months. Changes for size 2–3 years are in parentheses. (Shown in size 2–3 years.)

Knitted Measurements
Head circumference 14½ (16)"/37 (40.5)cm
Depth 8 (8½)"/20.5 (21.5)cm

Materials
■ 1 1¾oz/50g hank (each approx 136yd/125m) of Cascade Yarns *220 Superwash Sport* (superwash merino wool) each in #1941 salmon (MC) and #817 aran (CC)

■ Size 5 (3.75mm) circular needle, 16"/40cm long, *or size to obtain gauge*

■ One set (5) size 5 (3.75mm) double-pointed needles (dpns)

■ Stitch marker

Garter Ridge Stripe Pattern
Rnds 1 and 2 With MC, knit.
Rnd 3 With CC, knit.
Rnd 4 With CC, purl.
Rep rnds 1–4 for garter ridge stripe pat.

K1, P1 Rib
(over a multiple of 2 sts)
Rnd 1 (RS) *K1, p1; rep from * around.
Rep rnd 1 for k1, p1 rib.

Hat
With circular needle and MC, cast on 80 (88) sts. Join and pm for beg of rnds. Work around in k1, p1 rib for 1"/2.5cm. Cont in garter ridge stripe pat and work even until piece measures approximately 6¼ (6½)"/16 (16.5)cm from beg, end with rnd 4 (2).

Crown Shaping
Change to dpns (dividing sts evenly between 4 needles).

FOR SIZE 6 MONTHS ONLY
Next (dec) rnd With CC, *k9, k2tog; rep from * around—80 sts.
Next rnd With CC, purl.

FOR BOTH SIZES
Dec rnd 1 With MC, *k8, k2tog; rep from * around—72 sts.
Next rnd With MC, knit.
Dec rnd 2 With CC, *k7, k2tog; rep from * around—64 sts.
Next rnd With CC, purl.
Dec rnd 3 With MC, *k6, k2tog; rep from * around—56 sts.
Next rnd With MC, knit.
Dec rnd 4 With CC, *k5, k2tog; rep from * around—48 sts.
Next rnd With CC, purl.
Dec rnd 5 With MC, *k4, k2tog; rep from * around—40 sts. Cont with MC only as foll:
Next 2 rnds Knit.
Dec rnd 6 *K3, k2tog; rep from * around—32 sts.
Next rnd Knit.
Dec rnd 7 *K2, k2tog; rep from * around—24 sts.
Dec rnd 8 *K1, k2tog; rep from * around—16 sts.
Dec rnd 9 [K2tog] 8 times—8 sts. Cut yarn, leaving an 8"/20.5cm tail. Thread tail in tapestry needle, then thread through rem sts. Pull tog tightly and secure end. ■

Gauge
22 sts and 40 rnds to 4"/10cm over garter ridge stripe pat using size 5 (3.75mm) circular needle.
Take time to check gauge.

Button Panel Pullover

For a quick clean-up or a different look, simply switch out this sweater's clever button-on panel. Knit one in every color of the rainbow!

DESIGNED BY NANCY MACMILLAN

Sizes
Instructions are written for size 6 months. Changes for 12 and 18 months are in parentheses. (Shown in size 6 months.)

Knitted Measurements
Chest (closed) 20 (22, 24)"/51 (56, 61)cm
Length 10 (11, 12)"/25.5 (28, 30.5)cm
Upper arm 8 (9, 10)"/20.5 (23, 25.5)cm

Materials
■ 2 (3, 3) 1¾oz/50g hanks (each approx 136yd/125m) of Cascade Yarns *220 Superwash Sport* (superwash merino wool) in #900 charcoal (MC)
■ 1 hank in #1940 peach (CC) or #1910 summer sky heather (CC)
■ Size 6 (4mm) circular needle, 29"/74cm long, *or size to obtain gauge*
■ One pair size 6 (4mm) needles
■ Stitch markers
■ Eight ¹¹⁄₁₆"/17mm buttons

Note
Body is worked in one piece to the underarms.

Body
With circular needle and MC, cast on 83 (95, 107) sts. Work back and forth in garter st (knit every row) for 4 rows, end with a WS row.
Next row (RS) K4 (right front buttonband), pm, knit to last 4 sts, pm, k4 (left front buttonband).
Next row K4, sl marker, purl to last marker, sl marker, k4. Keeping 4 sts each side in garter st and rem sts in St st (knit on RS, purl on WS), work even until piece measures 6 (6½, 7)"/15 (16.5, 18)cm from beg, end with a WS row.

DIVIDE FOR FRONTS AND BACK
Change to straight needles.

RIGHT FRONT
Next row (RS) K4, sl marker, k8 (11, 14), pm, k2 (armhole band)—14 (17, 20) sts. Leave rem sts on circular needle for back and left front.
Next row K2, sl marker, purl to last marker, sl marker, k4. Keeping sts each side in garter st and rem sts in St st, work even until armhole measures 4 (4½, 5)"/10 (11.5, 12.5)cm, end with a WS row. Bind off all sts knitwise for shoulder.

BACK
Next row (RS) K2 (armhole band), pm, k51 (57, 63), pm, k2 (armhole band) from circular needle—55 (61, 67) sts. Keeping 2 sts each side in garter st and rem sts in St st, work even until armhole measures 3½ (4, 4½)"/9 (10, 11.5)cm, end with a WS row.

BACK NECKBAND
Next row (RS) K2, sl marker, k12 (15, 18), pm, k27 (neckband), pm, k12 (15, 18), sl marker, k2.
Next row K2, sl marker, p12 (15, 18), sl marker, k27, sl marker, p12 (15, 18), sl marker, k2. Keeping 2 sts each side and 27 sts in center in garter st and rem sts in St st, work even until piece measures same length as right front to shoulder, end with a WS. Bind off all sts knitwise for shoulders and back neck edge.

LEFT FRONT
Next row (RS) K2, pm, knit to last marker, sl marker, k4.
Next row K4, sl marker, purl to last marker, sl marker, k2. Cont to work as for right front.

Gauge
22 sts and 28 rows to 4"/10cm over St st using size 6 (4mm) circular needle.
Take time to check gauge.

57

Button Panel Pullover

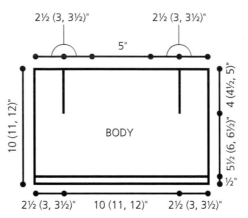

2½ (3, 3½)"   2½ (3, 3½)"

5"

10 (11, 12)"

BODY

4 (4½, 5)"

5½ (6, 6½)"

½"

2½ (3, 3½)"   10 (11, 12)"   2½ (3, 3½)"

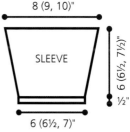

8 (9, 10)"

SLEEVE

6 (6½, 7½)"

½"

6 (6½, 7)"

Sleeves

With straight needles and MC, cast on 33 (36, 39) sts. Work in garter st for 4 rows, end with a WS row. Cont in St st, AT THE SAME TIME, inc 1 st each side on next row, then every 6th row 5 (6, 7) times more—45 (50, 55) sts. Work even until piece measures 6½ (7, 8)"/16.5 (18, 20.5)cm from beg, end with a WS row. Bind off all st knitwise.

Finishing

Block piece lightly to measurements. Sew shoulder seams. Place markers for 4

buttons along each buttonband, with the first ½"/1.3cm from lower edge, the last 2"/5cm below shoulder seams, and the others evenly spaced between.

BIB
With straight needles and CC, cast on 35 sts. Cont in garter st for 4 rows, end with a WS row.
Next (buttonhole) row (RS) K2, bind off next 2 sts, pm, k27, pm, bind off next 2 sts, knit to end.
Next row K2, cast on 2 sts, sl marker, purl to last marker, sl marker, cast on 2 sts, k2. Keeping 4 sts each side in garter st and rem sts in St st, cont to work 3 more buttonholes opposite markers each side, end with a WS row. Knit next 4 rows. Bind off knitwise. Sew sleeve seams. Set in sleeves. Sew on buttons. Button bib in place. ■

 **Quick Tip**
To customize the panel, knit it in stripes or a textured pattern. Be creative!

Argyle Cardigan

The classic argyle cardigan is perfect for pint-sized preppies when knit in fresh shades of pink, mint green, and coral.

DESIGNED BY KAREN GARLINGHOUSE

Sizes
Instructions are written for size 6 months.

Knitted Measurements
Chest (closed) 20"/51cm
Length 11"/28cm
Upper arm 6½"/16.5cm

Materials
■ 4 1¾oz/50g hanks (each approx 136yd/125m) of Cascade Yarns *220 Superwash Sport* (superwash merino wool) in #894 strawberry cream (MC)

■ 1 hank each in #1942 mint (A) #827 coral (B)

■ One pair size 5 (3.75mm) needles *or size to obtain gauge*

■ Size 3 (3.25mm) circular needle, 24"/61cm long

■ Four ¾"/19mm buttons

K2, P2 RIB
(multiple of 4 sts)
Row 1 (RS) *K2, p2; rep from * across.
Row 2 *K2, p2; rep from * across.
Rep rows 1 and 2 for k2, p2 rib.

Cardigan
BACK
With larger needles and MC, cast on 60 stitches. Work in k2, p2 rib for ½"/1cm. Change to St st (k on RS, p on WS) and work even for 6½"/16.5cm from beg, ending with a WS row.

ARMHOLE SHAPING
Cont in St st, dec 1 st each end of row every row 8 times—44 sts. Work even until armhole measures 4"/10cm, ending with a WS row.

SHOULDER SHAPING
Bind off 6 sts at beg of next 4 rows. Bind off rem 20 sts for back neck.

LEFT FRONT
With larger needles and MC, cast on 32 sts. Work in k2, p2 rib for ½"/1cm. Change to St st and work even for ½"/1cm.
Next row (RS) K1, work row 1 of 15-st chart rep twice, k1. Cont as set, working rows 1–15 of chart, then 3 rows MC, then rows 1–15 of chart. Work even in MC until piece measures 6½"/16.5cm, ending with a WS row.

ARMHOLE AND NECK SHAPING
At armhole edge, Dec 1 st every row 8 times—24 sts. At the same time, dec 1 st at neck edge (end of RS rows) every other row until 12 sts rem. Work even until armhole measures same as back.

SHOULDER SHAPING
Bind off 6 sts at beg of next 2 RS rows.

Gauge
24 sts and 32 rows to 4"/10cm over St st using size 5 (3.75mm) needles.
Take time to check gauge.

58
Argyle Cardigan

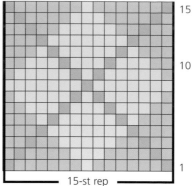

RIGHT FRONT
Work as for left front, reversing all shaping.

SLEEVES
With larger needles and MC, cast on 32 sts. Work in k2, p2 rib for ½"/1cm. Change to St st and work even until piece measures 2"/5cm from beg. Inc 1 st each end of row every 4 rows 4 times—40 sts. Work even until piece measures 6"/15cm from beg, ending with a WS row.

CAP SHAPING
Dec 1 st each end of row every row 6 times—28 sts. Bind off 4 sts at beg of next 4 rows—12 sts. Bind off.

Finishing
Sew shoulder seams. Set in sleeves, sew side and sleeve seams.

FRONT BAND
With RS facing, smaller needle, and MC, pick up and knit 77 sts along right front, 18 sts across back neck, and 77 sts along left front—178 sts. Work in k2, p2 rib

Color Key
▨ Strawberry Cream (MC)
☐ Mint (A)
▨ Coral (B)

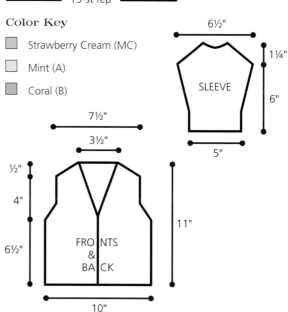

for 1 row, ending with k2.
Next row (RS) Work in rib pat for 3 sts, *yo, work next 2 sts tog in pat, work next 9 sts in pat; rep from * three more times, work in rib pat to end of row. Work 2 rows even in pat. Bind off. Sew buttons opposite buttonholes. ■

Colorblock Blanket

Gem-colored intarsia blocks frame a subtle tone-on-tone block pattern knit in a rich shade of teal.

DESIGNED BY KENNITA TULLY

■■■□

Knitted Measurements
Approx 32½" x 32½"/82.5cm x 82.5cm

Materials
- 7 1¾oz/50g hanks (each approx 136yd/125m) of Cascade Yarns *220 Superwash Sport* (superwash merino wool) in #811 como blue (MC)
- 1 hank each in #808 sunset orange, #849 dark aqua (B), and #841 moss (C)
- Size 6 (4mm) circular needle, 36"/91cm long, *or size to obtain gauge*
- Bobbins

Note
Use a separate bobbin of color for each color section.

Blanket
With MC, cast on 171 sts.
Row 1 (RS) With MC, sl 1 knitwise, knit to last st, p1. **Rows 2–14** With MC, rep row 1. **Row 15 (RS)** With MC, sl 1 knitwise, k6, [k13 with A, k5 with MC, k13 with B, k23 with MC, k13 with C, k5 with MC] twice, k13 with A; with MC, k6, p1. **Row 16** Keeping to color pat as established, work as foll:
Sl 1 knitwise, k6, *p13, k5; rep from *, end p13, k6, p1. **Rows 17–32** Rep rows 15 and 16 eight times more. **Rows 33–42** Rep row 1. **Row 43** With MC, sl 1 knitwise, k6; k13 with C, k131 with MC, k13 with B; with MC, k6, p1.
Row 44 Keeping to color pat as established, work as foll:
Sl 1 knitwise, k6, *p13, k5; rep from *, end p13, k6, p1. **Rows 45–60** Rep rows 43 and 44 eight times more.
Rows 61–71 Rep row 1. **Row 72** Sl 1 knitwise, k6, *p13, k5; rep from *, end p13, k6, p1. **Rows 73–88** Rep rows 71 and 72 eight times more.
Rows 89–98 Rep row 1. **Row 99** With MC, sl 1 knitwise, k6; k13 with B, k131 with MC, k13 with C; with MC, k6, p1.
Row 100 Keeping to color pat as established, work as foll:
Sl 1 knitwise, k6, *p13, k5; rep from *, end p13, k6, p1. **Rows 101–116** Rep rows 99 and 100 eight times more.
Rows 117–126 Rep row 1. **Row 127** With MC, sl 1 knitwise, k6; k13 with A, k131 with MC, k13 with A; with MC, k6, p1.
Row 128 Keeping to color pat as established, work as foll:
Sl 1 knitwise, k6, *p13, k5; rep from *, end p13, k6, p1. **Rows 129–144** Rep rows 127 and 128 eight times more.
Rows 145–154 Rep row 1. **Row 155** With MC, sl 1 knitwise, k6; k13 with C, k131 with MC, k13 with B; with MC, k6, p1.
Row 156 Keeping to color pat as established, work as foll: Sl 1 knitwise, k6, *p13, k5; rep from *, end p13, k6, p1. **Rows 157–172** Rep rows 155 and 156 eight times more.

Rows 173–182 Rep row 1. **Row 183** Rep row 1. **Row 184** Sl 1 knitwise, k6, *p13, k5; rep from *, end p13, k6, p1.
Rows 185–200 Rep rows 183 and 184 eight times more. **Rows 201–210** Rep row 1. **Row 211** With MC, sl 1 knitwise, k6; k13 with B, k131 with MC, k13 with C; with MC, k6, p1. **Row 212** Keeping to color pat as established, work as foll:
Sl 1 knitwise, k6, *p13, k5; rep from *, end p13, k6, p1. **Rows 213–228** Rep rows 211 and 212 eight times more.
Rows 229–238 Rep row 1.
Row 239 With MC, sl 1 knitwise, k6, [k13 with A, k5 with MC, k13 with C, k23 with MC, k13 with B, k5 with MC] twice, k13 with A, with MC, k6, p1.
Row 240 Keeping to color pat as established, work as foll:
Sl 1 knitwise, k6, *p13, k5; rep from *, end p13, k6, p1. **Rows 241–256** Rep rows 239 and 240 eight times more.
Rows 257–270 Rep row 1. Bind off all sts knitwise.

Finishing
Block piece lightly to measurements. ■

Gauge
21 sts and 34 rows to 4"/10cm over color block pat using size 6 (4mm) circular needle. *Take time to check gauge.*

Flower Motif Pullover

A chain stitch outline gives the oversized intarsia flower on this cheery pullover extra punch.
Buttons on one shoulder make for easy dressing.

DESIGNED BY HOLLI YEOH

Sizes
Instructions are written for size 6 months. Changes for 12 and 18 months are in parentheses. (Shown in size 6 months.)

Knitted Measurements
Chest 22 (24, 26)"/56 (61, 66)cm
Length 11 (12, 13)"/28 (30.5, 33)cm
Upper arm 9 (10, 11)"/23 (25.5, 28)cm

Materials
■ 3 (4, 5) 1¾oz/50g hanks (each approx 136yd/125m) of Cascade Yarns *220 Superwash Sport* (superwash merino wool) in #1946 silver grey (MC)

■ 1 hank each in #803 royal purple (A), #808 sunset orange (B), #802 green apple (C), #807 raspberry (D), #813 blue velvet (E), and #841 moss (F)

■ One pair each sizes 3 and 5 (3.25 and 3.75mm) needles *or size to obtain gauge*

■ Stitch holders

■ Three ⅜"/10mm buttons

Stitch Glossary
ssp (slip, slip, purl) Sl first st knitwise, then sl next st knitwise. Slip these 2 sts back to LH needle, then purl them tog tbl.

Back
With smaller needles and MC, cast on 74 (82, 88) sts. Work in garter st (knit every row) for 12 rows, end with a WS row. Change to larger needles. Cont in St st (k on RS, p on WS) and work even until piece measures 6½ (7, 7½)"/16.5 (18, 19)cm from beg, end with a WS row.

ARMHOLE SHAPING
Bind off 4 (5, 5) sts at beg of next 2 rows.
Dec row 1 (RS) K2, k2tog, knit to last 4 sts, ssk, k2.
Dec row 2 P2, ssp, purl to last 4 sts, p2tog, p2. Rep dec row 1 once more—60 (66, 72) sts. Beg with a purl row, cont in St st until armhole measures 2½ (3, 3½)"/6.5 (7.5, 9)cm, end with a WS row.

BEG CHART PAT 1
Row 1 (RS) With MC, k24 (27, 30), work chart over center 12 sts, with MC, k24 (27, 30). Cont to foll chart in this way to row 10, then cont to work with MC only. Work even until armhole measures 4½ (5, 5½)"/11.5 (12.5, 14)cm, end with a WS row.

SHOULDER AND NECK SHAPING
Next row (RS) K 15 (18, 20) sts, place these sts on holder for right shoulder, bind off next 30 (30, 32) sts for back neck, knit to end—15 (18, 20) sts.

LEFT SHOULDER BUTTONBAND
Change to smaller needles. Work in garter st for 7 rows. Bind off knitwise.

Front
Work as for back until piece measures 1¾ (2½, 3¼)"/4.5 (6.5, 8)cm from beg, end with a WS row—74 (82, 88) sts.

BEG CHART PAT 2
Row 1 (RS) With MC, k19 (23, 26), work chart over center 36 sts, with MC, k19 (23, 26). Cont to foll chart in this way to row 54, then cont to work with MC only.

Gauge
26 sts and 36 rows to 4"/10cm over St st using larger needles. *Take time to check gauge.*

Flower Motif Pullover

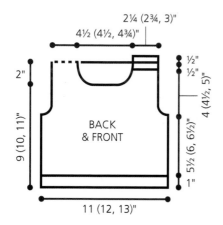

2¼ (2¾, 3)"

4½ (4½, 4¾)"

½"
½"

2"

4 (4½, 5)"

9 (10, 11)"

BACK & FRONT

5½ (6, 6½)"

1"

11 (12, 13)"

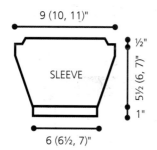

9 (10, 11)"

½"

SLEEVE

5½ (6, 7)"

1"

6 (6½, 7)"

AT THE SAME TIME, when piece measures same length as back to underarm, end with a WS row. Shape armholes as for back—60 (66, 72) sts. When chart is completed, work even until armhole measures 2½ (3, 3½)"/6.5 (7.5, 9)cm, end with a WS row.

NECK SHAPING
Next row (RS) K22 (25, 27), join a 2nd ball of MC and bind off center 16 (16, 18) sts, knit to end. Working both sides at once, bind off from each neck edge 3 sts once, 2 sts once, then 1 st twice—15 (18, 20) sts. Work even until armhole measures 4 (4½, 5)"/10 (11.5, 12.5)cm, end with a WS row.

LEFT SHOULDER BUTTONBAND
Change to smaller needles and work on left shoulder sts only. Work in garter st on 15 (18, 20) sts for 4 rows, end with a WS row.
Next (buttonhole) row (RS) K5 (6, 6), yo, k2tog, k4 (5, 6), yo, k2tog, k2 (3, 4)—2 buttonholes made (3rd buttonhole is on neckband). Work in garter st for 3 rows more. Bind off knitwise.

RIGHT SHOULDER
With larger needles, cont in St st on rem 15 (18, 20) sts until piece measures same length as back to shoulder, end with a WS row. Place sts on holder.

Sleeves
With smaller needles and MC, cast on 38 (42, 44) sts. Work in garter st for 12 rows, end with a WS row. Change to larger needles and St st.
Inc row (RS) K2, M1, knit to last 2 sts, M1, k2. Rep inc row every other row 4 (4, 3) times more, then every 4th row 7 (8, 11) times—62 (68, 74) sts.

Work even until piece measures 6½ (7, 8)"/16.5 (18, 20.5)cm from beg, end with a WS row.

CAP SHAPING
Bind off 4 (5, 5) sts at beg of next 2 rows.
Dec row 1 (RS) K2, k2tog, knit to last 4 sts, ssk, k2.
Dec row 2 P2, ssp, purl to last 4 sts, p2tog, p2.
Rep dec row 1 once more—48 (52, 58) sts. Purl next row. Bind off all sts knitwise.

Finishing
Block pieces to measurements.

EMBROIDERY
Work in chain stitch throughout. On back, outline center oval using D, then outline outer edge of oval using E. On front, embroider flower stem using C, then outline leaves using F. Outline center (B oval) using D. Outline A oval using E, then outline outer edge of oval using B. Join right shoulder using 3-needle bind-off.

NECKBAND
With RS facing, smaller needles, and MC, pick up and k 50 (50, 52) sts evenly spaced along entire front neck edge to right shoulder, 30 (30, 32) sts across back neck edge to left shoulder buttonband, then 4 sts across side edge of buttonband—84 (84, 88) sts. Knit next 3 rows.
Buttonhole row (RS) K2, yo, k2tog, knit to end. Knit next 3 rows.
Bind off knitwise. Sew on buttons. Button shoulder closed. Set in right sleeve. Set in left sleeve, sewing through all 3 layers at shoulder. Sew side and sleeve seams. ∎